800

DATE DUE

THE DIPLOMATIC HISTORY OF THE
CANADIAN BOUNDARY, 1749–1763

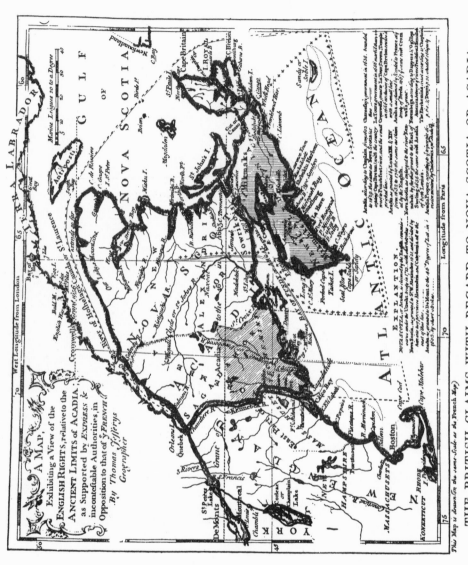

MAPS

BRITISH AND FRENCH CLAIMS TO ACADIA

THE FRENCH CLAIMS WITH REGARD TO ACADIA

From: "Mémoires des Commissaires du Roi et de ceux de sa Majesté Britannique, sur les possessions & les droits respectifs des deux Couronnes en Amérique; avec les actes publics et pièces justificatives. Tome premier, contenant les Mémoires sur l'Acadie & sur l'isle de Sainte-Lucie." A. Paris, de l'Imprimerie Royale. MDCCLV. Courtesy of Yale University Library.

THE
DIPLOMATIC HISTORY
OF THE
CANADIAN BOUNDARY
1749-1763

BY

MAX SAVELLE

NEW YORK / RUSSELL & RUSSELL

FOREWORD

THE war in Europe, by its challenge to the whole structure of the national state system there, gives added importance to this series of volumes dealing with American-Canadian relations. For it is not only in Europe that the Hitlerian Revolution is testing the realities of democracy. The impact of the attack reaches to every corner of the world, wherever free men have sought to embody their hopes of peace and justice in the institutions of self-government. Of all these experiments in the building of national states on the basis of liberty, a peculiar significance attaches to the two North American countries, which are the chief non-European inheritors of the great political traditions of France and Great Britain.

In similar but yet separate ways the United States and Canada safeguarded this heritage as they worked in friendly rivalry upon the one great common task confronting both countries, the conquest of the continent. But, until recently, neither Canadians nor their southern neighbors were seriously interested in the history of that interplay of interests which, in spite of boundary lines, gives to the political and economic evolution of each country its continental significance. This series of volumes deals with the background and present-day movement of these forces. Strangely enough, it is the first comprehensive attempt to do so. It was planned some ten years ago as a coöperative enterprise of Canadian and American scholars, when it seemed that there would be plenty of time and abundant opportunity for research. No one then could have foreseen the urgency of need for such an enterprise. But now it is abundantly evident that the leaders of the German and Italian peoples, not to mention others, have undertaken the overthrow of the process of three hundred years and more of European history, and that the threat extends deeply into the New World as well. For the process of national state building which the authoritarian leaders are set upon destroying reached its freest development here. It is therefore of very real importance that scholarship should add its sober illumination to the solution of problems of the past as well as of the present of both peoples, thus correcting while it enlarges their perspectives.

That this fundamental purpose can be achieved without doing violence to the exacting requirements of scientific work should need no proof, but if any were called for it can be found in the unshaken objectivity of these volumes.

The present study, the product of years of research in the United States, Canada, France, Spain, and Great Britain, reaches far back into colonial history, but the subject with which it deals is of vital interest still. Touched as it is with distance and the quaint formalities of the old regime in both France and England, it also brings upon the scene the realities of new world rivalries. Succeeding volumes in this Series, already published or about to appear, constitute a continuous and searching investigation of Canadian-American relations from the American Revolution to the present. Still other studies deal with the economic and social interplay of the two nations. And for those who may be led to the conclusion that war and diplomacy set the pattern for the political evolution of North America it is well to remember how under the new dispensation after the conquest of Canada in 1760, the French have not only maintained but strengthened their grasp upon the cultural and political life of Canada. The heritage of the New World was twice divided by war, but the common ideals of liberty within the law and of the dignity of self-government remain, nurtured by the arts of peace.

JAMES T. SHOTWELL

PREFACE

THE part played by American problems in the diplomatic intercourse between the colonizing nations of Western Europe was one of steadily increasing importance from the discovery of the continent to the war of American Independence. For Spain and Portugal, their colonies in the Western Hemisphere had an immense economic value almost from the beginning. For England, France, and Holland, on the other hand, interest in the colonial world was limited during the sixteenth century to a desire to profit from the seizure of Spanish and Portuguese ships engaged in colonial commerce, an illicit slave trade with the Spanish and Portuguese empires, and a half-dozen sporadic attempts of Frenchmen and Englishmen to settle colonies on the continent of North America.

Colonial questions did play an important part, nonetheless, in the diplomatic relations of the nations of Western Europe throughout the sixteenth century. Beginning even before the discovery of America the colonial question had reached the dignity of Papal consideration in the Bull of January 8, 1455; and colonial spheres of influence were recognized by Spain and Portugal in the Treaty of Alcaçovas in 1479. In the Treaty of Tordesillas, of 1494, Spain and Portugal arrogated to themselves possession of the entire New World, and it was only by way of challenge to this magnificent presumption that France and England injected their claims to a share of the new countries into the diplomacy of the sixteenth century.

Perhaps the most notable example of the influence of the colonial question upon diplomacy is to be seen in the negotiations preceding the Treaty of Cateau-Cambrésis in 1559. During these negotiations the French insisted that they had a right to go to the New World for the purposes of trade and colonization; the Spaniards, on the other hand, refused to admit this claim, on the ground that the New World belonged to Spain and Portugal by right of prior discovery and the Papal Bulls of 1493. No provision as to the colonial world was included in the treaty, but there seems to have been an oral agreement that the New World would be considered as a sphere of international law outside the European sphere, the effect being that European treaties were not to apply in America, and that violence in the New

World would not necessarily be considered a *casus belli* in Europe. In other words, if Frenchmen went to America, they did so at their own risk, and if they were caught and thrown into the sea by the Spaniards, France would not therefore consider that Spain had violated international law.

When James I came to make peace with Spain in 1604, England found herself in much the same position that France had occupied in 1559. England claimed that the terms of the *Intercursus Magnus* made between Henry VII and the Duke of Burgundy entitled Englishmen to the privilege of going to the colonial territories of the Spanish empire. The Spanish diplomats on the contrary insisted that the *Intercursus Magnus* was a treaty that pertained only to the territories of the Spanish and English rulers in Europe; that America constituted a "New World," and that, therefore, the terms of European treaties did not apply there. The result of the negotiations was an ambiguous clause in the Treaty of London, of 1604, which provided merely that English merchants might go to the places where they had been permitted to go prior to the war; which was immediately interpreted by the English to mean that they could go to America and by the Spaniards to mean that they could not.

It was not until 1648 that Spain in plain terms acknowledged the right of any nation, and specifically at this time the Dutch, to sail to the territories of the New World, whether America, Africa, or India, and then only for the purposes of trade with potentates not under the rule of the Spanish monarch. This recognition was extended to England in the Treaty of Madrid, of 1667, and was made more specific with regard to the actual possessions of England and Spain in America in a second Treaty of Madrid, that of 1670. In the latter treaty Spain and England mutually recognized each other's titles to the lands then actually occupied by them in America. No boundary lines were drawn; but English ownership of the Atlantic seaboard of North America, presumably as far south as the settlement at Charlestown, and of the islands in the West Indies occupied by Englishmen, including Jamaica, was clearly recognized by Spain. The terms of this treaty were renewed in an agreement between England and the Archduke Charles made at Barcelona in 1707, and in the Anglo-Spanish Treaty of Utrecht in 1713 they were again renewed. Not only that: England in the latter treaty agreed to guaranty the territorial *status quo* of the Spanish colonies in America against any change. These

terms were again renewed in the Anglo-Spanish Treaty of Madrid
in 1721.

Meanwhile England and France had fallen into competition for the
possession of the northern parts of America and this conflict had
found its way into the diplomatic correspondence of the two countries
as early as 1613, when France complained of Captain Argall's raid on
St. Sauveur. France also protested James I's grant of Nova Scotia to
Sir William Alexander; and after the conclusion of the short war of
1627–1628, Acadia and Canada, which the British had seized, were
returned to France in 1632 by the Treaty of St. Germain. Acadia
was again seized by the British in 1654 and the Treaty of Westminster of·the year following provided that the question of its ownership
should be submitted to a joint Anglo-French commission for decision,
failing which it was to be submitted to arbitration. This provision was
not carried out, but Acadia was returned to France under the terms
of the Treaty of Breda, in 1667. By the "agreement of Boston," in
1670, Sir Thomas Temple surrendered to the Sieur de Grandefon-
taine, Louis XIV's new governor of Acadia, all the territory from
Cape Breton southwestward to the Penobscot River. During the next
two decades Frenchmen and Englishmen began to struggle for the
possession of fur-trading posts around the shores of Hudson Bay,
while the governors of Canada and New York fell to quarreling over
the ownership of the lands south of the St. Lawrence River in the region of Lake Champlain and those lying along the shores of Lake
Ontario.

The quarreling of these French and English fur traders and colonial governors came to the ears of the monarchs of France and England at a most inappropriate time. Louis XIV had, only a few years
before, successfully seized the city of Strasbourg, and now found
himself faced by the League of Augsburg. He was laying plans for
the seizure of the Palatinate, and he was ardently desirous of preventing England from entering the war against him on the side of
the League. James II, for his part, had come to the throne of a
troubled England and he was more interested in asserting his authority at home than in the trackless forests of America. For these
and other reasons, in 1686 the two monarchs made an agreement at
Whitehall which is one of the most interesting documents in American
diplomatic history. It took cognizance of the struggles in the back-
woods of America and of the need of drawing a boundary line between

the respective possessions of the two countries in the New World. Provision was made for the settlement of this boundary line by joint commission; and, by a supplementary agreement of December, 1687, it was provided that all acts of violence should be suspended until the commission had had time to do its work. The most interesting provision of the treaty, however, was a new statement of the principle that acts of violence in America were not to be considered as cause for war in Europe. Nor, on the other hand, was a war in Europe to be considered cause for hostilities in America. Thus did the two kings think to rule out the American frontier quarrels as a *casus belli* between them. Thus, too, was the doctrine of the two spheres written down in clear and unequivocal language in a treaty between two major European powers.

But all to no avail. The situation in Europe was making for war. In England the "Glorious Revolution" brought to the throne William of Orange, the leading spirit of the League of Augsburg and the nemesis of Louis XIV. It was only to be expected that William would use every device at his disposal to justify his asking the English people to enter the war on the side of Holland and the League. But at the same time the local conflicts in America were sufficient to produce a war in the colonies regardless of the European situation. It would be a mistake to say that the American colonies were dragged into this, or any other intercolonial war against their will. For certain elements, at least, in the colonies, and particularly the New England fishermen and the merchants engaged in the fur trade, stood to profit from a war with the French, and they entered into it without protest, and even gladly. The situation in the Hudson Bay country was peculiar, however, because of the fact that the English merchants engaged in the fur trade of the Bay were residents of England and were men of tremendous political influence at court. It was probably as a result of their influence that the declaration with which England entered the War of the League of Augsburg, perhaps for the first time in the history of European expansion, mentioned a colonial conflict as being a cause for war in the Old World.

This is significant because it indicates that in the minds of Englishmen the colonies had now reached the point where they were worth fighting for; nor was this merely the result of the influence of one private corporation, the Hudson's Bay Company. The economic value of the colonies during the seventeenth century had increased enor-

mously. It is sufficient merely to note that whereas in 1660 the trade of
the colonies constituted only about one-tenth of the total trade of
Great Britain, by 1690 it constituted about one-seventh, and by 1721
it was responsible for approximately one-fifth of it. It was undoubtedly because of this rapid and striking increase in the value of its
colonies to England, to say nothing of those of Holland, Spain, and
France, that the colonies from this time on came to play an increasing
role in European international relations.

In the Treaty of Ryswick which ended the War of the League of
Augsburg and its American counterpart, known as King William's
War, it was provided that the question of the ownership of the posts
on Hudson Bay should be left to the decision of a joint Anglo-French
commission which should also be charged with the problem of establishing boundary lines for the territories to be restored elsewhere on
the American continent. A commission for this purpose did actually
meet in 1699, but it accomplished nothing; and the outbreak of the
War of the Spanish Succession threw the colonial situation and the
question of an Anglo-French boundary back into the uncertainty
where it had always been.

The Anglo-French Treaty of Utrecht, however, was a long step
toward the settlement of the question of colonial possessions. It provided that Hudson Bay should belong in its entirety to England. Newfoundland was also recognized as being British, although the French
retained the privilege of fishing and drying fish on and along the
northern and western coasts of the island. Acadia with its old boundaries, its *anciennes limites*, was ceded to England. St. Christopher in
the West Indies was similarly recognized as belonging wholly to England. The ownership of the Hudson Bay country, Acadia, Newfoundland, and St. Christopher was thus definitely settled. But the exact
boundaries of the Hudson Bay region and Acadia were not delimited;
and a provision was incorporated in this treaty providing for another
joint commission which should be charged with determining the
boundary lines between Hudson Bay and New France and in addition
those between the English and French colonies elsewhere on the continent. A joint commission met in Paris in 1719, as will be told in
greater detail later; but its work came to nothing, save for the establishment of the idea in the minds of interested Englishmen that the
forty-ninth degree of north latitude might be an appropriate southern boundary for the territories of Hudson Bay.

The most striking development in the story of the part played by America in European diplomacy is the fact that, at the Congress of Utrecht and later, English, French, Spanish, and Dutch diplomats, representing public opinion, such as it was, in their respective countries, were more conscious of the colonial problem than they had ever been before. In the diplomatic history of Europe during the following fifty years, colonial questions recur with steadily increasing frequency and emphasis in the correspondence between the courts of these four countries. Colonial questions seem to have furnished the most decisive consideration in the outbreak of war between Spain and England in 1739. But the War of the Austrian Succession, in which both France and England became involved, was almost purely a European conflict. What interest the combatants had had in its colonial counterpart became diverted, during the course of the war, from American to Old World issues.

The relative silence of the Treaty of Aix-la-Chapelle upon American questions is nevertheless hardly a sufficient indication of the importance of America to European diplomacy. The old conflicts between England and France, and between England and Spain, still remained to be settled; and the diplomatic intercourse of these three nations in the eight years between the Peace of Aix-la-Chapelle and the formal outbreak of the Seven Years' War was to an extraordinary degree devoted to American questions. So far as England, France, and Spain were concerned, the Seven Years' War was a colonial war fought for the solution of colonial and imperial questions. For the first time, probably, in the history of European international relations, three major nations were drawn into a major war in the prosecution of their imperial rivalries.

The issues in this conflict were numerous, but its chief interest, so far as England and France were concerned, was the question of where the boundary lines between their respective colonies should be drawn. Beneath this more obvious question there lay a deeper sociological conflict inherent in the competitive expansion of the British and French possessions on the continent of North America. The British colonies were rapidly expanding westward across the continent, and New France was slowly filling in the great interior valleys along a line running north and south. The French establishment lay directly in the path of the British expansion westward; and with the beginning of an English movement over the Allegheny barrier after the

Peace of Aix-la-Chapelle, the settlement of the century-old question of boundaries could no longer be postponed.

The real nature of this conflict was only vaguely realized in the chancelleries of Europe. English, French, and Spanish statesmen did realize, however, that the imperial conflict in America involved enormous stakes. And with the development of the idea of a colonial balance of power which might act as a decisive make-weight in the balance of power in Europe, they approached a realization of the fact that the colonies had now attained a position of importance in international affairs which made them, so far as the five great colonial powers were concerned, a new and enormously important factor in the determination of national destiny. Nearly all the statesmen of the time were dominated by the mercantilistic philosophy of national wealth and power. The strength of Great Britain, for example, was thought to have its basis and foundation in the wealth derived from her colonies. In the period just preceding the outbreak of war, the French diplomats in Spain made much of this argument in their attempt to win Spanish support against their English foe, by pointing out that if Great Britain were allowed to absorb the French colonies, her power both in America and in Europe would be greatly increased, and it would be only a short time before the British would move upon the Spanish colonies in America which, once absorbed into the British Empire, would make that Empire so overwhelmingly powerful as to place Britain in a position to dictate to the other nations of Europe. It is probably true that the French diplomats used this argument with their tongues in their cheeks, but there can be no doubt that it had much weight with Charles III, who ascended the Spanish throne in 1759.

The Seven Years' War in America then, fought as it was essentially to determine the question of what the boundaries between the British colonies and the French should be, constitutes a sort of climax to the crescendo of the colonial role in European diplomacy in the eighteenth century. The diplomatic question involved was a question largely of colonial boundaries; but underlying the grim and cynical diplomatic game there was a sociological conflict which was of profound and fundamental importance to the history of the future United States and Canada. For it is only necessary to imagine what would have been the result had France won the conflict over those boundaries, instead of England, to realize how different might have been the history of the continent and how pregnant with the ultimate course of North American history was the issue.

THE extensive travel and research that were necessary for the preparation of this essay were made possible by a series of generous grants from the Stanford University Council of Research in the Social Sciences. The work was completed under a grant from the Social Science Research Council, of New York City. It is a pleasure gratefully to acknowledge this assistance.

This monograph is based upon a study of manuscript materials in the Library of Congress in Washington, the William L. Clements Library in Ann Arbor, Michigan, the Canadian Archives in Ottawa, the British Museum and British Public Record Office, and the French *Archives du Ministère des Affaires Etrangères* and *Archives Nationales*. The author received most helpful coöperation and assistance in all these libraries, and he takes pleasure in making acknowledgment to the officials in charge of them.

The author wishes to express his gratitude to Thomas A. Bailey, Samuel Flagg Bemis, Chester B. Martin, Gustave Lanctot, and J. Bartlet Brebner, who read the manuscript in its entirety or in part and who made many helpful suggestions, and to Mrs. David Harris, Miss Frances Barney, and Mr. Harry Winton for indispensable editorial assistance. He is under very special obligation to Arthur E. McFarlane for his skilful and patient assistance in the preparation of the manuscript for the press. Finally, the author wishes to express his deep appreciation of the encouragement and assistance he has received from Dr. James T. Shotwell and the Carnegie Endowment for International Peace in connection with the publication of the volume in this Series, dealing with the past as well as the present of Canadian-American relations.

M. S.

Stanford University
June 1, 1940

CONTENTS

LIST OF ABBREVIATIONS

AE CP Espagne—*Archives du Ministère des Affaires Etrangères*, Paris. *Correspondance Politique: Espagne.*

AE Méms. et Docs. Amérique—*Archives du Ministère des Affaires Etrangères*, Paris. *Mémoires et Documents: Amérique.*

AN—*Archives Nationales*, Paris.

BM Add. MSS.—*British Museum*, Additional Manuscript Series.

BM Stowe MSS.—*British Museum*, Stowe Manuscripts.

CAO AE CP Ang.—*Archives of the Dominion of Canada*, Ottawa. Transcripts from the *Archives du Ministère des Affaires Etrangères*, Paris. *Correspondance Politique: Angleterre.*

CAO PRO FO 90 (France)—*Archives of the Dominion of Canada*, Ottawa. Transcripts from the Public Record Office, London. Foreign Office Papers, Series 90 (France).

CAO PRO FO 90 (BT MSS.)—*Archives of the Dominion of Canada*, Ottawa. Transcripts from the Public Record Office, London. Foreign Office Papers, Series 90 (Board of Trade Manuscripts).

CL Mildmay Papers—*William L. Clements Library*, Ann Arbor, Michigan. Personal Papers of William Mildmay.

CL Shelburne MSS.—*William L. Clements Library*, Ann Arbor, Michigan. Manuscripts of the Earl of Shelburne.

HL LO—*Henry E. Huntington Library*, San Marino, California. Loudoun Manuscripts.

LC Add. MSS.—*Library of Congress*, Washington. Transcripts from the Additional Manuscripts Series in the British Museum.

LC AE Méms. et Docs. Amérique—*Library of Congress*, Washington. Transcripts from the *Archives du Ministère des Affaires Etrangères*, Paris. *Mémoires et Documents: Amérique.*

LC AE Méms. et Docs. France—*Library of Congress*, Washington. Transcripts from the *Archives du Ministère des Affaires Etrangères*, Paris. *Mémoires et Documents: France.*

LC House of Lords MSS.—*Library of Congress*, Washington. Transcripts of Manuscripts in the Library of the House of Lords, London.

N.Y. Col. Docs.—E. B. O'Callaghan, ed., *Documents Relative to the Colonial History of the State of New York* (Albany, 1853–1887).

PRO Chatham MSS.—*The Public Record Office*, London. Chatham Manuscripts.

THE DIPLOMATIC HISTORY OF THE

CANADIAN BOUNDARY, 1749–1763

THE CANADIAN BOUNDARY, 1749-1763

CHAPTER I

INTRODUCTION: THE ISSUES DEFINED

THE Peace of Aix-la-Chapelle[1] in 1748 left unsettled every major boundary question that had troubled the relations of European powers on the continent of North America since the ejection of the Dutch from New Netherland in 1664. This peace took practically no cognizance of the colonial problem; it merely provided for the restitution of conquests made during the war, mentioning Cape Breton specifically as the most important. Yet it left embattled Englishmen and Frenchmen facing each other on a half-dozen fronts, in areas widely separated by vast stretches of forest, river, or sea. Separated as they were, these local conflicts were all parts of the single problem presented by the two-centuries-old race of Frenchmen, Englishmen, and Spaniards to settle and exploit the greatest possible colonial empires for themselves in the New World.

A generation earlier the Peace of Utrecht had, in 1713, recognized the British title to Rupert's Land, Newfoundland, and Acadia; and Great Britain had recognized the Spanish possession of Mexico and Florida in a blanket guaranty of the boundaries of Spanish possessions in America as they had existed in the time of Charles II. Yet neither of the Treaties of Utrecht specified any clear boundaries in America. The limits of Newfoundland alone, since Newfoundland was an island, were clear and recognizable. But even there the seeds of future diplomatic wrangling were planted, in the form of somewhat vague agreements between Great Britain on one side and France and Spain on the other with regard to the Newfoundland fishery.[2] What were the boundaries of Rupert's Land or Acadia? Nobody knew. To answer the question, provision was made, in Article X of the Anglo-French treaty, for the appointment of a joint commission to determine these points and "the limits between the other French and British colonies in those countries."[3] The Peace of Utrecht

1. In general, the word "peace"—as in "The Peace of Utrecht"—is used in this volume to indicate a general settlement of international problems in which several nations and treaties were involved; the word "treaty" is used to indicate one specific international agreement.

2. The texts of the Anglo-French and the Anglo-Spanish Treaties of Utrecht may be most conveniently found in Frances G. Davenport, ed., *European Treaties Bearing on the History of the United States and Its Dependencies* (Washington, 1917, 1929, 1934, 1937; Vol. IV edited by C. O. Paullin), III, 208–214, 223–231.

3. *Ibid.*, III, 211. Quotations from printed collections of documents where translations from foreign languages are already given reproduce verbatim the translation, in each case, as there given.

had thus recognized the existence of the boundary problem. But beyond the provision for a commission, which was eventually appointed only to accomplish nothing, that peace failed to face the issue in the other great areas of conflict—the St. Lawrence Valley, the Ohio Valley, and the valley of the lower Mississippi. The diplomats hardly realized, indeed, that any issues existed in those areas.

Before 1713, the problem of exact boundaries in America had never been very acute. Great stretches of primeval forest separated the French settlements from the English. It was only when Frenchmen and Englishmen actively entered the intervening areas and became competitors for the favor of the Indians in trade that they began to realize the fundamental nature of their rivalry, and to accuse each other of trespassing upon their respective lands. Frenchmen had clashed with New Englanders in the no-man's-land of Norumbega and Penobscot from the time of the settlement of Plymouth onward; French pioneers of the great west had clashed with English pioneer traders in the lands south of the present Ontario and along the portage around Niagara as early as the days of Governors Dongan and Denonville. The generation following the Peace of Utrecht was marked by a more rapid penetration of the interior by both sides, and a deliberate race to occupy the regions between the English frontier and the line of French settlements through the center of the continent. It was a race marked by the building of forts and the staking of claims, with the more or less conscious purpose of establishing actual possession, against the day when the delimiting of the boundary must inevitably be undertaken.

The period from 1713 to 1754, then, was one in which the question of boundaries became acute. But far from being limited to Canada, the problem must be considered as including a number of widely separated areas of friction, each presenting features peculiar to itself but all parts of a larger conflict, upon the issue of which depended the fate of the major part of North America. There were five of these areas, north of the Caribbean, in which Frenchmen had clashed with Englishmen over the ownership of the land. Farthest north was the shore of Hudson Bay, where the question of ownership had been settled in the Anglo-French Treaty of Utrecht, but where the boundary between Rupert's Land and Canada was still undefined. Newfoundland had been given to the English by the Utrecht agreement, but the French still claimed fishing rights along the coasts of that island—rights which involved the use of the land itself. This use meant contact, and contact meant conflict. Acadia, which was ceded "with its ancient boundaries" to England, immediately became a source of friction simply because no one knew what the "ancient boundaries" were. For Canada proper, the most acute problem was that involved in protecting the fur trade, which followed the Great Lakes and the St. Lawrence River system. To Englishmen this was the northern boundary of "New England"; to Frenchmen it was the heart of New France.

A fifth area of conflict and mutual distrust lay in the coastal plain of the Gulf of Mexico, where the competition was a three-cornered one for boundaries to separate Carolina and Georgia from Louisiana, and to define the line between Carolina or Georgia and the Spanish lands of Florida. Certain islands in the West Indies also constituted an integral part of the area of Anglo-French struggle for a definite settlement of ownerships in America; but with that part of the story this study can be only incidentally concerned.

The last of the disputed areas to become an actual sore spot in the diplomacy of England and France relative to North America was the Ohio River Valley. Frenchmen and Englishmen had been present in that region for a generation before the Peace of Utrecht. But it was only during and after the War of the Austrian Succession that the potential conflict there burst into flame. It was the spark that flashed beside the Ohio, nonetheless, which ignited the fires of the Seven Years' War, and brought on the struggle that settled the Anglo-French boundary question once and for all.

The cession of the lands about Hudson Bay to England by the Anglo-French Treaty of Utrecht had in that area settled the question of ownership, but not of boundaries. The building, therefore, of a trading post by the French Northwest Company on the upper waters of the Albany River in 1715 tremendously disturbed the Hudson's Bay Company, which promptly petitioned for the settlement of the boundaries as arranged for in the Utrecht treaty.[4] That document had provided that the boundaries separating Rupert's Land from New France, as well as other boundaries in America, should be determined by an Anglo-French joint commission. Largely because of the petition by the Hudson's Bay Company, the British government took steps to have this arrangement carried through. Commissioners were appointed on both sides in 1719, and actually met in Paris.

The British representatives, Martin Bladen and Daniel Pulteney, were instructed to demand a line from Grimington's Island on the coast of

4. Great Britain: *Journal of the Commissioners for Trade and Plantations* (London, 1920—), *November, 1718—December, 1722*, p. 96. Hereafter cited as *Journal of the Board of Trade*. Also Great Britain: *Calendar of State Papers, Colonial Series, America and West Indies* (London, 1922—), *1719–1720*, p. 209. Hereafter cited as *Cal. St. Paps. Col.: A. and W.I.*

Labrador through Lake Mistassini to the line of the forty-ninth degree of north latitude, and along that line to the westward.[5] But the joint commission accomplished nothing, and the British commissioners returned home in disgust.[6] The boundary between Hudson Bay and New France was thus left unsettled, and so it remained. When the Hudson's Bay Company proposed, in 1749, to expand its commerce with the Indians of the far western plains, France saw in the plan a British move to extend the boundaries of the Hudson Bay country to include territory rightfully belonging to New France, and demanded that the boundary be fixed. But Great Britain refused to discuss the matter, chiefly on the ground that the plans of the Hudson's Bay Company, a private organization concerned only with the improvement of its business, could not properly be a subject of French diplomatic concern.[7]

During the three decades following the Peace of Utrecht, the problem of Newfoundland was not an acute one. The Anglo-French treaty had recognized the British ownership of the island, and had granted to France only the privilege of fishing and drying fish along the northern coasts from Cape Bonavista to Pointe Riche. These privileges were the source of some trouble, for the French persisted in fishing south of Cape Bonavista, and the Frenchmen on the south coast, who had taken the oath of allegiance to the British Crown in order to retain their property, still

5. The British commissioners' instructions read as follows: "That the same begin from the Island called Grimington's Island or Cape Perdrix in the Latitude of 58½ North. . . . And further, That a Line be drawn from the South Westward of the Island of Grimington or Cape Perdrix (so as to include the same within the limits of the Bay) to the Great Lake Miscosinke alias Mistosseny, dividing the said Lake into two Parts . . . and that where the said Line shall cut the 49th Degree of Northern Latitude, another Line shall begin and be extended Westward from the said Lake, upon the 49th Degree of Northern Latitude. . . ." *British Diplomatic Instructions, 1689–1789,* II, *France 1689–1721* (Royal Historical Society, *Publications,* Camden Third Series, XXXV. London, 1925), p. 197. Hereafter cited as *Brit. Dip. Instrs.,* II, *France 1689–1721.*

6. *Cal. St. Paps. Col.: A. and W.I. 1722–1723,* p. 83, *et passim.* Beckles Willson, *The Great Company, 1667–1871* (London, 1920), I, 260–261.

7. There was an impression abroad in England, about 1750, that the Hudson Bay boundary had been definitely drawn, under the terms of the Treaty of Utrecht. At least two maps appeared in England during the year 1755 showing a line drawn approximately as described in the instructions to the commissioners of 1719. One map, in French, calls the line the *"Borne entre le Canada et les terres de la Comp: de la Baie de Hudson réglée par des Commissaires après le Traité d'Utrecht."* (*Carte des Possessions Angloises et Françoises du Continent de l'Amérique Septentrionale,* 1755. By "Thos. Kitchin Sculp.") The other calls the line the "Bounds of the Hudson's Bay Company according to the Treaty of Utrecht." (*A New and Accurate Map of the English Empire in North America . . .* By a Society of Anti-Gallicans, 1755.) Both these maps are in the collections of the William L. Clements Library, Ann Arbor, Michigan.

thought and acted as Frenchmen, greatly under the influence of the French establishment on Cape Breton. The British authorities were further annoyed by the development of Placentia as a center of illicit trade with the French colonies.[8]

The Spaniards, too, had been given a vague confirmation of "all such privileges as the Guipuzcoans and other people of Spain are able to claim by right" in the Newfoundland fisheries, and this ambiguous recognition was renewed in the Treaty of Madrid of 1721.[9] The precise meaning of the phrase was not clear; and, although the Spaniards sent very few ships to the Newfoundland fishing grounds, the ambiguity left open the door for much subsequent diplomatic recrimination.

Of all the French and British possessions in North America, it was Acadia that gave the two nations the most trouble. This area had been ceded to Great Britain by the Treaty of Utrecht, but in terms that were inevitably destined to give rise to contention.[10] For Louis XIV ceded "Nova Scotia, otherwise called Acadia, in its entirety, conformable to its former limits; as also the town of Port Royal, now called Annapolis Royal, and generally all the dependencies of the said lands . . ."; the terms of the treaty further stated that "it shall not be permitted to the subjects of the Most Christian King to engage in fishing in the said seas, bays, and other places within thirty leagues of the coasts of Nova Scotia, to the south east, commencing from the island vulgarly called Sable, inclusively, and drawing (a line) thence toward the south west."[11]

What a delectable tangle of terms for the disingenuous diplomat! The language of this article would seem to indicate that, in the minds of the treaty makers, the terms "Acadia" and "Nova Scotia" were synonymous. But the boundaries were not defined; and the ink was hardly dry before the question arose, in virulent form, as to what actually were the boundaries of the land thus vaguely ceded.

The French title to Cape Breton was, of course, clear; and that island furnished both the site for the new fortress of Louisbourg and the base of operations in a campaign of propaganda to conserve the loyalty of the Acadians on the mainland west of the Bay of Fundy and of the Indians residing in the forests between Acadia and New England. This territory was important to France as providing Quebec with a route and outlet to warm water; it was of great strategic importance because it might be-

8. *Journal of the Board of Trade, 1722–1723,* p. 51, *et passim; Cal. St. Paps. Col.: A. and W.I. 1722–1723,* p. 357, *et passim;* Ralph G. Lounsbury, *The British Fishery at Newfoundland, 1634–1763* (New Haven, 1934), pp. 246, 328–329; D. W. Prowse, *A History of Newfoundland* (2d ed. London, 1896), pp. 281–283.

9. Davenport and Paullin, *op. cit.,* III, 230; IV, 26.

10. *Ibid.,* III, 212.   11. *Ibid.*

come a point of easy attack upon Quebec in time of war.[12] Almost immediately after the peace, the English governors began to complain that the
Acadians north and west of the Bay of Fundy were being tampered with
by French priests and other agents, and that they refused either to take
the oath of allegiance or to leave the country, on the ground that it was
still, or soon would be, French.[13] The Indians living in the region of the
St. John River and the Kennebec River were recognized by the French as
holding the key to the region, and for this reason efforts were made to
hold them to the French interest. This was done by sending missionaries to
the Indians, by building posts and churches along the St. John River, and
by annual gifts to the Indians themselves.[14]

Protests were made by British colonial officials to the governors of
Canada against all this interference in British territory, and Lieutenant-
Governor Dummer of Massachusetts sent an "embassy" to Governor
Vaudreuil in 1725 to demand that the French refrain from aiding the
Abenaki Indians of that region in their wars against the British.[15] But it
was a useless mission. The French refused to refrain from inciting and
aiding the Indians against the British, and Vaudreuil prompted the In-
dians to demand that the British evacuate all the territory between the
Saco River and Port Royal.[16] The irregular Anglo-French struggle in the
Maine woods continued; but, despite French efforts to the contrary, the
British made an uneasy peace with the Indians, and the inevitable movement of their fur-trading stations, settlements, and lumber camps upward
along the Kennebec, the Penobscot, and the St. Croix went on.[17]

As the British development of this area continued, and as the realization of the strategic importance of the valleys of the Kennebec and the St.
John became clear, French colonial administrators and diplomats convinced themselves that the Acadia ceded to England by the Treaty of
Utrecht did not include the area between the isthmus and the borders of
New England. Louis XIV and his negotiators at Utrecht had certainly
understood Acadia to include all the coast from the Kennebec River to the
Gulf of St. Lawrence. But either the French colonial officials were now
ignorant of this fact, or they consciously ignored it, and French policy

12. *Collection des Manuscrits relatifs à la Nouvelle France* (Quebec, 1883, 1884),
III, 33, 34, 68, *et passim.* Hereafter cited as *Collection des Manuscrits.*

13. Thomas B. Akins, ed., *Selections from the Public Documents of the Province of
Nova Scotia* (Halifax, 1869), pp. 12 ff. Hereafter cited as *Nova Scotia Archives.*

14. *Collection des Manuscrits,* III, 5, 11, 16, 28, *et passim; Cal. St. Paps. Col.: A.
and W.I. 1719–1720,* pp. xxii–xxiii, *et passim; 1720–1721,* p. 158, *et passim.*

15. E. B. O'Callaghan, ed., *Documents Relative to the Colonial History of the State
of New York* (Albany, 1853–1887), IX, 941–946. Hereafter cited as *N.Y. Col. Docs.*

16. *Ibid.,* IX, 935, 943.   17. *Ibid.,* IX, 989, 1002–1006.

henceforth was aimed at preventing the British from expanding beyond the peninsula.[18]

Meanwhile, the Acadians living around the north end of the Bay of Fundy thought of themselves as Frenchmen, and directed their products and their allegiance along the beaten path that led across the isthmus of Chignecto to Louisbourg and Cape Breton. Early in 1718, a dispute arose between French and English fishermen as to the ownership of the island of Canso, in the course of which the French fishermen were driven from the island and certain French boats were seized.[19] This dispute came to the attention of the Board of Trade at about the time when the Hudson's Bay Company was urging the appointment of the boundary commission provided for by the Treaty of Utrecht; and this question, as well as the more general one pertaining to the limits of Nova Scotia, was included in the instructions to the British commissioners. On the basis of the charter of 1621 granted to Sir William Alexander, and in the light of subsequent occupations, the British negotiators were instructed to demand that Acadia be defined and described as all the land surrendered to the French by Sir Thomas Temple after the Treaty of Breda,[20] or, as somewhat vaguely stated in the instructions, all the land lying between the Kennebec and St. Lawrence rivers and the Atlantic.[21]

In this attempt to define the boundaries of Acadia the commission accomplished nothing. Because of their convictions as to the strategic importance of the Acadian mainland, the French commissioners took the position that Acadia was only the peninsula known by that name, lying east of the Bay of Fundy.[22] As for Canso, they produced maps showing the island in the middle of the strait, and not "depending" upon Acadia. They insisted that it was one of the islands in the Gulf of St. Lawrence clearly assigned to France by the Treaty of Utrecht. They even went so far as to claim the hinterland of Cape Canso, on the mainland, on the ground that it, too, was not properly a part of Acadia. The British com-

18. In 1712 the French negotiators at Utrecht were instructed to secure the restitution of Acadia to France, with "la rivière de Quinibiqui [Kennebec]" as a boundary. (*Archives du Ministère des Affaires Etrangères, Paris. Mémoires et Documents: Amérique*, XXIV: 25. Hereafter cited as AE Méms. et Docs. Amérique.) Louis XIV himself wrote to his plenipotentiaries that, if they succeeded in achieving the restitution, he would consent, as a demonstration of his generosity, to accept the St. George River instead of the Kennebec as a boundary (AE Méms. et Docs. Amérique, XXIV: 84).

19. *Collection des Manuscrits*, III, 29, 30, *et passim*. The island in question lay just to the north of the modern Cape Canso. See Frontispiece.

20. Davenport and Paullin, *op. cit.*, II, 183, 184.

21. *Brit. Dip. Instrs.*, II, *France 1689–1721*, pp. 198–200.

22. *Cal. St. Paps. Col.: A. and W.I. 1720–1721*, p. 135.

missioners, to their great discomfiture, were unable to produce an accurate map with which to counter the French claim.[23]

The question of the boundary of Acadia thus remained unanswered. Slowly, but surely, the British settlements in the region of the Kennebec were growing. The decision of Great Britain to establish a military colony in Nova Scotia gave dramatic emphasis to the French fear that British control of the Acadian mainland would surely mean, in winter, the cutting of communications between Quebec and the sea, and a constant threat of attack upon the heart of Canada in time of war.[24] It was no wonder, then, that immediately after the Peace of Aix-la-Chapelle, the French should have felt themselves on the defensive against an advancing and menacing British expansion in Acadia, or that they should have taken desperate steps to fortify the isthmus of Chignecto and the valley of the St. John before the English should arrive.

The country lying south of the St. Lawrence River and Lakes Erie and Ontario provided much occasion for diplomatic conflict. Here, too, differences arose out of the vagueness of the Anglo-French Treaty of Utrecht and the ever-increasing westward movement of the fur traders. The treaty had provided that the French in Canada should not "molest in the future the Five Nations or tribes of Indians subject to Great Britain, nor the other nations of America friendly to the crown." Similarly, the nationals of Great Britain were not to interfere with the Indians who were "subjects or friends of France"; but the subjects of both might frequent the Indian territories for the sake of trade. The commissioners who were to adjust boundary differences were to decide just which Indians were to be considered subjects or friends of Great Britain, and which were those of France.[25]

But the vague language of the treaty left a good deal to the commissioners who were to be appointed to determine boundaries. The Iroquois, too, refused to accept the European implications of "sovereignty" over

23. *Ibid.*

24. *Collection des Manuscrits,* III, 191–192; *N.Y. Col. Docs.,* X, 220–232.

25. "Les habitans du Canada et autres sujets de la France ne molesteront point à l'avenir les Cinq Nations ou cantons des Indiens soumis à la Grande Bretagne, ny les autres nations de l'Amérique amies de cette couronne. Pareillement les sujets de la Grande Bretagne se comporteront pacifiquement envers les Américains sujet ou amis de la France, et les unes et les autres jouiront d'une pleine liberté de se frequenter pour le bien de commerce, et avec la mesme liberté les habitans de ces regions pourront visiter les colonies Françoises et Britanniques pour l'avantage reciproque de commerce sans aucune molestation, ny empechement de part ny d'autre. Au surplus les Commissaires regleront exactement et distinctement quels seront ceux que seront ou devront estre censez sujets et amis de la France ou de la Grande Bretagne." (Article XV; Davenport and Paullin, *op. cit.,* III, 213.) This article was thought to bring to a final conclusion a long-standing dispute between the French and English over the control of the Iroquois and their lands.

them.[26] The essential stake in the race to control the routes to the upper lakes was the fur trade; and shortly after the Treaty of Utrecht the governors of New York and Quebec both took steps to corner the trade for their respective provinces. As early as 1716, the French revived the idea of an establishment at Niagara, and it became a reality in the post erected by Joncaire in 1720.[27]

This quarrel was not new. It had its beginning in the preceding century, after the defeat of the Iroquois by the Sieur de Tracy in 1666, and in the acrimonious exchanges of Dongan and Denonville over the Iroquois and their lands. At that time the French governor had taken the position that the entire valley of the St. Lawrence was French, by reason of the explorations of Cartier, Champlain, and their successors, and this argument was repeated by the French diplomats in the negotiations of 1686–1687. To this claim the governor of New York and the British diplomatists had replied that the lands of New York extended northward to the "Lakes of Canada" by conquest from the Dutch and by the submission of the Iroquois to the crown of Great Britain on July 30, 1684.[28]

The post-Utrecht struggle for control of the arteries of the fur trade in the region of the lakes was thus but a resumption of the inevitable conflict. The old dispute as to title to the country was renewed; the old arguments as to ownership were reaffirmed. The French laid down the basic principle that all the valleys drained by the rivers explored or settled by Frenchmen belonged to France; the British reasserted their sovereignty over the lands of the Iroquois up to, and even beyond, the lakes, and now cited the so-called Iroquois "deed" of 1701 to substantiate their claim.[29]

When news of the Niagara dispute came to England, the Board of Trade made a gesture toward having the question settled by the joint commission of 1719. But when the Board made inquiry as to what the boundaries of New York actually were, it found that they had never been determined.[30] It had to content itself, therefore, with reserving the right to call up the question later, and with the lame statement that the British crown would protest any "encroachments" upon its territory, and that nothing that might be decided with regard to the boundaries of Nova Scotia or Rupert's Land would be allowed to prejudice British claims to

26. *N.Y. Col. Docs.*, VII, 573; IX, 703. Cf. F. X. Garneau, *Histoire du Canada* (Paris, 1913, 1920), II, 39.

27. This fort was rebuilt in stone in 1726. *N.Y. Col. Docs.*, V, 550, 802–804, *et passim;* Garneau, *op. cit.*, II, 39–40; and H. E. Osgood, *The American Colonies in the Eighteenth Century* (New York, 1924), III, 364 ff.

28. *N.Y. Col. Docs.*, IX, 303–305, 355–356; III, 465–531, 796–797.

29. *Cal. St. Paps. Col.: A. and W.I. 1719–1720*, pp. 32–41; *Report of the Regents of the University on the Boundaries of the State of New York* (Albany, 1874, 1884), I, 106–107, 112–113; Garneau, *op. cit.*, II, 38.

30. *N.Y. Col. Docs.*, V, 530–532.

territory elsewhere on the continent. To anticipate any such "encroachments," the commissioners were instructed to demand that orders be sent
to the governor of Canada to prevent interference with the Iroquois by
Indians allied with the French, and to recall all French missionaries in
Iroquois territory.[31]

Meanwhile, suggestions had been coming from America that steps be
taken to counteract the expansion of the French.[32] The Board of Trade
had recommended, in its report of 1721, that forts be erected at the prin-
cipal passes over the Alleghenies to protect that natural barrier between
the French and the British, and, especially, that posts be built on the
shores of Lake Erie and Lake Ontario, to interrupt French communications between Quebec and Louisiana, and to divert to Albany the fur trade
of the western Indians.[33] The government did not act on this suggestion,
but in 1726 Governor Burnet actually began to build a fort at Oswego.[34]
This was the first British post west of the watershed between the great interior valleys and the Atlantic, the first invasion of those river basins
which, according to the French argument, belong to France by right of
prior discovery, exploration, and settlement. The French ministry made
a diplomatic protest against the building of Fort Oswego as promptly as
the British had protested against Fort Niagara, and linked this "aggression" of the British with their "aggressions" in Acadia. But the French
were not prepared to force the British from this foothold on the lakes, and
contented themselves with secretly inciting the Iroquois to drive the British out of the Indian lands.[35]

From the French point of view the failure to take strong measures
against Oswego was a fatal error. For the British could now present a *fait
accompli* to strengthen their claim to all the Iroquois territory up to, and
even beyond, the lakes ; and, in the Treaty of Albany, of September, 1726,
their position was buttressed by a special reaffirmation of the Iroquois
cession.[36] Moreover, they were now actually in a position easily to sever
the thin line of communications between Canada and Louisiana. Louis XV
thought of the fort at Niagara as of the utmost importance, and he himself had ordered that the log structure there be replaced with a fort of
stone.[37]

By 1730 conditions along the northern frontier of New York had be-

31. *Brit. Dip. Instrs.*, II, *France 1689–1721*, pp. 201, 203–204.
32. *Cal. St. Paps. Col.: A. and W.I. 1719–1720*, pp. 32–41; *N.Y. Col. Docs.*, V, 530–531.
33. *N.Y. Col. Docs.*, V, 602, 619–620, 624.
34. *Ibid.*, V, 802–804; Garneau, *op. cit.*, II, 41.
35. *N.Y. Col. Docs.*, IX, 959–985, 996–1007, 1014–1018.
36. *Report on the Boundaries of New York*, I, 112–113.
37. Garneau, *op. cit.*, II, 39–41.

come those of an armed truce; and the tense situation along the south shore of Lake Ontario was made even more acute by the decision of the governor of Canada, about 1731, to build a fort at Crown Point, near the southern end of Lake Champlain. The English settlements were slowly being extended beyond Albany, up the Hudson and the Mohawk, and the French governor was convinced that a grant had already been made to Peter Schuyler of Albany of lands around Lake Champlain. True to the French principle that the boundary was the watershed, Governor Beauharnois hastened to construct this new post to forestall the anticipated British advance.[38] Diplomatic protest was promptly made to France by the Duke of Newcastle, on the basis of the old argument that the lands about Lake Champlain had been ceded to Great Britain by the Iroquois, who were recognized as British subjects by Article XV of the Treaty of Utrecht.[39] But in vain. The French strengthened their position, and were even reported to be planning to settle Frenchmen along Wood Creek. Great Britain again protested, and seriously considered a plan to locate a colony of Scotchmen in the disputed territory to block the apparent Canadian expansion.[40]

South of the lakes, then, along the Hudson and the Mohawk, the British were expanding; they had built their fort at Oswego, and had established themselves in a position to break the life line of French communications in the interior. The French empire in North America was on the defensive; the British advance must be checked at all costs, if New France was to be preserved. And the place to check it was along the watershed. This had been done successfully by the fort at Crown Point; but the foothold the British had gained at Oswego was a sore threat to the safety of the French dominions. Inevitably, therefore, it was to become the first objective of French strategy in time of war.[41]

Before the outbreak, in 1740, of the War of the Austrian Succession, the Ohio Valley had not become an area of acute friction, for France and Great Britain hardly realized the importance of the great continental interior.[42] The French had, indeed, explored the Mississippi. They had established a chain of forts from Detroit to New Orleans, and had built towns in the Illinois country, and at Vincennes on the Wabash. But apparently they were not familiar with the upper reaches of the Ohio until

38. *N.Y. Col. Docs.*, IX, 1021–1023.   39. *Ibid.*, IX, 1034.
40. *Ibid.*, IX, 1061–1062; Osgood, *op. cit.*, III, 375–376.
41. *N.Y. Col. Docs.*, VI, 121–122, 143, 152; *Journal of the Board of Trade, January, 1734/35—December, 1741*, p. 290; Garneau, *op. cit.*, II, 41–42.
42. Clarence V. Alvord, *The Illinois Country, 1673–1818* (Chicago, 1922), p. 185; Albert T. Volwiler, *George Croghan and the Westward Movement, 1741–1782* (Cleveland, 1926), p. 56.

Léry's expedition in 1729.[43] The British likewise knew little about the "western waters," except that the French were there, and that the British should bestir themselves if they were ever to expand beyond the natural barrier of the Alleghenies.[44]

The colony of Pennsylvania took cognizance, about 1731, of the possibilities of conflict on the Ohio when it learned that the French were claiming "by Virtue of some Treaty," all the lands lying along the rivers of which they controlled the mouths.[45] This claim, if established, would bring the boundaries of French territory within the very frontiers of Pennsylvania and would completely block any British effort to penetrate the country west of the mountains.[46] Shortly afterward, it was reported that the French were building a log fort on the Ohio with a view to excluding British traders.[47] Apparently the Pennsylvanians were already going into this territory, trafficking particularly with the Shawnees.[48] From about 1730 the Pennsylvanians seem to have been going in increasing numbers into the valley of the Ohio, although it was not until about 1740 that British knowledge of the "western waters" became at all clear.[49] About 1743 the first Englishmen reached the French settlements in the Illinois.[50] The establishment of Pickawillany, on the Great Miami, which became a center of British trade and influence, is generally taken to mark the beginning of serious British penetration into the Ohio Valley.[51] Yet the French quickly came to see the significance of British competition. Governor Vaudreuil of Louisiana warned his superiors in 1745, and again in 1747, of the danger of British inroads into the valley, and of the necessity of establishing a fort on the River Wabash to check them.[52] Shortly after the Peace of Aix-la-Chapelle, the Marquis de la Galissonnière, governor of New France, ordered the French commandant at Detroit to oppose, by force if necessary, any and all enterprises that might be at-

43. Wm. M. Darlington, ed., *Christopher Gist's Journals* (Pittsburgh, 1893), p. 27.
44. *N.Y. Col. Docs.*, V, 623–624.
45. The French cited the Treaty of Ryswick as justifying their claims to all the lands drained by the rivers Frenchmen had explored. Cf. Justin Winsor, *The Mississippi Basin* (Boston, 1898), p. 350; *Cal. St. Paps. Col.: A. and W.I. 1719–1720*, p. 32.
46. *Pennsylvania Colonial Records*, III, 402–403.
47. *Pennsylvania Archives*, I, 309–310.
48. *Pennsylvania Colonial Records*, III, 402.
49. *N.Y. Col. Docs.*, IX, 1027; Charles A. Hanna, *The Wilderness Trail* (New York, 1917), I, 315 ff.; Winsor, *op. cit.*, pp. 175–177, 182–183.
50. Alvord, *op. cit.*, p. 186, 186 n.
51. *Ibid.*, p. 187; Volwiler, *op. cit.*, pp. 56 ff.; cf. Hanna, *op. cit.*, I, 315 ff.
52. Pierre Margry, ed., *Mémoires et documents pour servir à l'histoire des origines françaises des pays d'outre-mer. Découvertes et établissements des Français dans l'ouest et dans le sud de l'Amérique Septentrionale (1614–1754)* (Paris, 1879–1888), VI, 661–664.

tempted by the British along the Ohio or its branches.[53] According to La Galissonnière, they had never had any settlements west of the mountains, and must never be allowed to establish themselves there; for such a foothold in the Ohio region would be far more fatal than their establishment at Oswego.[54] In the face of an increasing British penetration into the valley of "la Belle Rivière,"[55] the French governors of Canada and Louisiana were on the defensive, here as elsewhere, and determined to hem in the British behind the Allegheny barrier—the only wall capable of restraining them.

In the south, along the foothills of the Alleghenies, in western Carolina and Georgia, Anglo-French rivalry had appeared not long after the settlement of Charleston. In this region, as in the north, Anglo-French competition was chiefly for the Indian trade, the most important item of which was deerskins, and this competition became particularly acute in the period following the Peace of Utrecht. Shortly after that Peace, the Yamasee War brought about a decline in British prestige and influence among the Indians; nevertheless, the British had already penetrated the Alabama and Tombigbee river basins, and were even reported to have sent envoys to the Natchez, in the neighborhood of the Mississippi River.[56] The Cherokee Indians, long the great friends of the British, were partially won away by the French, and it became one of the great objectives of British policy to win them back.[57] To block British penetration of the interior, the French in 1717 built Fort Toulouse, at the confluence of the Coosa and Tallapoosa rivers, in the country of the Creeks.[58] Shortly afterward, the Spaniards built Fort San Marcos, on San Marcos Bay, in western Florida, to watch both French and British and to maintain Spanish influence among the lower Creeks.[59]

The French government apparently realized the significance of British expansion toward Louisiana. In the generation following the Peace of Utrecht, France's chief concern in this area was to achieve an eastern boundary for Louisiana beyond which the British would not go. Pensacola was taken by the French in 1718, and, as it was regarded as being useless to Spain in any case, France generously suggested that the bound-

53. *Ibid.*, VI, 665. Roland-Michel Barrin, Marquis de la Galissonnière, Governor-General of New France from 1747 to 1749, and later director of the depot of maps for the ministry of marine and admiral in the French navy. He commanded the French fleet which assisted in the capture of Minorca from the British in 1756.

54. *Ibid.*, VI, 665 n.   55. The French name for the Ohio.

56. *Collection des Manuscrits,* III, 13.   57. Winsor, *op. cit.,* pp. 183–184.

58. V. W. Crane, *The Southern Frontier, 1670–1732* (Durham, N.C., 1928), pp. 254–256.

59. *Ibid.,* p. 258; Herbert E. Bolton, ed., *Arredondo's Historical Proof of Spain's Title to Georgia* (Berkeley, 1925), pp. 62, 67.

ary between Louisiana and Florida might be the Apalachicola River.[60] This proposition was refused, however, and the Spaniards returned to Pensacola in 1721, leaving the Perdido River as the *de facto* boundary dividing French Louisiana and Spanish Florida.[61] As between Louisiana and the British colonies, neither the governor of Louisiana nor his home government seems ever to have specified any definite line as a boundary. When the boundary commission of 1719 was being organized, however, the Board of Trade made inquiries as to the boundaries of the southern colonies. Dr. Daniel Coxe, who appeared before the Board several times during the summer of 1719, testified that the western boundary of Carolina was the Mississippi. On this same occasion, Joshua Gee, the economist, said the "natural bounds" of Carolina were formed by the Appalachian Mountains, although he had heard that the charter extended "as far as California."[62] A Mr. Byth, who had lived and traded among the Indians along the Coosa River, on which the French also had a settlement, testified that the British had traded with the Creeks for some thirty years, thus implying that British ownership extended at least that far.[63] The Carolina proprietors, however, claimed title to the lands of the Cherokees, along the Tennessee River, up to the Mississippi, and to the westward through the lands of the Chickasaws and the Creeks to the Gulf of Mexico. They asked that the frontier be fortified by military posts on the Altamaha and the Chattahoochee, and that the French be driven from Fort Toulouse, if possible.[64] It was hoped that the question of boundaries might be settled by the commission of 1719, but because of the lack of dependable information, the Board omitted any specific mention of Carolina in the commissioners' instructions, contenting itself with the general statement already cited.[65]

From all this it appears that a general fear of the effects of French colonial activity was aroused in British minds by such events as the settlement of Louisiana and the fortification of such posts as Niagara in the north—a fear which was expressed in the report of the Board of Trade in September, 1721.[66] At this time the British felt themselves distinctly on the defensive against French expansion; and the immediate result of the agitation for defense was the erection of Fort King George at the mouth of the Altamaha, in 1721. Ultimately, the founding of the colony of

60. France: *Recueil des Instructions données aux ambassadeurs et ministres de France depuis les Traités de Westphalie jusqu'à la Révolution Française*, XII, Espagne, pp. 374–376. Hereafter cited as *Recueil des Instructions*.

61. Crane, *op. cit.*, pp. 261–263.

62. *Journal of the Board of Trade, November, 1718—December, 1722*, p. 87.

63. *Ibid.*, p. 99.   64. Crane, *op. cit.*, p. 230.

65. *Brit. Dip. Instrs.*, II, *France 1689–1721*, pp. 196–205.

66. *N.Y. Col. Docs.*, V, 591–630.

Georgia was inspired, at least in part, by this same feeling. Fort King George was built "as a strategic move in the Anglo-French conflict for the West. Not Oswego in 1727, but Altamaha in 1721, saw the inception of the British eighteenth-century scheme of frontier posts to counteract French expansion."[67]

The colony of Georgia, with its sea-to-sea charter, was a slap in the face for both France and Spain; and Oglethorpe's treaty with the Creeks, Cherokees, Choctaws, and Chickasaws, in 1733, seemed to threaten French power in the lower Mississippi Valley. From this time on—indeed, from the erection of Fort King George—Spain's voice was joined with that of France in protest against the expansion of British settlements southward, and the Spanish troops at St. Augustine were made ready to check the British advance by *force majeure*, if necessary.

The Spanish government had vigorously protested against the building of Fort King George. Spain could appeal to the Treaty of Madrid (1670), by which England and Spain mutually recognized their respective holdings, and to the Anglo-Spanish Treaty of Utrecht (1713), by which Great Britain not only recognized, but also guaranteed, the boundaries of the Spanish colonies in America as they had existed at the time of King Charles II of Spain, or roughly, in 1700. England had not held a single foot of territory south of Charleston in 1670, nor had she acquired any since that time. The land south of Charleston, therefore, was Spanish, by right of exploration and a hundred years of actual occupation, and the British movement southward was clearly an invasion of Spanish soil.[68]

The diplomatic argument over Fort King George subsided after the accidental destruction of the fort by fire. Thereafter, various attempts were made to settle the Carolina-Florida boundary by joint commission, but without tangible results.[69] The Treaty of Seville (1729) provided for the establishment of limits in the colonies, but the provision was never carried out.[70] After the settlement of Georgia, the question of boundaries flared up again, both in Europe and in America. In 1736 James Oglethorpe came to an agreement with Governor Sánchez of Florida, by which Oglethorpe agreed to retire his troops from San Juan Island, just north of St. Augustine, an island which he had occupied, and to suspend further military action until the boundary could be settled by the home governments. But the agreement left the British in possession of practically all

67. Crane, *op. cit.*, pp. 233–234.

68. John Tate Lanning, *The Diplomatic History of Georgia* (Chapel Hill, 1936), pp. 11–27.

69. Manuel Serrano y Sanz, ed., *Documentos Históricos de la Florida y la Luisiana, Siglos XVI al XVIII* (Madrid, 1912), pp. 243–260; Bolton, *op. cit.*, pp. 70, 71, 177–188; Crane, *op. cit.*, pp. 235–253; Lanning, *op. cit.*, p. 233.

70. Davenport and Paullin, *op. cit.*, IV, 46–49.

the land they had occupied, and Sánchez's treaty was so little liked by his home government that he was reported to have been hanged for his pains.[71]

In 1739 another attempt was made by Great Britain and Spain, in the Convention of the Pardo, to agree upon a boundary by the agency of a joint commission. The commission actually met, but failed to accomplish anything, and the Georgia boundary question was left to the arbitrament of arms.[72] During the War of Jenkins' Ear, France and Spain agreed to join forces for the destruction of Georgia and the restoration of a boundary acceptable to themselves,[73] but the plan never reached the stage of action. The indecisive treaties that ended the war left the Georgia boundary question still unsettled; but, curiously enough, this issue failed to enter prominently into Anglo-Spanish diplomacy until, with the defeat of Spain in the Seven Years' War, there arose the proposal to cede Florida in its entirety to Great Britain. With that cession, the Florida boundary question reached a real, though temporary, settlement.

Thus the outbreak of the twofold third intercolonial war found many boundary controversies in North America crying for settlement. Specifically, these disputes existed in most acute form in the case of Rupert's Land, Acadia, the region of the Great Lakes, the Ohio Valley, the lower Mississippi Valley, and the Georgia-Florida frontier. Nor did the war, or the peace that ended it, bring any of these conflicts to a satisfactory conclusion. The War of Jenkins' Ear was essentially a colonial war, fought for colonial and commercial objectives; yet the colonial issues were in large measure forgotten when the attention of Spain was directed to the struggle for Italy, and that of Great Britain to the French threat in the Low Countries. The Anglo-French war that broke out in 1744 was concerned chiefly with the European balance of power; and Louisbourg was returned to France through the Treaty of Aix-la-Chapelle, by the clause that restored the international situation to the *status quo ante bellum*.

The treaty, therefore, left the colonial boundary situation untouched. But it had hardly been signed before the problem arose again in a new and doubly acute form. Both sides began to realize that the time had come to settle the question, once and for all. For immediately the British traders, land speculators, and colonists commenced to move over the divide into the valleys claimed by France, particularly in the region of the Ohio. As that movement got under way, British imperialists became acutely conscious of the French iron ring that hemmed them in, while French colonial statesmen became more than ever convinced that the only way to block penetration into New France was to confine the British behind the

71. Lanning, *op. cit.*, p. 48.   72. *Ibid.*, pp. 124–173.
73. Davenport and Paullin, *op. cit.*, IV, 65.

mountains and the height of land. And this conviction was supported by the age-old French contention that France owned in their entirety the river valleys explored by Frenchmen.

In the eyes of Great Britain the problem was one of maintaining for the British colonies a freedom of unhampered westward expansion. This concept had taken root among certain British imperialists at the time of the Peace of Utrecht, and it found classic expression in the report of the Board of Trade on the state of the British plantations in America, dated September 8, 1721.[74] The Board made a point of the recent establishment of French settlements in the neighborhood of Nova Scotia and Carolina, and recommended the building of forts in these two regions and on the Great Lakes. For Nova Scotia it proposed active colonization by four regiments of soldiers; similarly, for Carolina it suggested the building of forts at strategic points to guarantee British control of the rivers flowing into the Atlantic, and particularly the Altamaha. As for the great interior, the report recommended that immediate steps be taken to guarantee to Englishmen the Indian trade beyond the mountains:

Although these Mountains may serve at present for a very good frontier, we should not propose them for the boundary of your Majesty's Empire in America. On the contrary, it were to be wished that the British Settlements be extended beyond them, and some small forts erected on the great Lakes, in proper places, by permission of the Indian proprietors. . . .[75]

The forts thus proposed were to be built on Lake Erie, at Niagara, at the heads of the Potomac and the Susquehanna rivers, and on the Savannah, Chattahoochee, and Hagaloge rivers in Carolina.[76]

Here is expressed the idea, common to Englishmen and colonials of the generation following the Treaty of Utrecht, that the English settlements would sooner or later extend beyond the mountains. But this concept preceded the actual population movement. Georgia was founded, to be sure, as a part of an expansion of the old colonies that was at once aggressive and defensive. But it was not until after the War of the Austrian Succession that any considerable number of Englishmen began to move over the mountain barrier. When they did, and the movement came to be general, actual conflict with the French became inevitable. The settlement of Nova Scotia, the growth of the western Indian trade of New York and Pennsylvania, the land settlement schemes of the Grand Ohio Company of Virginia, as well as the revived Georgia and Carolina trade with the Creeks and the Cherokees, were all aspects of the same phenomenon. The British westward movement had reached the mountains and was sending the first small trickles of the oncoming flood down the other side.

74. *N.Y. Col. Docs.*, V, 591–630.   75. *Ibid.*, V, 624.   76. *Ibid.*, V, 625.

The French were not slow to realize what was happening. For them the North American problem had now become, more than ever before, one of defense; and the man who saw, more clearly perhaps than anyone else, the true significance of the impending struggle was La Galissonnière, the Governor-General. La Galissonnière returned to France in 1749, and wrote an able and penetrating report of the intercolonial situation in North America, which may be taken as expressing the basic principles of French colonial policy until the accession to power of the Duke de Choiseul.[77]

Beginning with a mercantilistic justification of the necessity of colonies for a great state, La Galissonnière admitted that Canada and Louisiana had been a net loss to the mother country and that they were at best very difficult to defend. Nevertheless, "motives of honor, glory and religion" demanded that they be not surrendered; and the anticipated profits to be derived from such rich and extensive territories made it both immoral and unpatriotic to contemplate allowing New France to slip out of French hands. But the weightiest argument for its retention lay in the fact that it furnished an effective barrier to the expansion of the empire of Great Britain,

whose power is daily increasing, and which, if means be not found to prevent it, will soon absorb not only all the Colonies located in the neighboring islands of the Tropic, but even all those of the Continent of America . . . if the rapid progress of the English Colonies on the Continent be not arrested, or what amounts to the same thing, if a counterpoise capable of confining them within their limits, and of forcing them to the defensive, be not formed, they will possess, in a short time, such great facilities to construct formidable armaments on the Continent of America, and will require so little time to convey a large force either to St. Domingo or to the Island of Cuba, or to our Windward islands, that it will not be possible to hope to preserve these except at an enormous expense.[78]

Thus La Galissonnière based his reasoning upon motives of honor, religion, and future profit, but chiefly upon the necessity of blocking the westward march of the British, both for the preservation of New France and for the establishment of an effective barrier between the British colonies and the Spanish possessions of Mexico.

But how were the British to be stopped? In the first place, said La Galissonnière, Louisbourg must be preserved and strengthened. The British in Acadia must be confined to the peninsula; the true boundaries of Acadia, he said, extended merely around the coast from Port Royal to

77. The report is printed in *N.Y. Col. Docs.*, X, 220–232.
78. *Ibid.*, X, 223.

Cape Canso. Furthermore, it seemed to him that it was of extreme importance to preserve the St. John River to France, for, as has been indicated, this was the only route from Quebec to the sea during the winter while the St. Lawrence River was frozen. To allow this important passage to the interior to fall into the hands of England would be seriously to jeopardize the safety of New France in time of war. Similarly, the passes over the mountain barrier must be fortified against the English, and forts must be maintained at Crown Point, at Niagara, at Detroit, and on the upper Ohio. Moreover, strong settlements should be made on Lake Champlain, at Detroit, in the Illinois, and in Louisiana. On the other hand, nothing should be left undone, he said, to destroy the British post at Oswego, and to prevent the British from establishing themselves on the upper Ohio. The natural boundary of New France was the Allegheny highland, and the French claim to this boundary was established by the French discovery, exploration, and possession of the river valleys to the westward, which went back to the time of Champlain and La Salle. La Galissonnière effectively demonstrated—to his own satisfaction—how untenable was the claim of the British to the lands of the Iroquois, and pointed out to his government that, were the British allowed to extend their posts or their settlements beyond the mountains, every such extension would be a threat at the heart of New France and would place the British in a position easily to cut the life line of communication between Canada and Louisiana. For him, the preservation of New France was vital to the preservation of the greatness of old France, and the preservation of New France depended upon stopping the expansion of the British, once and for all, at the mountains.

For such reasons France sought, immediately after the Peace of Aix-la-Chapelle, to clinch its possession of the St. John River and the Ohio, and to strengthen its positions on Lake Champlain, in the Gulf coastal plain, and along the long line of communications from Quebec to New Orleans. At the same time she prepared to seize, at the earliest possible moment and by any possible means, the British position at Oswego. In the eyes of the French the British colonies were on the march. New France was on the defensive, and, if it was to be preserved at all, the first line of defense must be established along the St. John River and the Allegheny divide.

Such, then, were the two sides in the conflict that existed between Frenchmen and Englishmen when, after the Peace of Aix-la-Chapelle, statesmen on both sides began to realize that the old, old boundary question must now be definitely and finally decided. In the fifteen years following the Peace of Aix-la-Chapelle, three distinct methods were used in the effort to decide where the Anglo-French boundary in North America should be. The first attempt was made by an Anglo-French joint commission created in 1749, which struggled with the problem intermittently from 1750 until the outbreak of war in 1756. The second attempt was made through the channels of direct diplomacy in 1754 and 1755. Meanwhile, both nations had attempted to improve their positions in America by military movements which precipitated armed conflict along the frontiers and forced the dispute to the arbitrament of war. It was this third method that finally carried the English frontier to the Mississippi.

CHAPTER II

DIPLOMATIC FUTILITY: THE ANGLO-FRENCH COMMISSION ON COLONIAL BOUNDARIES 1750–1754

The Treaty of Aix-la-Chapelle, signed October 18, 1748, had little to say of America, and less of the ominous friction being generated by the contact of two expanding colonial empires. It specified merely that conquered territory would be mutually returned, whether in Europe or in the Indies, East or West.[1] Far from settling the boundary conflicts in North America, it did not even mention them. It could be said to take cognizance of those matters only in so far as they might vaguely be affected by the renewal of the provisions of the Treaty of Utrecht.[2] The Treaty of Aix-la-Chapelle, as a matter of fact, could hardly do more than mark one of the "spells of rest in a great contest," however genuinely its makers may have hoped that it might be otherwise.[3] The one specific provision with regard to North America was that Cape Breton, taken from France during the war, was to be restored; England was to send two "peers of Great Britain" to Paris as hostages for the return of that important island. Otherwise, the *status quo ante bellum* in the colonial world was to be restored,[4] and debts incurred by prisoners of war, in whatever part of the world, were guaranteed by the signatory powers of which the prisoners were subjects.[5] Finally, in Article XVIII there was an omnibus proviso that certain European questions, "and other articles, which could not be regulated, so as to enter into the present treaty, shall be amicably adjusted immediately by the commissaries appointed for that purpose, on both sides, or otherwise, as shall be agreed on by the powers concerned."[6]

Even before the treaty was signed, however, the machinery of diplomacy was set in motion to iron out the wrinkles remaining in the fabric of peace. The Preliminary Articles, signed on April 30,[7] had provided for a cessation of hostilities, to take place, on land, within six weeks, and, at sea, within certain given periods that varied in different zones according

1. Article V. The treaty is printed entire in *A Collection of All the Treaties of Peace, Alliance, and Commerce, between Great Britain and Other Powers, from the Revolution in 1688, to the Present Time* (London, 1772), II, 68–85. Hereafter cited as *All the Treaties*.
2. Article III, *loc. cit.*
3. Cf. *Brit. Dip. Instrs., 1689–1789*, VII, *France 1745–1789*, p. xi.
4. Article IX, *loc. cit.*   5. Article IV, *loc. cit.*
6. Article XVIII, *loc. cit.*
7. Davenport and Paullin, *op. cit.*, IV, 68–69.

to their distance from Europe.[8] But for one reason or another the signature of the definitive treaty was delayed until October 18, long after the given periods fixed by the Preliminary Articles had elapsed. Some doubt was bound to arise in the minds of naval captains and commanders of privateers as to what their powers were after the expiration of the given periods, but before the signature of peace. Many of them actually again began to seize enemy shipping. For this reason the three contracting powers[9] agreed, in a separate joint statement of July 8, 1748, to appoint commissioners to go to St. Malo, to adjust the claims for restitutions and indemnities arising out of these seizures.[10] This commission duly met, not, apparently, within the two months provided in the declaration of July 8, but early in 1749. England was represented by a Mr. Allix and a Mr. Hinde, who went with instructions to negotiate both on prizes taken since the signing of the Preliminaries and on the exchange of prisoners made at sea during the entire war.[11] But when they began their conferences with M. Guillot, the French commissioner, they found that he was instructed to propose the restitution of prizes made during and even before the war. Difficulties also arose as to a definition of the limits of the English Channel, and because of the refusal of the French to negotiate with regard to prizes already adjudged by the regular courts of admiralty.[12] The result was that this abortive commission at St. Malo accomplished nothing.

The British government had by this time sent the Earl of Sussex and Lord Charles Cathcart to France as hostages for the restitution of Cape Breton under Article IX of the treaty of peace,[13] with instructions to exchange with the French foreign minister, M. de Puysieulx,[14] copies of the orders sent to French and English commanders and governors for the

8. According to Article III of the Anglo-French agreement for a cessation of arms, signed at Paris August 19, 1712; that is to say, within twelve days in the English Channel and the North Sea, within six weeks in the North Atlantic from the Channel to the Equator, and within six months in all parts of the world "beyond the Line." Davenport and Paullin, *op. cit.,* III, 165.

9. England, France, Holland.

10. Davenport and Paullin, *op. cit.,* IV, 72; CL William Mildmay Papers—"Memorials." The papers of William Mildmay in the William L. Clements Library are arranged in four sets, entitled "Memorials," "Conferences," "Letters from Paris," and "Private Letters from Paris." They will be cited hereafter as CL Mildmay Papers—"Memorials," etc.

11. The instructions are dated 27 Oct. 1748. CL Mildmay Papers—"Memorials."

12. "Extracts of Letters, from Messrs. Allix and Hinde," etc. CL Mildmay Papers —"Letters from Paris."

13. George Augustus Yelverton, Earl of Sussex, and Charles Cathcart, Baron Cathcart. *British Diplomatic Representatives, 1689–1789* (Royal Historical Society, *Publications,* Camden Third Series, XLVI, London, 1932), p. 20. Hereafter cited as *Brit. Dip. Reps.*

14. Louis-Philogène Brulart de Sillery, Marquis de Puysieulx, minister of foreign affairs, 1747–1751.

restitution of conquests, both in the East Indies and in America.[15] At the same time, permanent ambassadors were named by the two courts;[16] but as they did not take up their residences in London and Paris until late in July, 1749,[17] the diplomatic business of the two countries was carried on by *chargés d'affaires:* in London by M. Durand for France, and in Paris by Colonel Yorke for England.[18]

The old conflicts in America began to make trouble for these diplomats almost before the ink was thoroughly dry on the Treaty of Aix-la-Chapelle. The orders to colonial governors exchanged by the British hostages and Puysieulx had provided, in general, for the restoration of conditions to the *status quo ante bellum,* both in the West Indies and in North America. The restitution of Cape Breton made little difficulty,[19] but it was soon found that the two courts were at wide variance as to what the *status quo* actually was in the other areas of America.

The first difference of opinion arose over the situation in the West Indies, where, in accord with an agreement of 1730, the so-called "neutral islands," St. Lucia, St. Vincent, and Dominica, were to be evacuated by both nations and left in the possession of the natives.[20] For, immediately after the war, both French and British made plans to occupy the islands of St. Lucia and Tobago—the latter of which was not included in the agreement of 1730—and there took place an angry exchange of diplomatic charges and countercharges of bad faith.[21]

Out of these interchanges came the proposal immediately to settle all the American disputes by a joint Anglo-French commission. In several interviews that Yorke had with Puysieulx and the Count de Maurepas,

15. *Correspondence of John, Fourth Duke of Bedford* (London, 1842–1846), I, 561–562, 592–593. Hereafter cited as *Bedford Correspondence.*

16. For France, the Duke de Mirepoix, and for England, William Anne Keppel, Earl of Albemarle. *Ibid.; Brit. Dip. Reps.,* pp. 20–21; *Brit. Dip. Instrs.,* VII, *France 1745–1789,* pp. 1, 2.

17. *Archives of the Dominion of Canada,* Ottawa. Transcripts from the *Archives du Ministère des Affaires Etrangères,* Paris. *Correspondence Politique: Angleterre,* 426: 306, 396. Hereafter cited as CAO AE CP Ang.; *Brit. Dip. Instrs.,* VII, *France 1745–1789,* p. 5.

18. *Brit. Dip. Reps.,* p. 20; *Bedford Correspondence,* I, *passim.* CAO AE CP Ang. 426, *passim.* Copy of Yorke's credentials, January 24, 1748/49, *The Public Record Office,* London. Chatham manuscripts, LXXXV. Hereafter cited as PRO Chatham MSS.

19. *Collection des Manuscrits,* III, 426–436.

20. "Extrait de la Lettre écrite par M. [le] Comte de Maurepas à M. de Caylus, le 29 Novembre 1748," and copies of orders to the English Governor Grenville of Barbados and the French Governor Caylus of Martinique. CL Mildmay Papers—"Memorials"; *Brit. Dip. Instrs.,* VII, *France 1745–1789,* pp. 2, 3.

21. CAO AE CP Ang. 426:20–21; *Library of Congress,* Washington Transcripts from the Additional Manuscript Series in the British Museum, 32816:328. Hereafter cited as LC Add. MSS.; CL Mildmay Papers—"Memorials."

minister of marine, in April, 1749, both these statesmen intimated that France would like to settle the disputes in the West Indies by a joint commission.[22] This suggestion was received coolly by the British cabinet, but it was renewed in June, by Durand, now under instructions to include in it all the colonial disputes in America.[23]

The colonial conflict was rapidly spreading; and several developments were arousing the apprehensions of the French government. In England, a Mr. Arthur Dobbs was bringing forward a scheme to extend the trading activities of the Hudson's Bay Company into the great plains west and southwest of the bay. At about the same time, the establishment of a military colony at Halifax on Chebucto Bay, in Nova Scotia, was authorized as a counterpoise to the French fortress of Louisbourg. France was frightened. Dobbs' scheme had all the appearances of a plan to extend the lands of the Hudson's Bay Company into territories belonging to New France. The projected colonization of Nova Scotia raised the old specter of the British claim to an Acadia extending to the St. Lawrence. Indeed, in the West Indies, in Acadia, and in Rupert's Land the British seemed to have adopted a policy of aggressive expansion. On the other hand, French statesmen saw in the rising disputes an opportunity to revive the old French claim to Canso which had been left ungratified by the abortive conference of 1719.[24]

In view of this apparent British expansion in Nova Scotia and Rupert's Land, Durand was instructed to seek reassurance on the subject of Acadia and to demand that orders be sent to the British commanders in Nova Scotia and the ports about Hudson Bay restraining them from extending the settlements of those colonies into territory owned by France. With regard to Acadia, the French demanded that English settlements be not extended beyond the "anciennes limites" of the province, as provided by the Treaty of Utrecht. These boundaries were defined as including merely the peninsula of the present-day Nova Scotia up to the isthmus separating it from the mainland. The lands from the isthmus to the borders of New England were to be recognized as a part of New France, as was the island of Canso, which, as in 1719, the French claimed to be properly one of the islands of the Gulf of St. Lawrence reserved to France by the Treaty of Utrecht.[25]

22. LC Add. MSS. 32816:328.

23. CAO AE CP Ang. 426:171–174, 196–201; "Mémoire de M. Durand au sujet de la Nouvelle Ecosse de June 7, 1749," CL Mildmay Papers—"Memorials."

24. CAO AE CP Ang. 426:20–21, 196–201, et passim; "Mémoire de M. Durand au sujet de la Nouvelle Ecosse de June 7, 1749," CL Mildmay Papers—"Memorials." For the settlement at Halifax, see J. Bartlet Brebner, New England's Outpost (New York, 1927), chap. vii.

25. CAO AE CP Ang. 426:20–21, 171–174, 196–201. Supra, pp. 7–8.

In addition to these specific territorial assurances, Durand demanded that commissioners be appointed to arrange the boundaries of the possessions of the two nations in North America and to take up the task, as suggested by Maurepas and Puysieulx to Yorke, of deciding the ownership of Caribbean islands now in dispute between the two Crowns. These demands were based upon Article X of the Treaty of Utrecht and upon Article IX of the Treaty of Aix-la-Chapelle.[26]

The Duke of Bedford, British Secretary of State for the Southern Department, received Durand's communication with great coolness. Canso, he said, was obviously one of the "dependent isles" of Acadia ceded to England by the Treaty of Utrecht, and, therefore, not a subject for discussion between the two Crowns. The schemes of Mr. Dobbs in the Hudson Bay region were merely for the development of the commerce of a private English company within its own territory; the debate in parliament had to do only with the question of whether the trade of this great territory should be left in the hands of a private company or opened to all British subjects. As matters purely of internal concern to the British Empire, both these questions were ruled out of further diplomatic discussion.[27]

As to the possible usefulness of the proposed joint commission, Bedford was frankly skeptical. He had already expressed his doubts when a similar suggestion was first made for a solution of the West Indian question. If the commissioners already appointed, and now meeting at St. Malo, had been utterly unable to agree upon such inconsequential matters as prizes and prisoners of war, he asked, how would a new body be able to settle such an important issue as the ownership of territory which both nations had long looked upon as their own?[28] Yet the British government, he said, wishing to demonstrate its sincere desire for peace, was willing to appoint representatives to attempt to determine the ownership of the disputed islands.[29]

In July, 1749, then, the British government expressed a willingness to assign all the American disputes to a joint Anglo-French commission. To that end, the fruitless conference still working at St. Malo was to þe

26. CAO AE CP Ang. 426:200vo. The phrase in Durand's instructions reads, "These demands are founded . . . on Article IX of the Treaty of Aix-la-Chapelle, according to which nothing new is to be undertaken either in the West Indies or in the East Indies." The sentence in the treaty, upon which this expression is based, reads "And all things besides shall be restored to the condition that they were or ought to have been in before the present war." Davenport and Paullin, *op. cit.,* IV, 74. Apparently, the French consciously or unconsciously distorted the meaning of this article to suit the needs of the moment.

27. "La Réponse du D. de Bedford au Mémoire du Sr· Durand," CL Mildmay Papers—"Memorials."

28. CAO AE CP Ang. 426:209–210.

29. CAO AE CP Ang. 426:209–210, 306.

abandoned and another set of negotiators appointed to meet in Paris.[30] These new commissioners would have instructions to regulate the limits of the two empires in Acadia and the other parts of North America, and to determine the ownership of the disputed islands in the Caribbean, as well as new instructions for the settlement of the questions of prizes and prisoners that had been so troublesome at St. Malo. Bedford insisted, however, that discussion of Canso and Hudson Bay must be excluded.[31]

It was thus agreed to set up a new joint commission, with extended powers, to replace the one working at St. Malo. Obviously, the commissioners must come to their meeting prepared to deal with the same problems, and in the same terms; and there followed a painful discussion of just what they should be instructed to do. The first English memorandum was based upon the assumption that they would concern themselves with three problems: first, the disputes of the two countries over territories in America; second, the entire problem presented by the prisoners of war taken at sea during the war, and the money settlements to be made on their account; and third, the prizes taken at sea when hostilities had presumably ceased.[32]

The French were especially concerned about the powers to be given the commissioners with regard to the settlement of the North American boundary, a point lightly passed over in the English memorandum. According to the French view, the representatives of the two countries should be given ample powers to arrange the boundaries between the two nations in America and to decide the ownership of St. Lucia, Tobago, St. Vincent, and Dominica, "as well as all other lands in America which might be matters of contention between the two nations."[33] Yet this preliminary exchange was almost useless; for, when the commissioners fi-

30. "La Réponse du D. de Bedford au Mémoire du S^r· Durand," and Bedford to Yorke, July 6, 1749, CL Mildmay Papers—"Memorials"; CAO AE CP Ang. 426:396.
31. CL Mildmay Papers—"Memorials"; CAO AE CP Ang. 426:367.
32. "Sketch of a Plan for the Commissioners who are to meet at Paris," CL Mildmay Papers—"Memorials." In order to simplify the labors of the commission it was felt the two courts should agree upon certain other points which had made trouble for the negotiators at St. Malo. These were, first, a definition of the limits of the English Channel; second, an agreement as to the given periods within which hostilities should have ceased after the signature of the preliminaries, between Cape St. Vincent and the Line; and, third, the arrangement of a convention between the two Crowns to provide indemnities for the owners of ships taken by vessels of war since hostilities should have ceased. The French commissioner at St. Malo had proposed the discussion of prizes taken before the war; but the English memorandum again ruled this out, on the ground that Article IV of the Treaty of Aix-la-Chapelle made provision for the restoration only of prizes made after the expiration of the given periods agreed upon in the Preliminaries—which was true. This question of prizes made before the declaration of war was of great importance to France, and nearly wrecked the commission before it began its work.
33. "Mémoire de la Cour de France pour les Instructions à donner aux commis-

nally met, it was found that the actual instructions on both sides followed these memoranda without any sign of compromise. Apparently the only point agreed upon was the given period within which hostilities should have ceased between Cape St. Vincent and the Line![34]

Neither party to the many disputes in North America trusted the other. Each knew that the claims of its opponent in the period preceding the war had been such as greatly to reduce, were those claims granted, the extent of its own theoretical but as yet unoccupied empire. Even while the arrangements for peaceful adjustment were being made, therefore, steps were being taken in America to make sure that the unoccupied territory claimed on either side should be eliminated from diplomatic discussion—that the "disputed territories" should not include those regarded as "incontestably" belonging to one or the other. This meant that the conversations would refer only to the territories to which, as a matter of fact, one side did not even pretend to have a claim. Both litigants tried thus to evade the real issue; but it was a deliberate and systematic policy only on the part of France.[35] Her ministers and colonial officials, alarmed by the visible English threat to the natural boundaries that had for so long been the *de facto* frontiers between the two systems, put in motion a program of defensive occupations that was continental in scope. It was their hope that the *faits accomplis* that could be presented to the commission might prove useful in the business of wringing the desired concessions from the British.[36] All along the line French colonial governors began hurriedly to take such steps as might leave no room for doubt as to what France considered the unquestionable boundaries of its territory.

The Marquis de la Galissonnière, in his relatively short experience in America, had become convinced that the true boundaries between the British and the French in North America were the isthmus of Nova Scotia, the Kennebec River, the watershed between the St. Lawrence Basin and the Atlantic, and the Allegheny Mountains.[37] In Acadia, however, he saw the most vulnerable point in the French line of defense; for, again, the St. John River, which had its source within a day's march of

saires pour le règlement des Limites en Amérique et des Prises faites en mer," "Réponse au Mémoire intitulé Projet des Instructions pour les Commissaires qui doivent s'assembler à Paris," and "Mémoire d'Observations sur le Projet d'Instructions pour les Com^rs. Anglais," CL Mildmay Papers—"Memorials"; also CL Mildmay Papers—"Letters from Paris," *passim*.

34. "Memorial in Reply to the Answers and Objections of the French Court to the Plan of Instructions for the Commissarys to Settle Limits and Prizes," CL Mildmay Papers—"Letters from Paris"; *ibid*.—"Memorials"; *ibid*.—"Conferences," pp. 1–4.

35. *N.Y. Col. Docs.*, X, 220–232.

36. *Collection des Manuscrits*, III, 452–455; *N.Y. Col. Docs.*, X, 220–232.

37. *N.Y. Col. Docs.*, X, 220–232.

Quebec, furnished the only practicable overland route from Quebec to the sea—a matter of vital importance to New France during the long Canadian winters when the St. Lawrence River was frozen over. Because of the already-mentioned vital importance of this line of communication to the defense of Quebec, if for no other reason, La Galissonnière believed France must retain control of such a road to Louisbourg.[38] Even before the ministry realized what he was doing, the French governor began a series of moves calculated to make his policy of defense a reality before it should be too late. His action was the more acceptable to the ministry, however, as reports of the debates in parliament and the projected settlement of Nova Scotia seemed to indicate an aggressive program of British colonial expansion. Orders were sent to him and to Vaudreuil, governor of Louisiana, to watch the movements of the British in America with a view to forestalling them.[39] The year 1749 was thus marked by active efforts of the French to establish themselves in Acadia, to destroy the fort at Oswego through the secretly inspired agency of the Five Nations, to discourage the efforts of the British in the Ohio Valley, and by Vaudreuil's attempts to crush the Chickasaws, allies of the British, by using the pro-French faction of the Choctaws.[40]

This continental conflict first broke out in Acadia. Governor Mascarene of Nova Scotia, shortly after the Preliminary Articles had been signed, began to exact new oaths of loyalty from the Acadians on the isthmus, and sent Lieutenant Colonel John Gorham to exact the oath from the Acadians living on the west side of the Bay of Fundy. Gorham's boats were fired upon, and his actions called forth the immediate protest of La Galissonnière, who claimed that the St. John River lay entirely within lands dependent upon the government of Canada.[41] Mascarene, for his part, replied that the territory was a part of Acadia, that the French inhabitants of the St. John River valley were therefore subjects of the British Crown, and that he would continue to regard them as such until some settlement of the boundaries or orders from home should compel him to think otherwise. In this he was vigorously supported by Governor William Shirley of Massachusetts.[42]

This exchange, in the winter of 1748–1749, was quickly followed by

---

38. *Ibid.*, X, 226.

39. LC Add. MSS. 32817:118; *Report concerning Canadian Archives, 1905* (Ottawa, 1906), I, Part VI, p. 110. Hereafter cited as *Canadian Archives.*

40. "Instances of perfidious and dishonorable Hostility in the French in Time of Peace; being Matters of Fact, extracted .from the Letters of Mr. (*sic*) Vaudreuil, Governor of Louisiana, to the Court of France," *Henry E. Huntington Library,* San Marino, California. Loudoun manuscripts, 198 A & B. Hereafter cited as HL LO; *N.Y. Col. Docs.*, X, 219–220; Margry, *op. cit.*, VI, 662–665.

41. *N.Y. Col. Docs.*, VI, 478–481.   42. *Ibid.*, VI, 481, 482–484.

more warlike moves. La Galissonnière was determined that the British must not be allowed to get a foothold outside the peninsula of Nova Scotia, and almost immediately sent a detachment to build a fort on the St. John. At the same time, through the activities of the Abbé le Loutre and Père Germain, and with the approval of the ministry, he sought to induce the Acadians in the peninsula to leave their former homes and to move into the new French settlements along the St. John, on Cape Breton, and in Ile St. Jean (Prince Edward Island).[43] Meanwhile, at about the time when La Galissonnière began to build the fort on the St. John, Edward Cornwallis, under orders of May 2, 1749, sailed for Nova Scotia as its new governor, to plant English colonists there, and, specifically, to found a settlement on the St. John![44] Mascarene had already written Governor Shirley and the Board of Trade reporting the French activity on the St. John, and Cornwallis, on hearing of it upon his arrival, protested to the government of Canada and suggested to the Board of Trade the necessity of an immediate diplomatic protest.[45] These reports and protests at once became the subject of a vigorous diplomatic exchange,[46] and added fuel to the already smoldering disputes over the ownership of the "neutral islands" and the British occupancy of the island of Canso.

Early in January, 1750, news arrived in England that the French, far from withdrawing from their new positions, had taken others. The Marquis de La Jonquière, who had succeeded La Galissonnière as governor-general, had, in the autumn of 1749, sent the Chevalier de Lacorne to occupy Chipoudy, the region west of the Bay of Fundy between the St. John and the isthmus, and to keep the British from making any attempts to expand their new settlements beyond the peninsula.[47] Cornwallis protested to the French governor, and there ensued a fiery exchange of picturesque language,[48] while Albemarle, at Paris, was instructed to make a vigorous protest to the French ministry against La Jonquière's actions.[49] Cornwallis, however, was ordered to avoid forcible measures,[50] and he had to content himself with sending Major Lawrence with four hundred men to Beaubassin in April, 1750—only to find that

43. *British Museum*, Additional Manuscript Series, 32818:17–18. Hereafter cited as BM Add. MSS.; *Nova Scotia Archives*, pp. 178, 179 n, 183, 193–194; *Canadian Archives*, I, Part VI, p. 109; Garneau, *op. cit.*, II, 118.

44. *Canadian Archives*, II, Part III, Appendix C, p. 50.

45. *Journal of the Board of Trade, January, 1749/50—December, 1753*, p. 2.

46. BM Add. MSS. 32818:9–11, *et passim*.

47. *Journal of the Board of Trade, January, 1749/50—December, 1753*, p. 2.

48. LC Add. MSS. 32822:5 ff.; *ibid.*, 32821:103 ff.

49. LC Add. MSS. 32820:283–284.

50. CAO AE CP Ang. 428:231 ff.; *Canadian Archives*, II, Part III, Appendix C, p. 55.

the town had been burned, and that Lacorne had taken up a position at Beauséjour on the Missaguash, determined to resist by force any attempt by Lawrence to cross the river.[51] Whereupon Lawrence dug himself in at Fort Lawrence, on the English side of the little stream, to await developments. Both sides were now intrenched; the French had successfully forestalled British expansion beyond the isthmus; and both remained in a position of watchful waiting, hardly more than a cannon shot apart, until the outbreak of formal war.

The French proposal for the settlement of American disputes by a joint commission had been made and accepted before news of the skirmishing in Nova Scotia had arrived in Europe. When the news came, it had the effect of hastening the decision to make the proposed joint commission a reality. For upon receipt of the advices from Acadia Bedford in his turn made a vigorous protest, through the British ambassador, the Earl of Albemarle, and demanded that, as the St. John was in territory that was in dispute, all activity should there be suspended until the ownership of that territory could be decided by the commissioners who were to meet in Paris.[52] As a matter of fact, however, the French settlement on the St. John had been begun before the agreement to create a joint commission had been reached by the two sovereigns, and the instructions to Cornwallis himself, which certainly ordered him to make a settlement on that very river, antedated the agreement, having been given in May, 1749.[53]

The admission that this was disputed territory weakened the British case and gave logic to the French contention that they had a right to prevent Cornwallis from occupying it under the agreement to leave things as they had been before the war. After the virtual state of war that existed in April, 1750, on the Beaubassin front, news of which arrived in London in June, Bedford assured Puysieulx that Cornwallis had "neither yet made nor had any Intention of making any Establishment without the Limits of the Peninsula," and that "it never was the Kings Intention in settling His province of Nova Scotia, either to infringe upon the Right of His Most Christian Majesty, or to take forcible Possession of a Country (the right to which His Majesty had agreed should be referred to Commissaries to be named by each Court) before those Commissaries could have possibly met to settle the Boundaries of it."[54]

51. LC Add. MSS. 32821:334 ff.; *N.Y. Col. Docs.*, X, 216–217.
52. BM Add. MSS. 32818:9–11; *Brit. Dip. Instrs.*, VII, *France 1745–1789*, pp. 7–8.
53. The agreement to appoint commissioners was not reached until July. (CAO AE CP Ang. 426:306.)
54. LC Add. MSS. 32822:3–4. The first of these statements is belied by the original orders to Cornwallis; the second is true only if one accepts the British claim that

In his replies to Albemarle's strong protest against La Jonquière's latest coup, Puysieulx was at first disposed to think the governor had exceeded his instructions. He even went so far as to acknowledge that Chignecto and Beaubassin were on British soil and that some sort of reparation should be made.[55] His tone stiffened, however, after a conversation with Antoine-Louis Rouillé, Count de Jouy, minister of marine in charge of the colonies, and he suggested that La Jonquière, being perfectly familiar with the true boundaries of New France, certainly would not have invaded British territory. On the other hand, Cornwallis had probably exaggerated the facts; he must surely have attempted to invade French territory, said the minister, in order to have provoked such a firm resistance. In any case, he said, the events in Acadia only emphasized the advisability of proceeding at once to the organization of the boundary commission.[56] The fact was, of course, that military action had been taken on both sides before the appointment of the commission was decided upon. The French had correctly forecast the British expansion, and, perhaps with an eye to the possible reconquest of all Acadia, had managed effectively to block the English plan to settle the mainland. Now that this had been done, and after the building of Fort Lawrence at the site of the burned Beaubassin in the fall of 1750, both sides were intrenched and prepared to maintain the *status quo* until the larger issue should be decided, whether by arms or by diplomacy.

Thus within less than a year after the signing of the Treaty of Aix-la-Chapelle, the British and the French were at each other's throats over the boundaries of Acadia. But the conflict was not confined to Acadia. Within a very short time news came of disputes over ownership of territory on Lake Champlain, in the Iroquois country south of Lake Ontario, in the Ohio Valley, and in the Gulf coastal plain. And these contests became the subjects of a fruitless diplomatic correspondence that paralleled the discussions of the boundary commission and still further complicated the task of finding a peaceful solution to the intercolonial boundary problem. It seems clear that the French were actuated by a genuine desire to defend the territories that they had convinced themselves were theirs. For the British, however, the conflicts which were making the North American boundary problem increasingly acute arose out of the normal and irrepressible expansion of the British fisheries and fur trade and the settlements beyond the natural boundaries which, before 1721, the British had hardly thought of crossing. The American

Acadia included both sides of the Bay of Fundy—which the French, whatever may have been their position in 1712, certainly did not.

55. *Brit. Dip. Instrs.*, VII, *France 1745–1789*, pp. 10–11.
56. CAO AE CP Ang. 429:9–12, 15–16; 428:448.

problem that now presented itself to European diplomacy was one resting upon economic and social expansion, which gave point and direction, as in Nova Scotia, to military necessity.

Early in the year 1750, the commissioners who were to attempt a settlement of the North American boundary problem were finally appointed. For the French court, the negotiators were the Marquis de La Galissonnière[57] and Etienne de Silhouette, a rather colorless individual who was chancellor to the Duke of Orléans[58] and a minor official in the French court. On the English side, William Mildmay, a witty young man of good family but not too great intelligence, was appointed to act with William Shirley, governor of Massachusetts.[59] Mildmay arrived in Paris May 1, 1750, and Shirley late in August.[60]

Even then the British commissioners were still without adequate instructions. Preliminary instructions, dealing with prisoners of war and prizes, had been drawn up in April and delivered to Mildmay,[61] but the Board of Trade had asked for more time to prepare the data on the American disputes, for it had felt compelled to write to the governors for precise information as to the boundaries of the provinces.[62] Further instructions were sent to the British agents in July; but even these instructions, based upon those given to Pulteney and Bladen in 1719,[63] dealt chiefly with Acadia, the fisheries, and the disputed islands in the West Indies.[64] The Board of Trade was still unable to make up its mind as to what the boundaries in the interior of the continent were; the most it could say was that France had no title whatever to any lands south of the St. Lawrence River. Apparently the Board did not have the necessary and exact information for the presentation of an English case. But because there was "reason to believe" the French had made encroachments on English territories in the interior, the right was reserved, in the instructions to the commissioners, to call for a discussion of the inland boundaries after the more pressing questions of Acadia

57. It was he who had set the French "offensive defense" in motion in the forests of America.

58. CL Mildmay Papers—"Conferences," pp. 1-4.

59. *Brit. Dip. Instrs.*, VII, *France 1745-1789*, pp. 307 ff.

60. Mildmay to Bedford, May 6, 1750; same to Fitzwalter, August 22, 1750. CL Mildmay Papers—"Letters from Paris."

61. *Brit. Dip. Instrs.*, VII, *France 1745-1789*, pp. 307-308; Mildmay to Bedford, May 6, 1750, CL Mildmay Papers—"Letters from Paris."

62. *Journal of the Board of Trade, January, 1749/50—December, 1753*, p. 56; *N.Y. Col. Docs.*, VI, 560-561.

63. *Journal of the Board of Trade, January, 1749/50—December, 1753*, p. 56; *Brit. Dip. Instrs.*, II, *France 1689-1721*, pp. 196-205.

64. *Brit. Dip. Instrs.*, VII, *France 1745-1789*, pp. 309-313.

and the West Indies should have been disposed of.[65] Certainly the problem of Acadia was the most delicate matter in the negotiation, and the most pressing. As Newcastle put it, "I think it the most ticklish, and the most important Point, that We have almost ever had, *singly*, to negotiate with France."[66]

Furnished with but vague instructions and little precise information, the British commissioners, weakened by a lack of confidence in them in the councils of London, and hampered by the impossible conditions imposed upon them by their country's claims, found themselves confronted by an impossible task. After the necessary formalities and introductions, the commission held its first meeting on August 31, 1750, at the home of La Galissonnière.[67] This conference, begun with some *éclat* and not a little optimism, very quickly indicated to the participants how far apart the two nations were and how improbable it was that they should ever come to any agreement. The initial and fundamental difficulty was due to the commission's first official act, the exchange of instructions. The St. Malo conference, which had broken up a year before, had failed precisely because the commissioners there could not agree as to what they were supposed to do. Their instructions, which, under the Declaration of July 8, 1748, were supposed to deal with prizes made at sea after hostilities should rightly have ceased, and with the exchange of prisoners made at sea during the war,[68] had been found to differ radically. The fundamental difference between the two courts had been realized, and an effort had been made to bring them together. Yet, strange as it may seem, while the colonial disputes in the West Indies and North America had been added to the task of the new commission, no progress had been made, in a year of negotiation, toward an agreement as to what its instructions should be. The commission, meeting two years after the Treaty of Aix-la-Chapelle, found itself exactly where the commission of St. Malo had been when it had broken up, and with the even more difficult problem of colonial disputes also on its hands.

When the commissioners exchanged their instructions, it was found that the British were empowered to discuss only prizes made after hostilities should have ceased, whereas the French were instructed to discuss all prizes made as far back as 1738, at the beginning of the Anglo-Spanish War of Jenkins' Ear. What actually constituted the Channel

65. *Ibid.*   66. LC Add. MSS. 32822:305–307.
67. Mildmay and Shirley to Bedford, August 22–September 2, 1750, CL Mildmay Papers—"Letters from Paris"; CAO AE CP Ang. 430:123–128.
68. CL Mildmay Papers—"Memorials" and "Letters from Paris," *passim.*

and the North Sea had not been agreed upon;[69] and as to the West Indies, the British negotiators could not proceed because it was their understanding that the disputed islands were to have been evacuated by the French before discussion could take place, and this had not been done.[70] Orders for the evacuation of the islands had as a matter of fact been sent,[71] but it now appeared that, whereas the French commanders had carried out a military evacuation, the English had expected and still insisted upon the evacuation of the civil population as well.[72]

After finding these discrepancies in their instructions and agreeing to ask for clarifications from their governments, the commissioners turned their attention to methods of procedure. The British proposed first to settle the question of Acadia, as being the most important, and then to proceed to a discussion of the islands. The French, however, asked that the two questions be discussed alternately.[73] The French commissioners also voiced a desire that the commission proceed upon the principle that both sides should be disposed "to renounce anything that would give their respective colonists in America the temptation and the means to annoy, attack, or invade each other with ease and success, even in cases where a war might intervene and render such aggression legitimate."[74] This proposal, coupled with the insistence that Acadia and the islands be discussed concurrently, Mildmay and Shirley took to mean that the French were preparing to ask for a compromise in which a large Acadia might be given to Great Britain in return for the cession of St. Lucia to France. The British representatives therefore stiffly replied that they would defend His Majesty's just rights to the uttermost, no matter where they lay, because justice and amity went hand in hand.[75]

The stiffness of the British commissioners was reflected in the reaction of their government. Bedford was inclined to think that the position of the French indicated a lack of confidence in their claims to Acadia; their insistence, it seemed to him, grew out of their desire to be in a position to bargain for St. Lucia. On the other hand, he realized that the French might refuse to sign a convention on any of the problems at issue until

69. "Memorial in Reply to those of the French Court in Answer to the Sketch of Instructions for the Commissioners," CL Mildmay Papers—"Memorials."

70. Mildmay and Shirley to Bedford, August 22–September 2, 1750, CL Mildmay Papers—"Letters from Paris"; *ibid.*—"Conferences," pp. 1–4; La Galissonnière and Silhouette to Puysieulx, September 1, 1750, CAO AE CP Ang. 430:123–128. The "agreement" cited by the English commissioners probably was the French willingness to evacuate the islands expressed to Yorke by Puysieulx in April, 1749. (LC Add. MSS. 32816:328–331.)

71. CL Mildmay Papers—"Memorials"; *ibid.*—"Conferences," pp. 4–7.

72. CAO AE CP Ang. 430:123–128.

73. CAO AE CP Ang. 430:123–128; CL Mildmay Papers—"Conferences," pp. 1–4.

74. CAO AE CP Ang. 430:123–128.   75. CAO AE CP Ang. 430:123–128.

all were concluded, even if they were disposed of one by one, as the English wished. It was this consideration which led the Lords Justices[76] to authorize Mildmay and Shirley to accede to the French demand.[77]

Meanwhile, the commissioners had had a second meeting at Shirley's house on September 7, 1750. The French insisted that the evacuation of St. Lucia was not a prerequisite to a discussion of its disposition; the British insisted that it was. The French demanded alternate discussions, with the warning that no convention would be signed until all points had been settled; the British refused personally to proceed by alternate discussions, but promised to urge that permission be given them so to proceed.[78]

As yet nothing had been said as to the actual claims of either side. Two meetings had been wasted over powers and procedure, a circumstance which led the French commissioners to believe that the British were playing for time or for a tactical advantage. For, said they, if the French evacuate the islands before discussion begins, the British may then break off the negotiations and occupy the islands themselves.[79] The British, on their side, were suspicious of the French proposals, especially of their principle of mutual sacrifices, and refused to do more than approve it "in principle," because, as they said, "it may possibly preclude us hereafter, from availing ourselves of a Right, which upon Examination may turn out to be of great consequence."[80] The commission had thus begun its work in an uncompromising attitude of mutual distrust, and without authority to proceed along any line without prior instruction from the respective foreign offices. It is no wonder it accomplished so little.

It was decided at the second meeting that, while awaiting further instructions for the English members, the commission should proceed at the third session to a discussion of Acadia. Thereafter, the meetings were to be suspended until the desired instruction should arrive. The session of September 21, therefore, was devoted to a presentation of their respective claims to Acadia; and as both sides felt the futility of oral discussion, the cases were submitted in writing.

76. Acting in their capacity as a regency; the King and Newcastle were at the time in Hanover.

77. *Archives of the Dominion of Canada,* Ottawa. Transcripts from the Public Record Office, London. Foreign Office Papers, Series 90 (France), 238:142, 146. Hereafter cited as CAO PRO FO 90 (France). LC Add. MSS. 32823:243; Shirley and Mildmay to Bedford, October 10/21, 1750, CL Mildmay Papers—"Letters from Paris."

78. CL Mildmay Papers—"Conferences," pp. 4–7; Shirley and Mildmay to Bedford, September 8, 1750, *ibid.*—"Letters from Paris"; La Galissonnière and Silhouette to Puysieulx, September 7, 1750, CAO AE CP Ang. 430:143–145.

79. CAO AE CP Ang. 430:143–145.

80. CAO PRO FO 90 (France), 238:146.

The Treaty of Utrecht had ceded to Great Britain

Nova Scotia, otherwise called Acadia, in its entirety, conformably to its old limits ["anciennes limites"]; as also the town of Port Royal, now called Annapolis Royal, and generally all the dependencies of the said lands and isles of that country, with the sovereignty, propriety, possession and all rights acquired by treaty or otherwise, that the most Christian King, the Crown of France or their subjects have had up to the present . . . in such a manner that it shall not be permitted in the future to the subjects of the Most Christian King to fish in the said seas, bays and other places within thirty leagues of the coast of Nova Scotia, southeastwardly, commencing from the isle vulgarly called Sable and drawing [a line] toward the south-west.

The question now at issue was just what was to be understood by the phrase "anciennes limites." The British, in their memorial, submitted that it included all the land turned over to the French on the restoration of Acadia after the Treaty of Breda; that is to say, that the boundaries of Acadia should be delimited by a line drawn due north from the mouth of the Penobscot River to the St. Lawrence, and thence, following the shore, around Cape Rosier and across the Gulf of St. Lawrence southeast to the promontory of Cape Breton, whence it was to run to Sable Island and thence west to the point of beginning. This line would have included Cape Breton and Ile St. Jean (Prince Edward Island); but as Cape Breton was specifically ceded to the French by the Treaty of Utrecht, Acadia now included, in the minds of the English, everything within the line except Cape Breton.[81]

The earlier French memorial on the subject of Acadia had limited Acadia to the peninsula east of the Bay of Fundy. But La Galissonnière, doubtless influenced by strategic considerations, had already come to the conclusion that Acadia included even less than that, and that the cession made at Utrecht was, indeed, bounded by the coasts from Port Royal around to Cape Canso, and gave England no land facing upon the Gulf of St. Lawrence.[82] Following this line of reasoning, the French memorandum of September 21, 1750, asserted, despite the earlier admissions of the French government, that the "anciennes limites" of Acadia meant the boundaries it had had in the earliest times and included only a part of the peninsula; that the phrase "as also the town of Port Royal" indicated that Port Royal was not in Acadia; that the island of Canso, excluded from Acadia by this definition of the "anciennes limites," had not been ceded to England, and rightfully belonged to France. This

81. *Mémoires des Commissaires du Roi et ceux de Sa Majesté Britannique* (Paris, 1756), I, 1–6.
82. *N.Y. Col. Docs.*, X, 226–227.

statement made no attempt to define accurately the landward line of the boundaries it thus vaguely indicated.[83] But as though this were not enough, the French memorandum added an entirely new element to the discussion, by asserting that the boundary between New France and New England[84] had not been changed by the Treaty of Utrecht, but that all the land between their small Acadia and New England was part of New France.[85]

When asked to define the boundary of Acadia more exactly, the French commissioners replied only that as the English were the "demandants," "whatever we [the English] could not prove to belong to us would of course belong to them, *they being in possession*."[86] The English commissioners, of course, vigorously rejected the French idea of a boundary, as well as the French reference to Canso, the latter as having been ruled out by Bedford in the preliminary negotiations with Durand. But the French commissioners insisted that was not their understanding, whereupon the British commissioners had again to ask for instructions.[87]

This futile commission so continued, through six years, until a new war gave an excuse for its dissolution; these first meetings furnish an epitome of its entire history. Whether they dealt with prizes, the West Indies, or Acadia, both sides refused to modify, even slightly, their original demands. The British government was convinced that France realized she could not maintain her claim to continental Acadia, and expected the French agents to propose a compromise in which France would give up Acadia and Great Britain would give up St. Lucia. This the British were determined to refuse; Great Britain would stand upon the "real Right" of all the questions involved.[88]

Oral discussion was abandoned in October, 1750, and it was decided to submit all claims, arguments, and supporting documents in writing.[89] This made for delay, but it also made for more perfect preparation. The result was that both sides, far from weakening, became more and more convinced of the righteousness of their causes. The preparation of the British memorials was in large measure taken out of the hands of Mild-

83. CAO AE CP Ang. 430:160–161; CL Mildmay Papers—"Conferences," pp. 8–10.

84. Which they understood to be the Kennebec River (*N.Y. Col. Docs.*, X, 226–227).

85. CAO AE CP Ang. 430:160–161.

86. Mildmay and Shirley to Bedford, September 12/23, 1750, CL Mildmay Papers—"Letters from Paris."

87. *Ibid.*

88. LC Add. MSS. 32824:135 ff. The British seem never fully to have comprehended the strategic importance of the St. John Valley to France.

89. Mildmay to Fitzwalter, October 28, 1750, CL Mildmay Papers—"Private Letters from Paris"; CAO PRO FO 90 (France) 238:197.

may and Shirley by the Board of Trade,[90] and, to make matters worse, these commissioners themselves fell to quarreling. Mildmay complained of Shirley as "a slow mule that understands neither French nor English."[91] Each side complained of the apparently deliberate delays of the other, and the conferences continued in an atmosphere of increasing suspicion and cynical distrust.[92]

After the first exchange of memorials on Acadia, the British commissioners, challenged to show proof, presented, on January 11, 1751, a long and elaborate statement of their claims.[93] This memorial, prepared by the Board of Trade, reviewed the entire history of Acadia to show that the province had always been as the British claimed it. Referring first to French documents, it quoted the commission of the Sieur d'Aulnay (1647),[94] governor of Acadia, to the effect that Acadia included all the land between the St. Lawrence and New England. The memorial then cited the protests of the French ambassador against the seizure of Acadia by Oliver Cromwell.[95] But the strongest point made by the British commissioners was the fact that, at the time of the restoration of Acadia to France under the Treaty of Breda, in 1670, the distinction between Nova Scotia and Acadia claimed by Sir Thomas Temple was rejected by King Charles II, who defined Acadia as including the forts and towns of Pentagoët (Penobscot, now Castine), St. John, Port Royal, La Hève (now Lahave), and Cape Sable.[96] Many other documents were quoted to the same end, and particular emphasis was placed upon the negotiations preliminary to the Peace of Utrecht, during which the French agents repeatedly spoke of Acadia as extending to the St. George River, which flows between the Penobscot and the Kennebec.[97]

Turning then to English documents in support of its contention, the British memorial cited the grant of James I to Sir William Alexander in 1621, the warrant of Oliver Cromwell to Captain Leverett in 1656, and the language of the Treaty of Utrecht, which speaks of "Nouvelle Ecosse, autrement dite l'Acadie."[98] In conclusion, the British made these

90. CAO PRO FO 90 (France) 238:201.
91. Mildmay to Fitzwalter, October 28, 1750, CL Mildmay Papers—"Private Letters from Paris."
92. CAO AE CP Ang. 430:215, et passim; LC Add. MSS. 32824:131; CL Mildmay Papers, passim.
93. [William Mildmay and William Shirley], The Memorials of the English and French Commissaries concerning the Limits of Nova Scotia or Acadia [and St. Lucia] (London, 1755), I, 12–81. Hereafter cited as Memorials of the English and French Commissaries.
94. Ibid., I, 15.   95. Ibid., I, 17.
96. Ibid., I, 21. Davenport and Paullin, op. cit., II, 183–186.
97. Memorials of the English and French Commissaries, I, 33–37.
98. Ibid., I, 41–47.

claims: (1) that Nova Scotia and Acadia were one and the same territory; (2) that the "anciennes limites" included all the land between the
St. Lawrence River, the St. George River, and the Atlantic Ocean; and
(3) that these were the boundaries in the minds of the French negotiators at Utrecht. The territory between the Penobscot River and the
Kennebec, which remained in some doubt, the British memorial claimed
to be a part of New England.[99] The remainder of the document was devoted to a refutation of the historical and cartographical authorities
cited by the French commissioners, pointing out the well-known lack of
dependability of historians as guides to truth, and asserted that, in the
matter of the boundaries of Acadia, the present French claims were in-
consistent with their former notes.[100]

The French reply was not delivered until October 4, 1751, when, in a
still longer document, the French attempted to refute the British argument. Drawing a somewhat tenuous distinction between the "restitutions" of French territory by the British in the treaties of St. Germain
(1632) and Breda (1667) and the "cession" of Acadia by France in
the Treaty of Utrecht, the French commissioners based their argument
chiefly upon the contention that the Acadia that France "ceded" in
1713, as distinguished from the Acadia restored by England at other
times, was the Acadia France had settled "before the English had any
colonies in America." The "anciennes limites" of the Treaty of Utrecht
were the boundaries of this original Acadia, and France alone was judge
of what those boundaries were.[101] Beginning with this point of view, the
French memorial adverted to the prior French settlement of Acadia,
tracing the history of English and French exploration and settlement
of North America from Cabot to the colonization of Rhode Island, and
from the voyages of the Basque and Breton fishermen to the settlements
of Port Royal and Quebec.[102] The two provinces of Acadia, old and new
—that is, the province on the isthmus, and the one along the coast of
the Etchemins, west of the Bay of Fundy—were united, it said, under the
command of D'Aulnay by the commission of 1647, and D'Aulnay's
grant was even extended to the St. Lawrence. This did not, however, in
any way alter the boundaries of the old province of Acadia, which,
throughout the various changes that succeeded, remained only the southern half of the peninsula.[103] The allegation that England had "ceded"
Acadia to France in 1632 was false, in the opinion of the French; England had merely restored a territory, first occupied by France, that the
English had seized. Thus the assertion that England had merely reoc-

99. *Ibid.*, I, 47–53.　　100. *Ibid.*, I, 53–81.　　101. *Ibid.*, I, 83–89.
102. *Ibid.*, I, 89–91.　　103. *Ibid.*, I, 118.

cupied, after the Peace of Utrecht, territory that was formerly England's was also incorrect. The first real "cession" of Acadia was that of 1713. It had always been owned by France, and only France knew what Acadia really was.[104] One by one the French demolished, to their own satisfaction, the proofs adduced by the British memorial, drawing a distinction between Acadia and Nova Scotia, the latter of which, to them, had never really existed prior to 1713, but was only *un mot en air*. The French memorial cited various historical authorities, Champlain, Lescarbot, and even English authors, to support their contentions that Acadia was only a part of the peninsula.[105] Finally, the French elaborated upon their former textual argument, based upon Article XII of the Treaty of Utrecht, attempting to show that the prohibition of French fishing on the coast from Sable Island southwestward indicated that the negotiators considered this the entire coast of Acadia.[106]

While the French memoir may be said to succeed in demonstrating that the earliest use of the word "Acadia" designated the southeastern coast of the peninsula, just as the earliest use of the word "Canada" designated only a small strip of territory along the St. Lawrence, it is impossible to escape the conclusion that the French, in their use of the term during the seventeenth century, and very clearly in the negotiations preceding the Treaty of Utrecht, had understood it to mean substantially what the British now claimed it to be. It is impossible, moreover, to avoid the conclusion that the arguments of the French agents, and particularly La Galissonnière, were strongly colored by the realization that whoever controlled the valley of the St. John would inevitably be in a position to control all of Canada in winter.[107]

The opposing arguments of the French and British commissioners never went beyond the memorials of 1751. The British representatives submitted a lengthy reply on January 23, 1753;[108] but their case, while it went into much more detail and increased the number of the documents submitted in proof, remained substantially the same. The French commissioners prepared a rejoinder, but it was never delivered, on account of the outbreak of war in 1756.[109]

As a matter of fact, by the end of 1752, the commission had ceased

104. *Ibid.,* I, 125.   105. *Ibid.,* I, 203–216.
106. *Ibid.,* I, 216–220.   107. *N.Y. Col. Docs.,* X, 226.
108. *Memorials of the English and French Commissaries,* I, 233–543. This memorandum is signed by William Mildmay and Ruvigny de Cosné, who replaced Shirley in April, 1752. Mildmay to Fitzwalter, April 8/19, 1752, CL Mildmay Papers, "Private Letters from Paris."
109. It is printed in *Mémoires des Commissaires du Roi et de ceux de Sa Majesté Britannique, sur les Possessions et les Droits respectifs des deux Couronnes en Amérique; avec les actes publics et pièces Justificatives* (Paris, 1755–1757), IV.

to have any genuine reason for being. The English government had demanded, as early as the autumn of 1751, that the North American boundary question be taken out of its hands and negotiated directly through regular diplomatic channels,[110] and this demand was formally renewed in the spring of 1752.[111] But the French ministers opposed this,[112] and the British effectively paralyzed the commission's work in 1753 by refusing to submit its communications in French, because the French commissioners had objected to the vigor of the expressions in the English memorial of November 15, 1751, on St. Lucia.[113] The negotiators then used up a year in deciding whether the British documents should be submitted in French or English.[114] Only because the French refused to collaborate with Great Britain in arrangements for the commission's demise,[115] and because Great Britain herself was afraid to abandon this attempt at a peaceful settlement of colonial disputes, did this futile body continue to exist. It could not be abandoned by the British alone, because such a withdrawal might be taken as a confession of the untenable nature of the British claims, and because such a withdrawal would reflect unfavorably upon Great Britain, so far as public opinion went, both at home and in the neutral courts of Europe. On the other hand, as France seemed to have the advantage in the deliberations and might gain time enough to establish her line of American defenses by protracting the commission's existence, she refused to abandon it.[116]

Eventually, however, in the course of 1754, with the imminent approach of war, the two courts finally agreed to initiate direct negotiations, *de cour à cour*. As a concession to French insistence that the commission continue its work, both sides agreed that it should continue, as it had begun, and exchange views, in such fashion that its work would be considered as paralleling the work of the regularly accredited ambassadors in Paris and London.[117] The language difficulty was smoothed out by a compromise agreement that the British commissioners would sub-

110. LC Add. MSS. 32830:262; CAO AE CP Ang. 434:87–90.

111. Theodore C. Pease, ed., *Anglo-French Boundary Disputes in the West, 1749–1763* (*Collections of the Illinois State Historical Library*, XVII. Springfield, 1936), p. 36.

112. CAO AE CP Ang. 434:220–222, 258–259, *et passim.*

113. Conferences of March 18, May 2, 1752, January 23, 1753. CL Mildmay Papers —"Conferences."

114. CL Mildmay Papers—"Conferences," *passim;* CAO AE CP Ang. 434:333.

115. CAO AE CP Ang. 436:278–280.

116. LC Add. MSS. 32850:218–220, 301–303; cf. Richard Waddington, *Louis XV et le Renversement des Alliances* (Paris, 1896), p. 59. Hereafter cited as Waddington, *Louis XV.*

117. Albemarle to Robinson, August 14, 1754, CL Shelburne MSS. XXXVI:22; LC Add. MSS. 32851:82–84, 32835:261, 32836:94–95, 296–298,·300; CAO AE CP Ang. 437: 433–436.

mit their documents in English, but would check them with the translations made by their French colleagues.[118] Nevertheless, although the commission was apparently thus to enjoy a renascence, and although, on October 4, 1754, the French did, indeed, present a new note on St. Lucia,[119] the joint commission was never seriously considered of any use after the spring of 1752. The first genuine effort to settle the North American boundary by peaceful means had failed largely because neither side had any real confidence in the means employed. As a matter of fact, the commission seems only to have been employed by the French to gain time, whereas the British, although they had accepted it with great misgiving, seem to have expected that some sort of compromise would be the outcome. The near approach of war in 1754 and 1755 frightened both sides into resorting to a method of settlement in which they had more confidence—an appeal to direct diplomacy.

118. Albemarle to Robinson, August 14, 1754, CL Shelburne MSS. XXXVI:22; Robinson to De Cosné and Mildmay, September 19, 1754, CL Shelburne MSS. XXXVI:53.

119. *Memorials of the English and French Commissaries,* II, 157–244.

CHAPTER III

FRONTIER ACTION AND DIPLOMATIC STALEMATE, 1752–1754

IF, in the summer of 1749, the French under La Galissonnière had kindled backfires in Acadia with a view to forestalling British expansion there, this was only one part of a comprehensive plan to block the British all along the line. In general, it was La Galissonnière's conviction that the proper and most obvious line of demarcation south of Acadia was the watershed; and one of the most vital points in the defenses of that line was the fort on Crown Point, established by the French in 1731, at the south end of Lake Champlain. La Galissonnière believed that this fort should be strengthened and made the center of a firmly rooted French settlement that would effectively bar any possible British expeditions along this route to Montreal and Quebec.[1] Even before receiving news of the Peace of Aix-la-Chapelle, he took steps to carry his plan into action by building Fort St. John at the head of the rapids of the Richelieu River to give added support to Crown Point; and, immediately after the peace, he began to send settlers to Crown Point itself.[2]

This fort had long been a thorn in the side of the British, who had protested against its being built. From that time on its destruction had constituted a fixed objective, both military and diplomatic, of the British government.[3] With the establishment of the boundary commission of 1750, the Board of Trade inquired of Governor Clinton just what the boundaries of New York in that direction actually were.[4] Clinton referred the matter to Cadwallader Colden, who presented evidence to show that the Iroquois Indians had always claimed all the land south of the St. Lawrence. This information was eventually presented to the Board of Trade by William Shirley, and apparently formed the basis of the eventual British claims to the River St. Lawrence as a boundary.[5] Colden himself, however, recognized the practical validity of the French claim to the height of land as the boundary south of Lake Champlain.[6]

1. *N.Y. Col. Docs.*, X, 227–228, 231.
2. William Shirley to the Board of Trade, July 4, 1749, CAO PRO FO 90 (BT MSS.) LXXIII; *Brit. Dip. Instrs.*, VII, *France 1745–1789*, p. 8; *Journal of the Board of Trade, January, 1749—December, 1753*, p. 86.
3. *N.Y. Col. Docs.*, V, 933; VI, 125, *et passim*.
4. *Ibid.*, VI, 560–561.
5. *Ibid.*, VI, 569, 576, 577; *Journal of the Board of Trade, January, 1749—December, 1753*, p. 86.
6. *N.Y. Col. Docs.*, VI, 746.

Both the British commissioners at Paris were consulted on the question of the boundary in this region, but it was never placed in their hands for actual negotiation. Albemarle was instructed only to ask that La Jonquière, now the governor of Canada, be ordered to refrain from expansion there, and to keep the peace, pending a definitive settlement.[7] Later, the question of Crown Point became an important issue in the direct negotiations between the two governments.[8]

Another drainage area which La Galissonnière hoped to control for France was the land lying along the south shores of Lakes Ontario and Erie. The fort at Oswego he considered as standing upon French soil. This post, he felt, because of its strategic position on the route to the western fur trade, had been and always would be a threat of irreparable injury to the economic life of Canada. He felt very strongly that it must be destroyed at all costs and the British settlements confined to the territory east and south of the watershed.[9] It was for this reason that, as a part of his general plan, he began, immediately after the Peace of Aix-la-Chapelle, to carry his ideas into action.

La Galissonnière's program for the territory along the lakes was twofold. He would attempt to wean the Iroquois away from the British by trade, gifts, and the establishment of a mission on the south side of the St. Lawrence; and he would seek to induce them to destroy the fort at Oswego.[10] At the same time, he would be prepared to strike at Oswego from Canada as a "reprisal" for the first offense committed by the British, who, he expected, would soon give him the opportunity he desired.[11] On the other hand, he proposed to strengthen the French positions at Forts Frontenac and Niagara; and, in order to checkmate the influence of Oswego over the fur trade of the lakes, he proposed to build a post on the opposite side of Lake Ontario not far from the mouth of the Humber River. This post, Fort Rouillé (Toronto), he began to construct in the summer of 1749.[12]

Governor Clinton early took cognizance of the activities of La Galissonnière and his successor, La Jonquière.[13] In June, 1751, he wrote the French governor, protesting against the rebuilding of the fort at Niagara and the imprisonment of several British traders there. This territory, wrote Clinton, was British by virtue of the Iroquois cessions, and he demanded not only the liberation of the traders but that a stop be put to the building operations going on at Niagara.[14] To this La Jonquière

7. *Brit. Dip. Instrs.*, VII, *France 1745–1789*, p. 8.
8. *Ibid.*, p. 28; LC Add. MSS. 32837:238.   9. *N.Y. Col. Docs.*, X, 228, 229, 231–232.
10. *Ibid.*, X, 203, 228–232.   11. *Ibid.*, X, 229.
12. *Ibid.*, X, 201–202; cf. Garneau, *op. cit.*, II, 119.
13. *N.Y. Col. Docs.*, VI, 484–487, 505–507, 516–518, 529, 545, 602, *et passim.*
14. BM Add. MSS. 32833:389–390; *N.Y. Col. Docs.*, VI, 711–712.

replied that the Iroquois were an independent people, and that they had never ceded their lands to the British. On the contrary, he said, the post established by the French at Niagara was built with the knowledge and consent of the Iroquois themselves. The French, indeed, were the first discoverers of this territory; their right to it, therefore, was superior to that of the British. As for the traders taken on the Ohio, they were obviously trespassing on the lands of the Most Christian King in violation of the King's ordinances forbidding the British to trade there. They must be punished accordingly.[15]

News of the friction along the lakes came to England early in 1752, when British confidence in the boundary commission was rapidly fading; and, like the Lake Champlain boundary question, this quarrel was never referred to it for discussion. A vigorous protest was lodged with the French government through Albemarle, however, who was instructed to see that La Jonquière was restrained and that the British traders were released.[16]

Another drainage area included in the comprehensive defensive plans of La Galissonnière was the Ohio River Valley. British traders had begun to cross the mountains into it before the war, and the French governors of both Louisiana and Canada recognized the menace of this movement to the French control of the Illinois country and the communications between the northern and southern French colonies.[17] The Miami chieftain, La Demoiselle, had established his village at Pickawillany on the Great Miami, and this had become the center of a thriving British fur trade. Now, at the close of the war, news came to the French of the formation of the Ohio Company of Virginia, whose purpose was the settlement of the lands south of the Ohio and the control of the Indian trade. Again it appeared to the French that the British were expanding westward, and that they were actually on the march.

La Galissonnière had already recommended, in the fall of 1748, the settlement of the Illinois country as a barrier against the British.[18] He was determined to keep them out of the entire Ohio Valley, and gave orders that, although the two nations were at peace, the British were to be opposed by force if necessary.[19] In his memorial to his government, delivered on his return to Europe, he emphasized the importance of this valley to France for the blocking of British ambition and for the preservation of communication between Canada and Louisiana. French ownership he based upon the discoveries of La Salle and subsequent actual settlement and use.[20]

15. *N.Y. Col. Docs.*, VI, 731–734.
17. Margry, *op. cit.*, VI, 661–664, 665.
19. Margry, *op. cit.*, VI, 665.
16. BM Add. MSS. 32853:387–388.
18. *N.Y. Col. Docs.*, X, 134–136.
20. *N.Y. Col. Docs.*, X, 229.

It was because of his strong convictions that La Galissonnière had sent Céloron de Blainville to the Ohio in the summer of 1749; and had given him orders to reassert French ownership, to drive out the British traders, and to win the Indians back to the French influence. On his way down the Allegheny and Ohio rivers, Céloron had stopped from time to time to bury leaden plates reasserting the French king's ownership "of the said River Ohio, and of all the lands on both sides, up to the sources of the said rivers," a claim based upon prior ownership, maintenance by arms, and its recognition by the treaties of Ryswick, Utrecht, and Aix-la-Chapelle. He had summoned the British to leave, and had written to Governor Hamilton of Pennsylvania to restrain the traders from entering this territory, "with regard to which England has never had any pretensions."[21]

This expedition awed neither the Indians nor the British, and Céloron himself confessed its failure.[22] He even doubted whether the French could ever hope to restrain the British in the Ohio Valley, except by an establishment that would involve tremendous difficulty and expense.[23] Céloron's pessimism was shared by La Galissonnière; yet both the latter and Vaudreuil recommended the establishment of posts along the Ohio, particularly toward its source;[24] and La Jonquière carried out his plans here as elsewhere with the approval of the French ministry. The British trading stations must be destroyed, and the British must be discouraged from going into the Ohio Valley; the French title to it seemed so clear that it was not expected that Great Britain would make any vigorous protest.[25]

The first blow struck by the French was the destruction of the pro-British village at Pickawillany, in June, 1752, where four British traders were arrested and sent to France.[26] But La Jonquière died before he could do more to strengthen the French position. Duquesne, who succeeded him, came with instructions to carry forward the projects of La Galissonnière,[27] and immediately began the construction of a line of forts from Lake Erie to the Ohio. This program elicited a complaint from Lieutenant-Governor Dinwiddie of Virginia, and the result was the famous race for the seizure of the forks of the Ohio that culminated in the fight at Fort Necessity in 1754. In Dinwiddie's protest against the French occupation of the valley, carried by George Washington to

---

21. Margry, *op. cit.*, VI, 667–726; *N.Y. Col. Docs.*, X, 189; VI, 532.

22. Margry, *op. cit.*, VI, 725.   23. *Ibid.*, VI, 726.

24. *Ibid.*, VI, 661–664, 727; *N.Y. Col. Docs.*, X, 229–230; Vaudreuil to La Jonquière, March 4, 1750, HL LO 205.

25. *N.Y. Col. Docs.*, X, 239–240.

26. *N.Y. Col. Docs.*, X, 240–241; LC Add. MSS. 32836:173; cf. Volwiler, *op. cit.*, pp. 78–79.

27. *N.Y. Col. Docs.*, X, 243.

France's newly built Fort Le Boeuf, the governor took the position that the lands along the Ohio were "notoriously known" to be the property of Great Britain, and that the building of forts by the French constituted an invasion of British territory.[28] Legardeur de Saint-Pierre, the French commander, replied that he was there by the orders of Duquesne, and that there he would remain, unless ordered by his governor to do otherwise.[29]

Here, then, in the valley of the Ohio, was a situation similar to that in Acadia, on Lake Champlain, and along the shores of Lakes Erie and Ontario. The French, moved by their conviction that the true boundary was the watershed, were determined to prevent the expansion of the British beyond it. The latter, on the other hand, irresistibly expanding, but without much logic in their claims, were just as determined as the French to do the very thing the French had made up their minds the British must not be allowed to do. Both sides were convinced of the righteousness of their positions; both sides, foreswearing all aggressive designs on the territory of one another, proclaimed that they were merely on the defensive, to protect their own obvious vested interests.

In one other area the French were on the defensive before an expanding British empire. That was the Gulf coastal plain, in the valleys drained by the Chattahoochee and Alabama river systems, between the French colony of Louisiana and the English colonies of Carolina and Georgia. Here the English had been expanding westward, as elsewhere on the continent; the plan of William Livingston, toward the end of the war, to settle Protestant families in his proposed grant of 200,000 acres on the frontier of South Carolina was comparable to that of the Ohio Company in Virginia.[30] But the French had been on guard here, also, and had taken active steps to block any British movement before it could get well under way.[31] Vaudreuil, governor of Louisiana, had reported that the British were more active than ever.[32] Spain, who might have been expected to resist the British expansion from Georgia and Carolina, had seemed to be more complaisant than before.[33] Therefore, while urging La Jonquière to destroy the British allies at Pickawillany,[34] Vaudreuil had instructed his lieutenant in the Illinois country to do everything possible to block the reported activities of the British along the Ohio and on the Tennessee, by

28. *Ibid.*, X, 258. 29. *Ibid.*, X, 258–259.

30. *Journal of the Board of Trade, January, 1741—December, 1749*, pp. 4, 5, 39, 455.

31. B. R. Carroll, ed., *Historical Collections of South Carolina* (New York, 1836), pp. 432–433.

32. *N.Y. Col. Docs.*, X, 219–220.

33. Vaudreuil to the Count de Maurepas, August 28, 1749, HL LO 191; cf. Bolton, *op. cit.*, pp. 98–101, and Lanning, *op. cit.*, chaps. x, xi.

34. Vaudreuil to La Jonquière, March 4, 1750, HL LO 205.

force if necessary, and to coöperate with La Jonquière's commander at Detroit to the common end.[35] At the same time, he had exerted his influence to hold the Choctaw Indians in the French interest, and to prevail upon them to exterminate the Chickasaws, friends of the British.[36] At home, the French ministry had hoped that the decision of the boundary commission might put a stop to the British enterprises westward; but in the meantime, both Vaudreuil and La Jonquière had been instructed to watch the British and "prevent their undertakings."[37]

Thus in Louisiana, too, France was on the defensive. No definite proposal had as yet been made for a boundary between the British and the French, although the presence of Fort Toulouse on the Alabama River would strengthen a French claim to a boundary east of that river; yet observers recognized the Louisiana frontier as an integral part of the problem of frontiers throughout the continent. It was also recognized that it would be a long time before the North American empire could be made profitable for France. But it was not for immediate profit that France must keep and defend it. Pointing in true mercantilist fashion to the wealth of England, which was derived largely from the British colonies, La Galissonnière had given warning that if Great Britain succeeded in taking Canada and Louisiana the British, "by the wealth they would draw thence, to the exclusion of other Nations, would most certainly acquire the superiority in Europe."[38] This was the fear that had led France to determine at all costs to block British expansion; and La Galissonnière, the man who was the chief exponent of this French attitude, had been one of the commissioners named to adjust the American boundary disputes between France and England!

The Anglo-French joint commission had begun its work by discussing the boundaries of Acadia and the ownership of the disputed islands of the Caribbean; it was expected that the commission would later take up the other boundary questions in North America.[39] But events in America were moving too rapidly. By 1752 the tardiness, if not the complete futility, of the commission had been demonstrated, and the British government felt no inclination to turn over to it these new conflicts along the lakes and in the Mississippi Valley that were so insistently pressing for solution.[40]

35. "Ordre de Commandement pour M. de Macarty, Major du pais des Illinois, du 8 août, 1751," HL LO 325.

36. *N.Y. Col. Docs.*, X, 219–220; Carroll, *op. cit.*, pp. 432–433.

37. *N.Y. Col. Docs.*, X, 219–220; *Canadian Archives*, I, Part VI, p. 110; cf. Alexander Franz, *Die Kolonisation des Mississippitales bis zum Ausgange der französischen Herrschaft* (Leipzig, 1906), pp. 240–248.

38. *N.Y. Col. Docs.*, X, 232.

39. *Brit. Dip. Instrs.*, VII, *France 1745–1789*, p. 312.

40. LC Add. MSS. 32835:145.

The British government had, in fact, never had any real enthusiasm for, or confidence in, the commission. While incident after incident took place along the extended North American frontier, the commissioners in Paris were finding more and more excuses for delay. The British commissioners themselves had quarreled,[41] both sides quarreled over procedure,[42] and by the end of 1751 the British were convinced of the futility of such wrangling with the French.[43] In December, 1750, before the commission had been at work more than three months, Bedford had complained to the Duke de Mirepoix, French ambassador in London, of the delays of the negotiations and brought up the expediency of abandoning the attempt to settle the American boundaries on the basis of rights which were, at best, shadowy and conflicting. Instead, he had suggested the drawing of an arbitrary but negotiated boundary line which would end this dangerous North American conflict once and for all.[44] Not having received any response to his suggestion, he returned to his new plan in February, 1751. As a preliminary measure, he proposed that both sides evacuate the lands in actual dispute until a satisfactory line could be drawn.[45] The suggestion was received with suspicion in France,[46] and was not taken up again until the fall of 1752. In the meantime Holdernesse[47] had succeeded Bedford, and Saint-Contest[48] had succeeded Puysieulx. Holdernesse and Newcastle again raised the question with Mirepoix in October, 1751, by suggesting that the "national" points might be settled by direct negotiation. Mirepoix responded favorably, but laid it down as a principle that neither nation should possess any position in America that would endanger the possessions of the other. Newcastle objected to this principle as being unduly favorable to the French. The British minister proposed, in his turn, that the Anglo-French Treaty of Utrecht might be made the basis for the negotiations, and to this Mirepoix agreed

41. LC Add. MSS. 32825:29; CL Mildmay Papers, *passim*.

42. LC Add. MSS. 32830:262; CL Mildmay Papers—"Conferences," *passim*.

43. Mildmay to Fitzwalter, December 4/15, 1751, CL Mildmay Papers—"Private Letters from Paris"; "Memorial concerning the most probable Method of coming to an amiable Determination upon the Disputes relating to the Limits of Nova Scotia and the Right to St. Lucia, etc.," *ibid.*

44. CAO AE CP Ang. 429:335. This had already been suggested by Rouillé, in a conference between himself, Puysieulx, and Mirepoix. CAO AE CP Ang. 429:335; 434:187–192.

45. CAO AE CP Ang. 431:120–123.   46. CAO AE CP Ang. 431:120–123.

47. Robert Darcy, fourth Earl of Holdernesse, Secretary of State for the Southern Department, 1751–1754; Secretary of State for the Northern Department, 1757–1761. (The Secretary of State for the Northern Department was charged with the conduct of relations with the states of Northern Europe. The Secretary of State for the Southern Department had in his charge relations with Southern Europe and the Colonies.)

48. François-Dominique Barberie, Marquis de Saint-Contest, Minister of Foreign Affairs, 1751–1754.

—with the remark, however, that it might be difficult to agree as to the meaning of that treaty.[49]

Hitherto the British had had but little encouragement for their proposal. But by this time the situation in America had come to be such that Newcastle insisted upon the "indispensable necessity" of a prompt conclusion, if war was to be avoided. Mirepoix, while convinced of the sincerity of the British minister, refused to give him any hope that France would agree to take the American questions out of the hands of the commission.[50] In this he was supported by Saint-Contest, who interpreted the proposal of the British commissioners as being a confession of the weakness of their claims;[51] or, he asked, if it meant only that the British ministry had no confidence in their commissioners, why did they not discharge them and get others?[52]

It was Mirepoix's personal opinion that the questions at issue could never be settled by commissioners. Such questions were too complicated; and, he said, "Il n'y a point de tribunal ou se jugent les procès entre le Roy de France et le Roy d'Angleterre[53]—there is no tribunal where questions at issue between the King of France and the King of England can be brought to judgment." Saint-Contest was not convinced, and refused to consider bringing the work of the commission to an end; it seemed to him that the apparent lack of confidence of the British in their claims was all the more reason why it should not be ended. On the other hand, he said, the existence of the commission did not preclude direct negotiations if the British so desired.[54]

This was the opening the British wanted. The ministry promptly instructed Albemarle to approach Saint-Contest again with a proposal to negotiate the points at issue directly. Holdernesse had gathered from Mirepoix the impression that if France could be assured of the uninterrupted possession of Canada and the free navigation of the St. Lawrence the other matters in dispute might easily be settled. And as to Acadia, Mirepoix had apparently acquiesced in the British claim to all the lands surrounding the Bay of Fundy, with satisfactory land communication between Nova Scotia and New England. Upon the basis of these preliminary assumptions, England hoped that, while the commission's work need not be interrupted, all the points at issue, including Acadia and the West Indies, might be adjusted. Holdernesse did insist, however, upon the prior evacuation, by the French, of both the "neutral islands" and Acadia.[55]

49. LC Add. MSS. 32830:262.   50. CAO AE CP Ang. 434:87–90.
51. CAO AE CP Ang. 434:180–184.   52. CAO AE CP Ang. 434:232.
53. CAO AE CP Ang. 434:187–192.
54. CAO AE CP Ang. 434:220–222, 232; LC Add. MSS. 32835:145–146.
55. LC Add. MSS. 32835:145–148.

Mirepoix shortly afterward returned to Paris, and presented to Saint-Contest his reasons for believing that direct negotiations would be success-ful. As a result, he was empowered to begin a series of conversations with Albemarle in Paris, the two ambassadors to be the channels for the com-munication of the claims of their respective governments. The French ambassador indicated that, to serve as his basis for negotiations, he would be given a set of instructions which he would show to Albemarle.[56] The British ambassador was advised not to expect any detailed instruc-tions until he had seen and reported upon the French proposals, for New-castle thought a set of preliminary detailed instructions would be more binding than useful in the trading of concessions that must of necessity take place.[57] In the meantime, however, Albemarle was advised to act upon the general principle that the rights of the two sides should not be too strictly adhered to, but such concessions were to be made as would guarantee "the mutual security of the undisputed Possessions of each Crown."[58] As it was expected that the "favorite Object" of French de-sires would be the recognition of the French title to St. Lucia, Great Brit-ain was prepared to concede that island to France in return for a clear title to Nova Scotia, to which was now to be added, as a further considera-tion, the demolition of the French fortress at Crown Point, on Lake Champlain.[59] Great Britain also claimed the territory up to the St. Law-rence River, however, and even though she might admit a proposal to establish a neutral zone between the river and her own colonies, it was to be made perfectly clear that such a concession must not be used by the French as their authorization to make settlements in that territory.[60]

These instructions reflect what seems to have been a genuine desire on the part of the British government to settle the boundary disputes peace-ably. Even Mirepoix seems to have believed that an arrangement on the basis of this general plan was possible. This French ambassador, had he been given full powers to negotiate, might probably have brought the quarrel to a successful conclusion. But, apparently, he had already com-mitted himself to concessions greater than his superiors were prepared to make, and he found himself unable to continue the negotiations with Albe-marle along the lines to which he had himself agreed. The instructions he had expected from Saint-Contest were not forthcoming, because the Brit-ish ambassador was not given detailed instructions which he could pre-sent to the French court, and the negotiations came to naught.[61] The ex-

56. LC Add. MSS. 32835:261.
57. LC Add. MSS. 32836:94–95, 296–298.
58. LC Add. MSS. 32836:300.
59. LC Add. MSS. 32836:94–95, 97–99, 296–298, 300–301.
60. LC Add. MSS. 32836:94–95, 97–99, 296–298.
61. LC Add. MSS. 32837:98–99; CAO AE CP Ang. 435:236–240, 243–246.

change of ideas is important, nonetheless, as it forecasts the line of reasoning followed by the British in the negotiations which actually took place early in 1755.

The British government had overlooked a real opportunity in its naïve attempt to get Saint-Contest to lay down his cards first; for the result was that French distrust of British sincerity increased. Mirepoix insisted, on his return to London in the fall of 1752, that France was prepared to negotiate as soon as Albemarle received his instructions, and suggested that the British ministry draw up a statement of their claims. On the other hand, Newcastle feared a partial settlement; he therefore proposed to Saint-Contest that the preliminary agreement provide for the settlement of all the points in dispute.[62]

It was easy for the French ministers to agree to this proposal, for this was the very position they had taken in the negotiations of the boundary commission. Rouillé, however, to whom Saint-Contest turned for advice, insisted that the respective rights of the two sovereigns must be known before any direct negotiations could be successful; it was therefore desirable that the commission continue its discussions. The first step was to clarify the rights of both sides, and this was logically the duty of the commission. Afterwards, he thought, it might be possible to recognize those respective points where each might be asked to forego certain of its claims. This was especially important to France, Rouillé admitted, as, apparently, the French would have to make greater concessions than the British.[63] On the surface of things it appears that the two courts were not too far apart to hope for an agreement. But, aside from the mutual distrust which led both to use every trick known to diplomacy to win any tactical advantage over the other, however slight, they were in fact miles apart in their ideas as to what their rights were, and as to the concessions one side might expect from the other. "But even supposing [Newcastle] genuinely intends to work effectively for a termination of these disputes," wrote Rouillé, "may one flatter oneself that he dares to take it upon himself to make an arrangement . . . such as we should be able to adopt, relative to the convenience, the security, and the tranquility of our respective Colonies?"[64] The French Minister of Marine was probably entirely correct in his realistic assumption that neither France nor Great Britain would ever surrender such "unquestionable rights" as would satisfy her opponent. This being true, the only way to settle the question was by force; and force meant war.

62. LC Add. MSS. 32841:354, 356–357; CAO AE CP Ang. 435:235–240, 243–246.
63. ". . . ce qui est d'autant plus important pour nous, que vraisemblablement nous aurons plus à céder que les Anglais." CAO AE CP Ang. 434:258–259.
64. CAO AE CP Ang. 434:258.

Throughout the year 1753, indeed, France and England drifted farther and farther apart.[65] While the boundary commission was wasting the year over the question whether the British commissioners might submit their memorials in their native language, the ministries let the year pass without making any progress toward a peaceful settlement. Late in 1753, France sent a force to the East Indies.[66] Meanwhile, the American forest fire was spreading. The French had built Fort Rouillé and rebuilt Fort Niagara; and now they were establishing themselves upon the upper waters of the Ohio. In August orders went out from England to prevent encroachments by the French, to warn them to keep out of British territory, and, if they did not, to oppose force with force.[67] In fact, in the autumn, in pursuance of these orders, George Washington made his way through the Allegheny wilderness to Fort Le Boeuf to call upon Legardeur de Saint-Pierre, the French commander there, to retire from the "western parts of the Colony of Virginia."[68] In October Newcastle again raised the question of direct negotiations, this time to be conducted by Mirepoix in London;[69] but without result. It seemed to Newcastle that the French probably desired peace, but that they were presuming upon the British desire for peace to encroach upon the British possessions around the world, "in Europe, Asia, Africa, and America, without any ill Consequences from it."[70] This was a dangerous state of affairs; and Newcastle expressed the hope that the nations of Europe really desirous of peace might be brought into a sort of league against France to maintain it.[71] Perhaps it was this view which led him, a little later, to make public to the interested courts of Europe an account of the French negotiations which was calculated to win sympathy and support for Great Britain.

The year 1754 dawned with no appreciable change in the positions of the two powers as to the question of American boundaries. Yet the attention of Anglo-French diplomacy was suddenly focused upon the new center of frontier activity in the Ohio Valley. Governor Dinwiddie of Virginia replied to Legardeur de Saint-Pierre's refusal to retire by sending an expedition to build a fort at the confluence of the Allegheny and Monongahela. This famous expedition, also under the command of George Washington, reached the neighborhood of the Ohio only to find itself forestalled by the enterprising Governor Duquesne.[72] The resultant skirmish, followed by the battle of Fort Necessity, furnished the shock

65. Mildmay to Fitzwalter, February 7, 1753, CL Mildmay Papers—"Private Letters from Paris"; same to same, January 23, 1754, *ibid.*

66. LC Add. MSS. 32848:142 ff. 67. *N.Y. Col. Docs.*, VI, 794–795.

68. *Ibid.*, X, 258–259. 69. CAO AE CP Ang. 436:335–337.

70. LC Add. MSS. 32848:142 ff. 71. LC Add. MSS. 32848:142 ff.

72. LC Add. MSS. 32850:221.

that set in motion two trains of events, the revival of negotiations for a peaceful settlement of the American disputes, and the succession of forcible measures on both sides that made a peaceful settlement progressively more difficult.

Mirepoix returned to Paris in June, 1754, carrying with him Newcastle's warning that if the French king really desired peace he must give his colonial governors such orders as would restrain them from occupying territory claimed by the British Crown. With the news of the defeat of Washington at Fort Necessity, Newcastle realized the success of the French in blocking British expansion all along the line, and the effectiveness of the French plan to confine the British colonies to the seaboard. "All North America will be lost," he wrote, "if these Practices are tolerated, And no War can be worse to this Country, than the Suffering Such Insults, as these."[73] The French had long advanced, and were now successfully maintaining by force, the argument that the true boundary between the two empires was the Appalachian watershed. The British Empire, only now really awakening to a consciousness of its own need to expand beyond that line, found the French intrenched and ready to block its passage at every important point. To Newcastle, indeed, it seemed that it would be relatively easy for the French, from these posts as bases, to drive the British out of North America altogether. "But that," he wrote, "is what We must not, We will not, suffer." Measures were already being taken to prevent it.[74]

The French, on their side, were evasive but clearly determined to maintain their position. Rouillé tried to reassure Albemarle and called for a revival of the negotiations of the commission. But the British ministers were skeptical. "I own, I am quite sick of Commissaries," wrote Newcastle, "tho' I don't well know how to get rid of them. I am sure, they will do no Good, and therefore hope, We shall not be so far amus'd by their Conferences, as to suspend, or delay, taking the proper Measures, to defend Ourselves, or recover our lost Possessions."[75]

The British attitude was clearly stiffening. Albemarle likewise privately scoffed at "commissarys," and recommended sending "Officers, and good ones," to discipline and lead the colonial militia against the French.[76] Sir Thomas Robinson,[77] had succeeded Holdernesse as Secretary of State, and he was more specific. He voiced his appreciation of Rouillé's expressions of peaceful intention, but he made it clear that they would carry more weight if accompanied by more friendly action. This

73. LC Add. MSS. 32850:218.   74. LC Add. MSS. 32850:218–220.
75. LC Add. MSS. 32850:218–220.   76. LC Add. MSS. 32850:289.
77. Sir Thomas Robinson, later Baron Grantham, was Secretary of State for the Southern Department from March, 1754, to November, 1755.

would mean the complete evacuation of the "neutral islands," the abandonment of the French forts built in Acadia since the peace, and the withdrawal of French forces from the Ohio. Great Britain, he said, could not be directed by a joint commission while the French troops were in possession of British territory.[78] On October 3, 1754, he advised Albemarle that the government had decided to send General Braddock and two regiments of soldiers to Virginia.[79]

The French ministers were now disturbed, and Rouillé protested against this military action as being an aggression. The French, said Rouillé, proposed only to resume possession of their own lands and to confine the British within their natural boundaries, which they had violated by going to the Ohio.[80] A little later Rouillé asked Albemarle if he thought the boundary dispute in America could be settled peaceably. Albemarle said that a prerequisite would be the withdrawal of French troops from the "English Side" of the Ohio. But Rouillé felt this could not be done, as it would be a confession of weakness and tantamount to a surrender of territory that was French. When Albemarle asked for a definite proposal, Rouillé could give none, and announced that France, too, must now send soldiers to America.[81] The focus of tension over America had shifted from Acadia to the Ohio Valley. But the issues in the West Indies and Acadia and the Gulf coastal plain were far from forgotten. Any settlement calculated to be satisfactory must include them all; and the statesmen of France and Great Britain knew it.

78. LC Add. MSS. 32850:301–302; CL Shelburne MSS. XXXVI:48; *Brit. Dip. Instrs.*, VII, *France 1745–1789*, pp. 47–48.
79. LC Add. MSS. 32851:14; CL Shelburne MSS. XXXVI:61; *Brit. Dip. Instrs.*, VII, *France 1745–1789*, pp. 48–49.
80. CL Shelburne MSS. XXXVI:69.   81. CL Shelburne MSS. XXXVI:86.

CHAPTER IV

THE DIPLOMATIC CRISIS OF 1755

WAR seemed now to be inevitable;[1] and both sides began to look around for possible allies. The eyes of both had long since turned to Spain, not only because Spain was directly interested in the colonial quarrel, but also because she held the balance of power in the colonial world. France, ever since the Peace of Aix-la-Chapelle, had cultivated the friendship of the Spanish court, and had done everything possible to prevent a *rapprochement* between Spain and Great Britain.[2] Duras, the French ambassador at Madrid, was instructed to call the attention of the Spanish ministers to the British expansion, and to point out the danger to Mexico and other Spanish possessions in America inherent in a movement that threatened the destruction of the French empire in North America. In view of their common colonial interests, Duras suggested a common defensive program to prevent a disturbance of the American balance of power.[3]

This appeal to Spanish distrust of the British was well calculated, for Great Britain had long given Spain trouble in the colonial world. British ships were trading with Spanish colonial ports, and logwood (dyewood) cutters on the coasts of Campeche and Honduras had established settlements in territory which was admittedly Spanish—settlements that threatened to become permanent. Spanish coast guards were stopping British vessels on the high seas, and periodic raids by the Spanish colonial governors upon the British logwood cutters intermittently threatened to bring on an out-and-out conflict.[4] French influence at the Spanish court was increased, moreover, by the pro-French sympathies of the chief minister, the Marquis de Enseñada, whose belligerent orders to the commanders of Spanish ships at Havana in April, 1754, almost precipitated war between Spain and England.[5] But a war between Spain and England would throw Spain back under the domination of France, and His Catholic Majesty did not relish that thought. In addition to this, Sir Benjamin

1. Mildmay to Fitzwalter, December 15, 1754, CL Mildmay Papers—"Private Letters from Paris"; BM Add. MSS. 32851:315–316, *et passim.*
2. *Recueil des Instructions,* XII *bis, Espagne,* pp. 294, 295, 315–317, *et passim; Archives du Ministère des Affaires Etrangères,* Paris. *Correspondance Politique: Espagne* 510:165–175. Hereafter cited as AE CP Espagne.
3. AE CP Espagne 510:387.
4. "Notes of a Council at Kensington, July 19, 1744," PRO Chatham MSS. XCVIII; LC Add. MSS. 32829:163, 32837:86, 284, 32839:24, 32842:152, 32843:147, 32847:177, *et passim.*
5. BM Stowe MSS. 256:221–231, 236–242, 244–247, 274–276, *et passim;* LC Add. MSS. 32849:441–452, 465–468.

Keene, the British ambassador in Madrid, was so far successful in winning the confidence of the Spanish sovereign, by the power of intrigue and his own good graces, as to expose and bring about the disgrace of Enseñada, who was replaced by the pro-British Ricardo Wall.[6]

In the autumn of 1754, when the Anglo-French negotiations seemed to have failed, Louis XV wrote to his Spanish cousin explaining the course of the negotiations and expressing a grave fear that Great Britain's "ambition" might force France into war, to prevent the projected British intrusion upon the glory of "our house."[7] He sent his royal cousin a note in which great emphasis was laid upon British expansion from Georgia and Carolina toward the Gulf of Mexico—an emphasis calculated to arouse the Spanish court to join forces with France to resist the British menace.[8] But Ferdinand's reply was evasive. All honor was to be done to the ties of blood, and to Louis' desire for peace, he said; but the king and his ministers believed that Spain's quarrels with Great Britain could and should be liquidated by diplomacy rather than war.[9]

On the British side, Newcastle had been "frightened out of his Wits" by the Enseñada crisis, and he wrote Wall a personal letter appealing for a peaceful adjustment of the Anglo-Spanish disputes.[10] Keene lost no time in playing up certain French movements in the West Indies, notably the occupation of Turks Island, and in capitalizing the favorable turn events had taken.[11] He was instructed to explain the Anglo-French negotiations from the British side, to call attention to obstacles thrown in the way of the negotiations by France, and to voice Great Britain's determination to achieve a settlement on the basis of "right."[12] Keene reported that France had invited Spain to mediate the Anglo-French disputes in America, but that the invitation had been declined. Spain, Wall was reported to have said, could not mediate a quarrel in which she had interests so similar to those of the disputants, and Great Britain would certainly resent any attempt at mediation by a member of the house of Bourbon.[13] In any case, Wall expected to settle the Spanish differences with England by negotiation; but the most weighty reason for Spanish caution was probably the fear of falling under the domination of France.[14]

6. BM Stowe MSS. 256:130–137, 236–242, *et passim;* Great Britain, Royal Commission on Historical Manuscripts: *Reports,* III, Lansdowne MSS. p. 141; Sir Richard Lodge, ed., *The Private Correspondence of Sir Benjamin Keene, K.B.* (Cambridge, 1933), p. 38.

7. AE CP Espagne 516:83.   8. AE CP Espagne 516:920.
9. AE CP Espagne 516:542.   10. LC Add. MSS. 32849:309.
11. LC Add. MSS. 32851:110, 319.   12. BM Add. MSS. 32851:315–316.
13. LC Add. MSS. 32850:362, 32851:110.

14. LC Add. MSS. 32850:362, 381, 32851:110; BM Add. MSS. 32851:315, 32848:155; AE CP Espagne 517:143; Wall to Keene, September 15, 1754, PRO Chatham MSS. XCII.

The appeal of France and Great Britain to the good opinion of the Spanish King was intensified as the Anglo-French dispute continued,[15] and was soon extended to every important court in Western Europe.[16] Meanwhile, Mirepoix returned to London; Albemarle had died, in December, 1754, and Lord Hertford had been named as his successor.[17] Another effort was to be made to effect a settlement of the American boundary disputes by peaceful diplomatic negotiation. Mirepoix's instructions, however, were scarcely calculated to bring about the desired accommodation. Somewhat belligerent in tone, and expressing indignation at the warlike utterances of the British King at the recent opening of Parliament, the instructions had little to offer that was new. The joint commission had made no progress, according to this document, because of British delays; and the direct negotiations proposed by the British government in 1752 had not materialized because of the failure of the ministry to send the ambassador in Paris instructions to that end. Now, the French had been attacked[18] in territory which unquestionably belonged to the French Crown, and the King felt he must protest against the warlike measures of the British governors. If the British assurances of peaceful intention meant anything, the American disputes should be referred to the joint commission already established for that purpose. But if the British ministry still desired direct negotiations, Mirepoix might undertake them.[19]

The French ambassador began his negotiations about the middle of January, 1755. He found Robinson rather better informed on the actual geography of America than he was. The British minister was prepared to point out that the French had historically followed three different routes between Canada and Louisiana, the shortest being via the Wabash, and that all of them were rather distant from the mountains. The French, said Robinson, had never claimed the territory lying along the upper waters of the Ohio.[20] On the contrary, this territory had been conquered by the Iroquois Indians, who were recognized by the Treaty of Utrecht as allies and subjects of Great Britain, and they had subsequently sold it to the British.[21] The British title, therefore, was based upon Article XV of the Treaty of Utrecht, the conquest of the west by the Iroquois, and the pur-

15. AE CP Espagne 517, 518, et passim; LC Add. MSS. 32853:179.

16. LC Add. MSS. 32851:148, 32849:154, 32853:179, 193, 205, 429, 486; LC AE Méms. et Docs. Amérique 24:200–240; CAO AE CP Ang. 438:38.

17. CAO AE CP Ang. 438:100. Hertford never actually went to Paris.

18. By the Washington expedition.

19. Pease, op. cit., pp. 60–83. LC AE Méms. et Docs. France 525:186–199.

20. Pease, op. cit., pp. 87–88.

21. Ibid. The purchase referred to is apparently that made at the Treaty of Lancaster, in 1744.

chase of these lands by the British colonies. The King of England was entirely within his rights, said Robinson, in granting lands in this region to a company of Englishmen, and in sending a detachment of soldiers to fortify the forks of the Ohio. The American colonies naturally looked upon the French intrusion in that region as an invasion of British territory, and the attack upon Washington's little army as an unjustifiable act of violence in time of peace.[22]

Mirepoix pleaded his lack of instructions for a discussion of the bases of the French title, but said the differences as to title should have been referred to the commission in Paris. Meanwhile, he said, the British colonial governors should never have interfered with arms in a disputed territory.[23] Nevertheless, in order to avoid further incidents and to bring about a spirit of conciliation as quickly as possible, he laid before Robinson a memorandum containing four propositions. First, before entering upon a discussion of their respective rights, orders should be sent to the colonial governors to avoid all further action; second, the situation in the valley of the Ohio should be restored to what it had been before the last war; third, the question of actual possession should be referred to the commission in Paris; and, fourth, His Most Christian Majesty should be informed as to the destination of the military expedition then preparing in England.[24]

These propositions were unacceptable to the British cabinet. The British were willing to have affairs in the Ohio Valley restored to the condition they were in, not at the beginning of the last war, but at the time of the Peace of Utrecht.[25] This restoration was to be similarly applied in regard to all the other changes that had taken place since the date of that treaty, and specifically to the forts built by the French at Niagara, on Crown Point, the St. John River, and the isthmus of Nova Scotia. As for the armaments then preparing, the French might rest assured of their purely defensive nature; the King of England had no aggressive designs on the territory of any of his neighbors. He must, however, protect his just rights. At the same time, moreover, he now asked to be informed of the intentions of the French with regard to the naval force then being made ready in the harbors of Brest and Toulon.[26] In Robinson's note embody-

22. *Ibid.*, pp. 88–91.
23. *Ibid.* It apparently did not occur to him that the French were doing precisely the same thing; for them, of course, it was really French territory, and open to no question.
24. *Ibid.*, pp. 93–95, 95–97.
25. The distinction is important; if the *status quo* of 1713 were restored, France would have had to demolish Crown Point, Niagara, Fort Toulouse, and the forts in Acadia. England would have lost only Oswego.
26. Pease, *op. cit.*, pp. 85–86.

ing these ideas, he tactfully omitted any specific reference to the French establishments at Niagara, Crown Point, and on the St. John River, but proposed that "the other" possessions in North America be restored to the *status quo* at the time of the Peace of Utrecht; and, without directly mentioning the proposal to submit the dispute to the Paris commission, he proposed negotiations *"de cour à cour"* in the matter of the orders to be sent to the colonial governors.[27]

Mirepoix pointed out in reply that France still had no clear information as to what Great Britain claimed on the Ohio; the French had possessed the valley since 1679, when La Salle had discovered it, and the Treaty of Utrecht did not even mention it. What France now proposed was entirely conformable to the Treaty of Aix-la-Chapelle. Consequently, France again proposed that orders to the colonial governors be sent immediately; that the *status quo* be restored throughout North America, as provided in Article IX of the Treaty of Aix-la-Chapelle; that, conformable to Article XVIII of the same treaty, the disputes in America be referred to the commission in Paris for a discussion of the rights involved; and that the ministers of the two courts be authorized to negotiate a settlement.[28] This note was accompanied by full powers for Mirepoix to negotiate the settlement directly with the British government.[29] But as to the Ohio Valley, Rouillé insisted that it had always formed a part of the territory of the French King and that the British had only recently raised a claim to it. To admit even the slightest pretense of a British claim to occupy that valley would be to admit the British into the center of his dominions and to place them in a position quickly to possess themselves of Canada and Louisiana. The burden of proof, he said, was upon the British.[30]

The final authorization of Mirepoix to negotiate on the question of a boundary was the opening for which the British had been waiting throughout this interlude of diplomatic sparring, and the British ministers now prepared to make a definite proposal. On February 7 the cabinet authorized Robinson to enter into negotiations with Mirepoix and to propose an immediate evacuation of the lands along the Ohio; all the forts in that area were to be demolished.[31] When Robinson met with Mirepoix, he expressed the willingness of the British government to send orders to the colonial governors for such evacuation, but with the qualification that they must be instructed as to the exact limits of the territory they were to evacuate. As the commissioners in Paris gave little hope of an early agreement on this point, he proposed an immediate understanding between the

27. CAO AE CP Ang. 438:38–39; Pease, *op. cit.,* pp. 99–101.
28. Pease, *op. cit.,* pp. 102–106.   29. CAO AE CP Ang. 438:114.
30. Pease, *op. cit.,* pp. 106–108.   31. *Ibid.,* p. 109.

two governments. Mirepoix demurred, falling back on the old French contention that any permanent settlement must be based upon rights rather than expediency, and he proposed a provisional arrangement which would provide for an armistice and the precise orders to be sent to the colonial governors while the commission in Paris should be charged with the task of arriving at the rightful claims of the contestants. Robinson asked how they were to reach such a provisional agreement, and Mirepoix referred to the French principle proposed in 1752, that neither side should be allowed anywhere to own forts which would menace or disturb the possessions of the other. As a mode of clarifying this principle, Mirepoix distinguished between "useful possession," under which the land was actually settled and exploited by the owner, and "exclusive ownership" of territory, which procured for the owner little beside the ability to prevent his enemies from establishing themselves there. In other words, proceeding upon this principle, the frontiers to be defined would be the limits of actual settlement by the French and British, but between the British frontier and the French frontier there would be a sort of unoccupied zone, stretching from Acadia to the Ohio. Within this zone, the nationals on both sides would be permitted to go for trade, but they would not be allowed to build forts or set up any other sort of establishment.[32]

On February 9, 1755, Robinson reported to the cabinet, and was authorized to negotiate upon the basis of Mirepoix's proposals; the Ohio Valley was to be evacuated and left as a neutral country, in which both British and French should be allowed only to trade. He was authorized to agree upon a suspension of arms for an unspecified number of months, while negotiations on the various points should proceed, during which neither side was to send ships of war or soldiers to America.[33] As a definition of the boundaries which were to be regarded as having prevailed at the time of the Treaty of Utrecht, Robinson agreed that "the limits of the English colonies should terminate at the mountains, and that all the land beyond, as far as the lakes and to the Ohio and Wabash rivers, should remain as formerly free to the natives of the country and to the French and English for the purpose of travel and commerce only." All forts within this territory were to be demolished. As soon as these "limits" were agreed upon the negotiators should proceed to the other points in dispute; and as soon as an agreement should be reached with regard to any area the necessary orders would be immediately dispatched to the colonial governors. If all this seemed satisfactory to the French ministry, they were invited to send a detailed plan for an agreement.[34]

32. CAO AE CP Ang. 438:114.
33. Pease, *op. cit.,* pp. 109–110; CAO AE CP Ang. 438:119.
34. CAO AE CP Ang. 438:120–122.

In transmitting these proposals to his superiors, Mirepoix expressed the belief that the British were sincere in their desire for peace, and he was optimistic as to the outcome. He thought there was not a moment to lose, however, for the English nation was aroused, the government was weak, and the ministers might be dragged by public opinion into warlike measures from which they could not withdraw. He therefore urged that the instructions necessary for further negotiation be sent to him promptly. The entire North American problem, it seemed to him, reduced itself to three points—the Ohio frontier, the New York–Great Lakes boundary, and the boundaries of Acadia. Time was of consummate importance; but if the ministry could give him, now, such instructions relative to the Ohio as would make it possible to settle that point, the tension would be relaxed, and one might then proceed at greater leisure to the others in dispute. This did not seem difficult, for the territory between the mountains and the Wabash fell within the classification he had defined as "exclusive ownership"; and he thought both sides might be satisfied with an arrangement there that would guarantee the security of their settled territories east of the mountains and west of the Wabash.[35]

Robinson apparently felt it was safe to proceed further, for at a cabinet meeting following this exchange, the proposed neutral area was defined as "the River Ohio, with the Countries on Each Side of The sd River, from the Allegheny Mountains to The Lake of Ontario, The River of Niagara, The Lake of Erie, and The River Oubach [Wabash], or St. Jerome." This area was to be evacuated, but left open to subjects of both kings for trade.[36] As for the other areas, Robinson was to demand the free navigation of the Niagara River and of Lake Ontario and Lake Erie for Englishmen, with the demolition of Crown Point and any forts there might be on the "Western Side" of the Niagara River. The isthmus of Nova Scotia, together with an undefined strip of land along the shore of the Bay of Fundy from the isthmus to the borders of New England, was to be British; the land between this strip and the St. Lawrence was to be left neutral, as was that in the upper Ohio.[37]

The promise of peace now seemed fairly good. Even Newcastle believed the matters in dispute would be successfully compromised.[38] But this optimism was unjustified; for the ministers had not reckoned upon the opposition of the imperialists, chief of whom were the Earl of Halifax in England, and Rouillé, apparently influenced by La Galissonnière, in France.[39] Halifax had not been present at any of the three cabinet meet-

---

35. CAO AE CP Ang. 438:122–124.   36. Pease, *op. cit.*, p. 110.
37. *Ibid.*, pp. 110–111.   38. LC Add. MSS. 32852:529.
39. Mirepoix has been accused of weakness and docility when faced with the English demands. But he seems to have realized, more than any other Frenchman, that,

ings that had authorized Robinson's plan,[40] and when the plan of February 10 was submitted to him for comment, this fiery empire-builder found much in it to criticize. He pointed out the vagueness of the proposed line to be drawn from the mountains to the lakes and the fact that, however drawn, it would cut off considerable parts of Pennsylvania or New York, or both; and he doubted the legal right of the Crown to interfere with the territorial status of those provinces. He appealed also to the British claim to the lands of the Iroquois, pointing out that the proposed line would exclude the British from the Iroquois lands south of the lakes. How, he asked, could the British right to traverse the lakes be maintained if the British were to abandon their means of protecting it? As a matter of fact, he said, the Iroquois possessed the lands to the north of the lakes, and the proposed arrangement, that is, to leave the French in possession of their forts in that region, would be tantamount to a complete surrender of it, when, according to Halifax, it was recognized as British by the Treaty of Utrecht. Finally, he pointed out the vagueness of the terms which dealt with the Niagara River, Lake Champlain, and the proposed boundaries of Nova Scotia. Great Britain's right to the latter, he said, was so clear and indisputable that any concession there should be made only in consideration of some equal concession by the French elsewhere.[41]

Halifax's objections to the Allegheny Mountains as a boundary were convincing to Robinson and Hardwicke,[42] and at a cabinet meeting on February 20 the earlier plan, so big with potentialities for subsequent North American history, was revised. In the new scheme, arbitrary lines were to be substituted for the natural boundaries; the British colonies were to be bounded by a line which, starting at Canagahogue or Cuyahoga Bay, on the south side of Lake Erie, was to run due south to its intersection with the line of the fortieth degree of latitude, and thence southwest to the line of the thirty-seventh degree of latitude. The French territory was to be limited by a line which, starting from the mouth of the Maumee River, on Lake Erie, would run directly to the source of the Wabash River, thence down that river to its confluence with the Ohio, and thence due south to the line of the thirty-seventh parallel of latitude. The territory between these lines was to be left to the natives, but should be open to

even though the logic of geography and history might be on the side of France, some sacrifice must be made for the sake of peace. Especially was this true in the face of a British determination which no other French minister seems to have appreciated; certainly the sacrifices that Mirepoix would have made in 1755 were infinitesimal when compared to those that France was compelled to make as the final result of the trial by war. Cf. Pease, *op. cit.*, p. xlix, *et passim*, and Waddington, *Louis XV*, pp. 77, 78, *et passim*.

40. Pease, *op. cit.*, pp. xlvii, 109, 110.   41. *Ibid.*, pp. 111–114.
42. BM Add. MSS. 32852:505–506.

Frenchmen and Englishmen for trade. With regard to the lakes region, this new plan proposed that the forts at Crown Point and Niagara be demolished, and that the French agree never to build any other forts along the lakes. These waterways were to remain open for trade to the subjects of both Crowns. The boundary of Nova Scotia was to be the Penobscot River and a line drawn due north from its source to the St. Lawrence; but a straight line was to be drawn from a point some distance up the Penobscot to a point on the Gulf of St. Lawrence north of Cape Tourmentin, and the lands between that line and the St. Lawrence were to be left unpossessed by either France or Great Britain, although the nationals of both might go there for trade.[43]

With regard to the Ohio, this plan was clearly a withdrawal from the offer already made by Robinson to Mirepoix in accord with the earlier decisions of the cabinet, and could hardly have been expected to meet with French approval. Rouillé had, indeed, already drawn up a project for a preliminary convention, based upon Mirepoix's report of his conferences with Robinson, which was forwarded to the French ambassador on February 19. Rouillé's project accepted the British proposal to restore the *status quo* when the Treaty of Utrecht was signed, and took Robinson's willingness to use the mountains as a boundary for the British colonies as an admission that the land beyond the mountains did not belong to Great Britain. Rouillé was therefore able to make much of the sacrifice of the French King in evacuating the region of the upper Ohio and consenting to the demolition of the forts that had been built in this area which His Most Christian Majesty considered as incontestably his. The demolition of forts must be reciprocal, said Rouillé, and must include on the part of the British the demolition of the forts at Oswego on Lake Ontario, and at Chignecto, Beaubassin, and Minas, in Acadia. But France could never consent to the inclusion of lands west of the Ohio in the proposed neutral zone, for the course of the Ohio was necessary to the maintenance of communications between Canada and Louisiana; the neutral zone must be the land between the upper Ohio and the mountains. The proposal to leave the neutral zone open to the traders of both nations Rouillé found to be impracticable: if the traders went into the country they would have to establish trading posts, these posts must be protected by palisades against the temperamental Indians, and this would make them military forts. France therefore proposed, even at great sacrifice to herself, that the subjects of both Crowns be forbidden to enter the neutral territory. The proposed convention was to remain in force for two years, during which time both governments should instruct their ministers and their commissioners

43. Pease, *op. cit.*, pp. 135–138.

in Paris in such a fashion as to make it possible, within that time, to come to a definitive agreement upon all the boundaries in North America.[44]

Both governments had been unwilling to make the concessions suggested by their negotiators, which made their work increasingly difficult. The British insisted upon a neutral zone in the Ohio Valley that would extend to the Wabash, although they were willing to leave the French completely free on the east bank within a few miles of that river. Now, too, conformably to their plan of February 20, the British began to find fault with Robinson's earlier line. The mountains, they said, could not serve as a boundary for the British colonies, because the mountains were not parallel with the Ohio, and, whereas at certain points the British might find themselves very close to it, at others mountain irregularities would push them far away from it. Moreover, in the valleys there were many British settlements of long standing which would be cut off by the proposed line, thus encroaching upon the provinces of New York, Pennsylvania, and Virginia. So, far from accepting the French claims to the ownership of the Ohio Valley, the British ministers professed to see in those claims a threat to the success of the entire negotiation, and promised to submit compromise proposals.[45]

This shifting of their position by the British seemed to justify Rouillé in his fear that they were simply playing for time while preparing for war. The French minister displayed a righteous indignation at the fact that, instead of appreciating the sacrifices his sovereign had made for the sake of peace, the English were now demanding still greater ones and quibbling over the proposed line along the mountains. This line, he said, might be drawn along the mountain chain nearest the French, and would thus leave the British settlements in the valleys intact. The British pretension to the lands about the lakes, based upon Article XV of the Treaty of Utrecht, Rouillé considered equally preposterous, but he would not enter into details on this claim, as this was a matter to be decided by subsequent negotiation. For the present, the important thing was to arrive at an arrangement that would bring to an end hostilities on the Ohio.[46]

The climax of the negotiations was reached early in March. For when, on March 7, Robinson laid before Mirepoix the formal British counterproposals to the French plan of February 19, the impossibility of harmonizing the views of the two governments became clearly apparent. This

44. *Ibid.*, pp. 126–129.
45. *Ibid.*, pp. 138–143. The English who traded with the Indians had begun to build houses and settlements in the mountain valleys, and even on the westward slopes. Such, for example, were Christopher Gist's settlement on the Monongahela and Draper's Meadows on the New River.
46. *Ibid.*, pp. 143–148.

document outlined what was expected to be the preliminary articles of a definitive settlement instead of the armistice desired by the French. It proposed that the lines described in the plan of February 20 rather than the natural boundaries be used to define the limits of the two empires, and again insisted that the neutral zone between these lines be open to the traders of both. Further, it specified that the French forts on the Niagara River and at Crown Point must be demolished, leaving Lakes Champlain, Ontario, and Erie, together with the Niagara River, open to the traders of both nations. With regard to Nova Scotia, the British still proposed that the boundary be the Penobscot River and a line drawn due north from the source of that river to the St. Lawrence, with a neutral zone along the St. Lawrence to the Gulf of St. Lawrence, as suggested by Halifax.[47]

These Halifax-inspired counterproposals reaped the whirlwind. The demands of the English were inadmissible, wrote Rouillé, and the French council refused to reply to them in writing; the mere acceptance of such a document by the French ambassador, indeed, was to be regarded as evidence of the extreme desire of France for peace.[48] In the "observations" on the counterproposals sent to Mirepoix, it was pointed out that the arbitrary lines proposed by Robinson would make for more dispute and confusion, whereas mountains and rivers had ever been the most satisfactory lines of demarcation. Further, the French minister pointed out that the British had had no establishments in the valley of the Ohio, and had advanced a claim to that territory only since the Peace of Aix-la-Chapelle. The British traders who had gone there had been private individuals; when France, in the exercise of her sovereignty, arrested some of them in 1750, Great Britain had acquiesced,[49] and Albemarle had simply asked that they be released, a request which France had generously granted. The demand for the demolition of the forts placed the burden of sacrifice entirely upon the French, as the British had no forts on the Ohio; further, Robinson's stipulations would also involve the demolition of the fort at Presqu'Isle, on Lake Erie, "*où les anglais n'ont jamais mis le pied*"— "where the English have never set foot," and of Vincennes, dependent on Louisiana, which was located on the eastern shore of the Wabash.[50] The British demand for the demolition of the forts at Niagara and Crown Point and for freedom of commerce on the Great Lakes, it was maintained, would involve a great sacrifice by France, which would not in any way be compensated for by England. Both these forts had been built long

47. BM Add. MSS. 6862:58–62.   48. Pease, *op. cit.*, p. 161.
49. This was not true; Albemarle had protested vigorously, and had demanded both the release of the traders and the restoration of their goods.
50. CAO AE CP Ang. 438:139–142.

ago, without any protest by Great Britain.[51] The British had likewise mentioned to Mirepoix a fort on the north side of Lake Ontario, of which he did not recall the name, which they would expect to be razed. This Rouillé took to be Fort Frontenac,[52] and one might with as much justice, he said, demand the demolition of Quebec. As for granting freedom of commerce on the lakes, one might as well demand the cession of Canada, in its entirety, since these waters passed directly through the colony. Any claim the British might have to territory granted by the Indians Rouillé also thought absurd. The Indian lands had no defined limits; and, since they were a migrant people, the British contention implied that, wherever the Iroquois Indians happened to go, any land they set foot upon immediately became British! In any case, Article XV of the Treaty of Utrecht was useless, because the provision for determining which Indians were the allies of France and which of Great Britain had never been acted upon; nor could it be, because of their fickle and unreliable character.[53]

France was equally disturbed by the British demands with regard to Acadia. The line proposed as a boundary cut the south shore of the St. Lawrence into two parts; the lower part Great Britain would leave neutral, but from the silence of their counterproposals with regard to the upper part, which would lie opposite Quebec and Montreal, Rouillé professed to believe the British would soon demand that territory in full ownership. This would make the St. Lawrence the boundary between Canada and the English colonies, and thus give Great Britain a continuous strip of territory along the St. Lawrence and the lakes from Acadia to the north and south line proposed by Robinson as the eastern limit of the Ohio region. This would split Canada in half. As for the neutral zone proposed by Great Britain between Nova Scotia and the St. Lawrence, it would destroy the land communications between Quebec and the Atlantic, or Cape Breton, and so leave Canada completely defenseless during a great part of the year, when the St. Lawrence was frozen over. In the face of these considerations, Rouillé felt it was hardly useful to discuss the British demand for a *lisière* along the Bay of Fundy.[54] Finally, Great Britain proposed to make this a definitive settlement of American disputes, instead of the provisional convention proposed by France; yet at the same time the British counterproposals were silent as to the West In-

51. The British ambassador had, on June 13, 1732, protested against the building of Fort St. Frédéric, at Crown Point. (*N.Y. Col. Docs.*, IX, 1034.) Governor Dongan of New York had protested against the original fort at Niagara (*ibid.*, III, 516, *et passim;* IX, 389), and Governor Burnet had protested upon the building of the new fort there in 1721 (*ibid.*, IX, 899).

52. The English really meant Fort Rouillé, known to them as Toronto, near the mouth of the Humber. Pease, *op. cit.*, p. 197.

53. CAO AE CP Ang. 438:142–144.   54. CAO AE CP Ang. 438:145.

dies, where there still existed problems which must be settled before France would consent to any definitive arrangement in North America. France would be willing to make such a settlement on reasonable terms; but if Great Britain did not desire war, she must abandon her desire to acquire possession of Canada by treaty. It was not merely a question of a little more or a little less territory in the American wilderness, said Rouillé; both nations might easily give up much, in the name of peace. The most important consideration to each contestant was that of assuring strategic security for the territory it possessed.[55] The value of the entire trade of the Ohio Valley was not worth a thousand pistoles a year. But the Ohio River flowed through the heart of New France; it was for that reason that France was determined, at all costs, to maintain herself in its possession. Neither would France consider the opening of the lakes to the British, or their equally excessive claim to the south shore of the St. Lawrence.[56]

These eloquent "observations" were probably written with an eye to the other courts of Europe. But the full pressure of French wrath and indignation appeared only in the private letter accompanying them. "We see with regret, Monsieur," wrote Rouillé, "that war alone can terminate our discussions."[57] It appeared to him that the British ministry, having unwisely taken precipitate measures of force, now found themselves under the necessity of justifying their policy in the eyes of their country, and he predicted their early fall. From now on, France would consider the negotiations as broken off, unless the British made some more conciliatory gesture. Should they make any proposal, Mirepoix was to transmit it to his court, but he was not to make any overtures on his own account. Europe, said Rouillé, was deeply concerned and must surely see with surprise and alarm that such an unimportant matter as the territory of the Ohio should give rise to the "monstrous" pretensions of the British, and that Great Britain, to satisfy her "unjust visions of ambition and conquest," wished to destroy the "balance of power" in the New World, thus exposing all Europe to the dangers of a new war.[58]

The British counterproposals of March 7 and the French reply mark the real failure of the negotiations and the beginning of their end. They dragged on until summer, to be sure, as each side tried with apparently desperate earnestness to convince the other. But both sides apparently realized the truth of Rouillé's conviction that only the trial by war could now decide the American boundary questions in dispute between them. As early as March 11, four days after the British counterproposals had been delivered, and before the French replied, Robinson wrote to Sir Benjamin

55. This was La Galissonnière's idea.   56. CAO AE CP Ang. 438:146–147.
57. Pease, *op. cit.*, p. 161.   58. *Ibid.*, pp. 159–165.

Keene, in Madrid, stating his conviction that the French had never desired more than a mere cessation of arms;[59] and on the same day George II issued a proclamation which offered bounties to recruits for the navy. A wave of warlike fervor began to run through England. The King's speech from the throne, on March 24, was distinctly belligerent in tone, and it was followed by the voting of a million pounds in war credits.[60] Braddock had sailed for America early in January, and, to forestall him, the French had begun to prepare, at Brest, a far stronger expeditionary force for Canada. The British ministry knew of the French preparations, of course, and on March 18, before the receipt of Rouillé's "observations" on the counterproposals, the cabinet had decided that the French fleet must be intercepted and prevented from landing any troops in Canada.[61]

Strange as it may seem, and despite his positive orders to the contrary, a little later Mirepoix entered into a new series of conversations with Robinson in which he not only took the initiative but also went far in the direction of compromise.[62] He now agreed to meet the British demands as to Acadia, in return for one of the West Indies ; when asked what he would do with the proposed neutral zone along the St. Lawrence, he suggested the possibility of arranging it in such a way as to leave France a line of communication overland between Quebec and Ile St. Jean (Prince Edward Island). He intimated that Fort St. Frédéric might be moved from Crown Point to a location farther down the lake ; but Robinson got the impression that he would be willing to concede its entire demolition, if the British insisted. South of the lakes and the St. Lawrence, Mirepoix proposed that there be a *lisière* twenty leagues in breadth, in which the French might have no establishments except in that part of it that lay along the St. Lawrence. East of the Wabash, likewise, he proposed a *lisière* twenty leagues in width. As for the line marking the boundary of the British colonies, he proposed that it be drawn from Venango, on the Allegheny, to the mountains, and then along the mountains to their southern end. Robinson was especially impressed by the advantages this boundary would have for the British colonies in the south. "If the top of our line can be adjusted, I should humbly think the mountains stretching as they

59. LC Add. MSS. 32853:185.

60. Julian S. Corbett, *England in the Seven Years' War* (London, 1907), I, 31, 40–42.

61. CAO AE CP Ang. 434:335–339; Corbett, *op. cit.,* I, 31, 40–44.

62. LC Add. MSS. 32853:437–438. Robinson and Newcastle both apparently believed Mirepoix had secret instructions from Louis XV, over the heads of the French ministers, which would have made the English negotiations comparable to Louis' contemporary secret negotiation with the court at Vienna. It is difficult to account for his new concessions otherwise. Cf. Waddington, *Louis XV,* p. 162; Pease, *op. cit.,* p. 191 n., and p. 200.

do far to the West would be a very advantageous boundary for our Carolinas."[63]

Robinson was skeptical of Mirepoix's authority to make any such far-reaching proposals, but the French ambassador reported to his superior that the British minister had accepted most of them. And Robinson, skeptical though he was, submitted to the cabinet a set of proposals which embodied them, with slight modification. Now the line in the Ohio region was to be drawn from Lake Erie to the mountains, and thence along the mountains to the thirty-ninth degree of northern latitude, and the French were to have both sides of the Wabash. The territory along the lakes was to be restored to its *status quo* after the Treaty of Utrecht, which apparently meant that it would be restored to the Indians, and the natives were to be free to go and come on the lakes and the Niagara River. But Lake Champlain was not to be French: a line would be drawn from Newburgh Bay (Sackett's Harbor?) through the lower end of Lake Champlain, thence to the western source of the St. John River, and thence straight to the shore of the Gulf of St. Lawrence. The territory north of this line was to be French, and to the south, British.[64]

These propositions continued to be the basis of the conversations between Mirepoix and Robinson. But neither government was any longer in a mood for serious negotiations. On March 27, Rouillé wrote proposing a cessation of warlike measures and a renewal of the negotiation. "How would it be possible to negotiate fruitfully," he asked, "if the incidents in America continue, and if they begin to take place on the high seas?" But he made no specific proposal, asking only that the British ministers submit definite proposals to Mirepoix in writing.[65] Robinson showed Rouillé's letter to the King; but George II was in a belligerent mood and was not impressed. Robinson himself was now thoroughly skeptical of French sincerity and saw in Rouillé's proposal merely a trick to induce Great Britain, now ahead in the preparedness race, to suspend military action long enough for France to catch up.[66] The King was willing, nevertheless, to have Robinson "humor" Mirepoix by submitting a written memorandum of the British demands; but he rather hoped it might do no good— "France being so low, we so Superior at Sea and such the alacrity of the whole nation—England would never have such an opportunity."[67]

Accordingly, Robinson handed Mirepoix another communication, on April 5. This document was noncommittal, carrying only the British re-

---

63. Pease, *op. cit.,* p. 190.
64. *Ibid.,* p. 198. I have been unable to identify the "Newbur Bay" mentioned by Robinson.
65. LC Add. MSS. 32853:515, 522.   66. Pease, *op. cit.,* p. 199.
67. *Ibid.,* p. 200.

fusal to agree to an armistice, on the ground that Great Britain could not consent to a cessation of military activity without a definitive agreement upon the disputed points. Informally, Robinson convinced Mirepoix of the sincerity of the English King and government in their desire for peace. "Our dispositions being the same," wrote this deluded minister, "it is a very unhappy circumstance that, for such insignificant objects, we are come, on one side and the other, to the brink of the most extreme measures."[68] He felt that matters were now out of the hands of the British ministry, and that they would be able to save themselves only by a successful and definitive settlement. To this end Robinson indicated that the whole problem might be solved if France would accede to the British demands in Acadia. But Great Britain would demand that the St. Lawrence and the lakes be recognized as the boundary, consenting only to refrain from establishing posts within a certain distance of these shores, and that the territory between the shores and the line to be established be left entirely to the savages. The British would accept the mountains as a boundary in the west, Mirepoix reported, and would allow France the proposed *lisière* on the left bank of the Wabash.[69]

This proposal, submitted to Mirepoix to "humor" him, marks a further extension of the British claims in the direction of the lakes and seems to indicate that the British were playing the French ambassador's complaisance for all it was worth. "The ambassador must either have private instructions to go to such a length, or must be the weakest of ambassadors; In either case nothing so right as to lay hold of the advantage of one, or the other."[70] But this could not be said of Mirepoix's superior, who lost no time in rejecting this proposal to make a line through the center of Canada its boundary. There were three points, he said, on which France could not and would not recede: this preposterous claim of the British to make the lakes the boundary, their demand for a *lisière* along the Bay of Fundy, and the territory between the Ohio and the Wabash. It would be totally useless, therefore, to enter upon any further discussion of the bases proposed by the British government. "We differ," he said, "too fundamentally in our interests and our views upon the points which the English ministers regard as a necessary base for the negotiations."[71]

The two governments were indeed far apart. Robinson and Newcastle, under the influence of Halifax, had now advanced to the lakes. Rouillé, apparently influenced by La Galissonnière, had fixed upon the watershed as the *sine qua non* of a peacefully arranged colonial boundary. The British ministers having themselves recognized the mountains as the limits of their establishments, French policy indicated that this rule should be ap-

68. *Ibid.*, p. 203.
70. *Ibid.*, p. 200.
69. *Ibid.*, pp. 201–206.
71. *Ibid.*, p. 210.

plied to the entire boundary problem, so that the watershed, from New England to Georgia, should be recognized as the dividing line. Under such an arrangement the British would own the lands drained by the rivers that flow into the sea, while the lands watered by the tributaries of the St. Lawrence and the Mississippi would belong to France. It would be easy to establish an unoccupied territory along the frontier, and to agree not to build any posts that would constitute a threat to the colonies of either. But there was one exception: France must retain the St. John River as a route of winter communication between Quebec and the sea, although the boundary of New England might be brought reasonably close to that river. This was the extreme compromise beyond which France could not go; and there could be only two possible motives for its rejection by the British: the pretended prejudice to their commerce beyond the mountains, which was not worth the hundredth part of the cost of these unhappy negotiations, or a desire of the British to get into a position to invade French territory. Moreover, this extreme offer could be made only as a consideration for some equal concession by the British in the West Indies or in India.[72]

The memorial in which this policy was expressed is the clearest and most dramatic expression of the French position. The ultimate consideration that ran throughout the French argument was, in 1755 as in 1749, the security of the French possessions in North America before an advancing line of British expansion. This vital consideration centered upon three points: the winter communication between Quebec and the sea, the security of Quebec from attack by way of the lakes and the St. Lawrence, and the line of communications between Canada and Louisiana via the Ohio Valley. Let the British desist from their pretensions on these three points, said Rouillé, and France would negotiate on all the rest in such a way as to assure to the British the security both of their possessions and of their commerce.[73]

Unfortunately, events were now moving too rapidly to permit of hope for the success of this policy. On April 10 the British cabinet reaffirmed its decision of March 18 to send a fleet to America to intercept the French expedition preparing at Brest;[74] yet on April 21 Mirepoix still "firmly believed" that the military movements of the British were purely defensive, and that "their commanders have very precise orders to undertake nothing aggressive." He had talked to Robinson about the three points regarded by the French minister as vital, and was again optimistic. Although Robinson refused to concede all this in writing, Mirepoix believed

72. CAO AE CP Ang. 438:371–382.
73. CAO AE CP Ang. 438:397–403; BM Add. MSS. 6862:71–73.
74. Pease, op. cit., pp. 206–207.

Great Britain would not insist on the twenty-league *lisière* along the Bay of Fundy, if France would consent to leave it neutral, and he even thought the English would admit French sovereignty over the lakes and the territory between the Ohio and the Wabash.[75]

But even this incorrigible optimist was beginning to have his doubts. Robinson talked to the ambassador vaguely about the "three points"; but when pressed for an official proposal he declined to make it, and Mirepoix broke off the discussion. He now had to report that the British government was yielding to the public clamor for war. The decision had been taken, and the warlike preparations of Great Britain were being made in anticipation of an open rupture. George II was shortly to leave for Hanover, and would leave the Duke of Cumberland, arch Francophobe, as head of the regency. "There is no longer any hope for a conciliation," Mirepoix wrote. Nevertheless, he said, the British would still play for time.[76] Two days after this was written, Admiral Boscawen sailed for America, with orders to establish his position off Louisbourg and take possession of any French ships that might appear bearing troops or warlike stores.[77]

The next move in what was now hardly more than a diplomatic game for time was made by the British. Robinson, noticing Mirepoix's reticence, asked for further discussion, and, protesting that his government persisted in the firm resolution to avoid a rupture, he delivered himself of a convincing explanation of the British position, which represented a decided tempering of the demands of March 7 and April 5. With regard to Acadia, he said the line proposed in the counterproposals of March 7 was only a suggestion, made with a desire to emphasize the necessity for fixing the boundaries in that region. The real object of the British, he said, was to prevent the French from establishing themselves on the Bay of Fundy; and if France would agree to desist from her operations there, Great Britain would accept a prohibited zone along the coast and opposite the isthmus. With regard to the right bank of the St. Lawrence, Robinson insisted that the British had never denied French sovereignty there; all they desired was a delimitation of that area. Similarly, he assured the French ambassador that Great Britain would not contest the sovereignty of France over the south shores of Lakes Ontario and Erie; but Indians friendly to Great Britain were established there and, if not given freedom of navigation on the lakes, they would become entirely dependent upon the French. As to the Ohio Valley, Robinson expressed a willingness on the part of Great Britain to grant France the territory between the Ohio and the Wabash, provided the Ohio Valley was left neu-

75. CAO AE CP Ang. 438:418–423.   76. CAO AE CP Ang. 438:442–449.
77. Corbett, *op. cit.,* I, 45.

tral. The land between the river and the mountains should be closed to the subjects of both Crowns. Robinson assured Mirepoix that, although he could not say so "ministerially," these were the true sentiments of his government, and he was prepared to conclude an agreement on these bases if France was willing.[78]

This overture, as reported by Mirepoix, certainly has the ring of sincerity, and did go far indeed toward meeting the French objections. Mirepoix was encouraged. But he was still disturbed by the silence of the British ministry as to Boscawen's destination, and asked Lord Granville to explain the nature of the admiral's orders. Granville avoided an answer, and Robinson hinted that he had gone to defend the shores of Acadia from attack by Macnémara's French fleet from Brest.[79]

Mirepoix was still skeptical. Rouillé had suggested that La Galissonnière be sent to London to aid Mirepoix, perhaps to make the latter less compliant. Mirepoix was willing, but he doubted whether it would do any good, at that stage of the game;[80] and a few days after Robinson's new overture, on May 5, Mirepoix was writing Rouillé that no attention should be paid to the British proposal, as England was determined to make war. Either Robinson was trying to gain time, he said, or was misled by his own personal desire for peace. The French ambassador now knew that Boscawen had orders to attack the French fleet.[81]

Nevertheless, the French government saw fit to reply at length to Robinson's advances, in a note which was delivered by Mirepoix on May 14. This note reviewed the entire American problem, but, while making slight concessions in Acadia and the West Indies, it added little to the previously stated French position. As it is the last summary of the French case, however, it merits careful consideration. It presents the problem under four heads, the first of which is the question of Acadia. Referring to the statement submitted by the French commissioners in Paris, on October 4, 1751, the author of this communication claimed that the arguments there submitted were unanswerable; that Acadia was in truth only a small part of the peninsula of Nova Scotia, and that Great Britain had neither title nor need for the land between Acadia and New England. France, on the other hand, not only had a title to this region, but was compelled, by geographical considerations, to retain as much of it as might be necessary to preserve the line of communications between Quebec and the sea in winter. Because of her desire for peace, France would cede to Great Britain the territory between the Sagadahoc (Kennebec), the boundary of New England established by the Massachusetts charter of 1691, and the Penobscot River. For the assurance of its line of com-

78. CAO AE CP Ang. 439:4–13.
80. CAO AE CP Ang. 439:2–3.
79. CAO AE CP Ang. 439:10–11.
81. CAO AE CP Ang. 439:24–26.

munication, however, France must be given the isthmus, Beaubassin, and the coast of the Bay of Fundy as far as the Penobscot River.[82] With regard to Canada, the French ministry definitely rejected the British pretension that the St. Lawrence and Lakes Ontario and Erie constituted the boundary. The British must recognize the fact that the St. Lawrence River ran through the center of Canada; once this principle was agreed upon, one might proceed to a consideration of the question whether the conveniences of the two nations demanded a special local arrangement. The British claim to sovereignty over the Iroquois and their lands by virtue of Article XV of the Treaty of Utrecht was rejected as absurd. These Indians were free and independent; not only that, but on the basis of the British argument the French would have just as much right to build posts in the northern part of Acadia on lands owned by the Micmacs, friends and allies of France, as Great Britain had for the building of Oswego. According to the French view, the question resolved itself into two considerations, security and commerce, and it ought to be easy to arrive at some agreement that would satisfy both opponents on these two points.[83] As to the Ohio, France claimed complete ownership. Here, too, Great Britain had neither title nor establishments, nor any need of any, while France not only had a title to the territory, but was under compulsion to retain it for the security of the two parts of New France. Despite her superior claims, however, France offered to leave unoccupied the territory between the Ohio and the mountains, and to agree to bar it to both French and English.[84] Finally, this note reviewed the claims of France to the disputed islands in the West Indies, which, it maintained, clearly demonstrated their French ownership. But for the sake of peace, if Great Britain would agree to recognize the French title to St. Lucia and Tobago, France would agree to leave St. Vincent and Dominica to the natives, to remain unoccupied though under her protection.[85]

The final British reply to the French memorial was not handed to Mirepoix until June 6. When it was delivered, it was found that, despite the slight concessions made by France, Great Britain remained unmoved on all four major points. If France referred to the French statement of October 4, 1751, as establishing the French title to Acadia, Great Britain referred to her own reply as refuting it. Great Britain, it was claimed, must retain the entire shore line of the Bay of Fundy; and the British reply cited historical examples to show that small areas such as the Bay of Fundy could not successfully be occupied in common by France and

82. LC AE Méms. et Docs. Amérique 24:218–220.
83. LC AE Méms. et Docs. Amérique 24:221–222.
84. LC AE Méms. et Docs. Amérique 24:223–224.
85. LC AE Méms. et Docs. Amérique 24:225.

Great Britain. The lines already proposed for the division of Acadia ought to satisfy the exigencies of the situation for both nations; the British certainly could not surrender the isthmus to France. Great Britain was no less intransigent on the question of the St. Lawrence and the lakes. Far from being in midmost Canada, the river and the lakes lay in the territory of the Iroquois, and Great Britain's answer advanced a lengthy argument to show that not only the region south of the lakes, but also the Ohio Valley, belonged to the said Indians, and that they had transferred their lands to the British. Based upon Article XV of the Treaty of Utrecht, the British argument was at great pains to show that the commerce of the lakes had always been open to both French and British, and that Forts Niagara and Presqu'Isle, and the post on the Rivière aux Boeufs, were all on British soil. Nevertheless, the British ministry, "*pour l'amour de la paix*," would consent to enter upon a discussion of the limits of the territory south of the lakes, without prejudice to the rights and possessions of the Iroquois. In the Ohio Valley the British had built establishments from the sources of the river to Pickawillany, and had done so prior to any French occupation, a *de facto* occupation which strengthened the British title derived from their purchase from the Indians. Nevertheless, the British ministry had already offered, and now again offered, to leave the territory of the Ohio neutral and to negotiate in a friendly manner as to what the precise boundaries of that territory should be. Finally, as to the Caribbean islands, the British reply rejected the French claim to ownership, but indicated a vague willingness to come to a friendly accommodation in the matter. The implication was that if France would give in on the other American points Great Britain would give in there. But just what the British would surrender in that region was not specified.[86]

This unbending statement hardly advanced the argument, and the French prepared to reply in kind.[87] Rouillé now agreed with Mirepoix that the British were playing for time; and, while sending them a noncommittal answer, he authorized Mirepoix to return to France. He was to assure the British ministers, however, that he would always be ready to return to London, whenever it should seem desirable.[88]

By a coincidence that might have been expected, the day after Rouillé's final letter to Mirepoix was written, and two days before it was received, news arrived in London—on July 15, 1755—that Boscawen had intercepted the French fleet off Newfoundland on June 10, and, after an engagement treacherously begun, had taken two French men-of-war, the

86. LC AE Méms. et Docs. Amérique 24:227–232; BM Add. MSS. 6862:90–96.
87. CAO AE CP Ang. 439:242–245.   88. CAO AE CP Ang. 439:239–241.

Alcide and the *Lys*, with eight companies of soldiers and 200,000 livres in money.[89] Robinson hastened to assure Mirepoix that the fight had been the result of a "misunderstanding," but the French ambassador refused to discuss the matter, and left London without taking the customary leave.[90]

These negotiations had lasted much too long. There had been little or nothing to justify their continuance after the presentation of the British counterproposals of March 7; for it was at that time that the irreconcilable positions of the two powers had become clear. There was undoubtedly going on in Britain's American colonies an expanding westward movement which had begun to flow over the Allegheny watershed in the period following the Peace of Utrecht. The French ministry, guided by such students of colonial affairs as La Galissonnière, had recognized this movement westward, and, convinced of the justice of the French claim to all the lands between the Allegheny watershed and the Spanish possessions in the Far West, had determined to block it. Basing their claim upon prior discovery and occupation, they were determined, despite the slight value of the disputed areas, to establish the security of New France once and for all by wringing from Great Britain a recognition of the watershed as the boundary between the French and British empires in North America. France was on the defensive: not, indeed, in defense of a profitable empire—for profitable New France never was—but in defense of a colonial possession upon which depended the balance of power, not only in America, but in the Old World as well. Judged on the basis both of its historical antecedents and of the logic of geography, the French position, save as it concerned Acadia, seems to have been the sounder of the two. In Acadia, however, the French insistence upon possession of the valley of the St. John River was based upon expediency alone.

The British, on the other hand, were driven by other forces. The land speculators, the Indian traders, and the squatters of a community of British colonies bursting with robust expansiveness were moving over the mountains, and they had the support of the Board of Trade and its imperialistic president, the Earl of Halifax. In Acadia, now established as the military counterpoise for Cape Breton, Great Britain seems to have been justified, legally and historically, in her claim to at least all the lands that gave upon the Bay of Fundy. But elsewhere on the continent the French were right in their contention that, aside from an occasional trader, prior to 1740 few people in Great Britain or her colonies had been interested in the Mississippi Valley. Great Britain was therefore

89. CAO AE CP Ang. 439:250, 254.
90. CAO AE CP Ang. 439:252–253, 255–256.

compelled to fall back, in attempting to justify her claims to lands west of the divide, upon the vague and indecisive Article XV of the Treaty of Utrecht, which, however sound it may have been for the purposes of eighteenth-century diplomacy, had little to validate it in either logic or historical fact.

CHAPTER V

THE APPEAL TO EUROPEAN OPINION

GREAT BRITAIN and France were now effectively at war. They had broken off diplomatic relations, and British ships began to seize French ships on the high seas. In America, British plans were laid for a military campaign against Forts Duquesne, Niagara, and Crown Point. And yet, there was no war. The two litigants preferred not to fight alone. They must have allies. Great Britain began to make approaches to Prussia, while France executed the *volte face* that resulted in an Austro-French alliance. Until these maneuvers were completed, until Great Britain and France had attached to themselves additional strength to bolster them against the stress and strain, there must be no formal war. Therefore, they must play for time; and to gain the needed time, one more step in their negotiations had to be taken.

The two countries that were, perhaps, most obviously interested in the Anglo-French dispute were Prussia and Spain; Prussia, chiefly because of interests peculiarly European; Spain, because of interests peculiarly American. Frederick II had watched the previous negotiations with his habitual insight. As early as February 14, 1755, he had put the odds on war at ten to one;[1] and, early in March, he expressed his belief that a rupture was inevitable.[2] Until summer, he sympathized with France, and he gave the French ministry a great deal of free advice—advice "which shows at once his sympathy for the French cause and his poor opinion of the French ministers."[3] But after the return of Mirepoix to Paris in July, Frederick entered upon negotiations with Great Britain looking toward a *rapprochement* between that country and Prussia which culminated in the Treaty of Westminster, of January 16, 1756.[4]

In Madrid, Duras, the French minister, was instructed to call the attention of the Spanish court to the British threat to the balance of power in America, and to press for a renewal of the Family Compact.[5] But Duras could make no headway, because, he reported, Ricardo Wall was

1. J. Holland Rose, A. P. Newton, and E. A. Benians, eds., "The Cambridge History of the British Empire": Vol. I, *The Old Empire from the Beginnings to 1783* (New York, 1929), p. 469.

2. LC Add. MSS. 32853:228.   3. Waddington, *Louis XV*, p. 47.

4. *Ibid.*, pp. 192, 193, 196.

5. AE CP Espagne 517:143, 518:85–89. Emmanuel-Félicité de Durfort, Duc de Duras. The First Bourbon Family Compact between France and Spain was made in 1733; the second was signed in 1743.

completely dominated by Sir Benjamin Keene, the British ambassador. Spain would not take sides.[6]

Still the opponents did not declare war. Great Britain, in the summer of 1755, began seizing French merchant vessels in the English Channel and elsewhere,[7] but France hesitated to undertake reprisals for these or for Boscawen's actions, apparently in the forlorn hope that the new British parliament might take a less belligerent attitude than its predecessor, and that the American disputes might still be settled peaceably—a policy that elicited from Frederick the sarcastic comment that "Louis XIV never waited to make a decision until he could know what an English parliament might say, but, very much to the contrary, the parliament was obliged to adjust its deliberations to the enterprises of Louis XIV."[8]

Whether simply to gain time or because France still clung to the hope that Great Britain could be brought to modify her extreme demands, Anglo-French conversations through devious channels continued throughout the year 1755 and well on into 1756. Joshua van Eck, an Anglo-Dutch banker, approached the British ministers,[9] and had a number of conferences with them. But he was compelled to report to M. Vernet,[10] his Paris correspondent, that he could not bring the British to concede the essential points of the French demand in the matter of Acadia, although they did apparently show a willingness to leave the French in possession of the St. John River.[11]

But this private and abortive sounding-out of the British ministry was not entirely without results. For the British ministers assured the French of England's desire for peace; and on the basis of these assurances,[12] and despite the belligerent attitude of Parliament, on December 21 Rouillé

6. AE CP Espagne 517:198, 518:98–103; Waddington, *Louis XV*, p. 192.

7. *N.Y. Col. Docs.*, X, 385–386.

8. Frederick to Knyphausen, November 11, 1755; quoted by Waddington, *Louis XV*, p. 187.

9. Waddington, *Louis XV*, pp. 185–187.   10. Or Wernet.

11. CAO AE CP Ang. 440:86, 90–91. To deal with the problem in America, Vernet formulated a project for a treaty that is of academic interest; and because he felt sure it would be acceptable to the British, he submitted it to Rouillé on March 1, 1756. According to his proposal, Great Britain would be given a twenty-league *lisière* along the coast of the Bay of Fundy from the St. John River to the borders of New England: the land between this *lisière* and the St. Lawrence would be left neutral, although recognized as belonging to France; the St. John River would be left open to the French for communication with Quebec, but might not be fortified; and the French might also cross the isthmus to Baie Verte. On Lake Champlain, from the site of Fort St. Frédéric, which was to be destroyed, a straight line would be drawn to Oswego, whence it would be continued straight to the source of the Ohio, and from there the boundary would be the Ohio itself. On the lakes, the French forts, except Frontenac, would be demolished; and the Indians (but neither the English nor French) would be free to navigate the lakes. (CAO AE CP Ang. 440:90–92.)

12. BM Add. MSS. 15915:53–54.

sent a would-be conciliatory note and statement, through Colonel Yorke, the British ambassador at The Hague, to Henry Fox, who had succeeded Robinson at the Foreign Office. In this note he assured Fox of France's desire for peace and Louis XV's willingness to reopen American negotiations if Great Britain would restore the prizes already made at sea.[13] But the tone of Rouillé's note was ill-calculated to promote peace; it bluntly stated that if Great Britain refused, France would regard this "denial of justice" as a declaration of war.[14] It was, in fact, probably written for the purposes of French diplomatic propaganda in the courts of Europe.

The offer was refused. The British ministry felt that France had been the aggressor ever since the Treaty of Aix-la-Chapelle—the invader of territory that they were convinced was British. British arms on land and sea had been used, they felt, only in defense and as a last resort against French acts of war in America; and Boscawen's seizure of French transports at sea was as purely defensive as the building of Fort Lawrence or the expedition of Braddock to the Ohio.[15] But in any case popular feeling was now aroused to the point where war could hardly be avoided. It offered stakes too great to be lightly waved aside. For not only might Great Britain win a great empire by war, the French marine would likewise be swept from the sea,[16] a great added gain for Britain.

Fox's reply, of January 13, 1756, was therefore short and discouraging. He flatly refused the restitution of the prizes and simply asserted that all the military actions taken by the British had been forced upon them by the aggressions of France.[17] The French gesture, indeed, was thought by the British ministry to have been made only for the purpose of arousing sympathy for France; and, as copies of the French notes had been handed to the diplomatic corps in Paris, Fox sent a circular letter to British diplomatic agents to counteract such propaganda.[18]

Here was a good opportunity for a war. But no war was declared, yet. For whatever may have been the intentions of France when she sent England the note of December 21, the French ministry realized that, for the time, the diplomatic situation made war impossible. Three days after Fox's reply to Rouillé, the Anglo-Prussian defensive Treaty of Westminster was signed, which deprived France of her great ally in the Germanies.[19] News of this treaty apparently came as a shock and a complete surprise to the French government, and hastened the negotiations be-

13. *Archives Nationales,* Paris, K-1351:121. Hereafter cited as AN. BM Add. MSS. 6862:106, 15915:53–54; CL Shelburne MSS. XXII:5–24; *N.Y. Col. Docs.,* X, 378–379.

14. AN K-1351:121.

15. CL Shelburne MSS. XXII:1–3; *N.Y. Col. Docs.,* X, 388.

16. Waddington, *Louis XV,* p. 186.   17. BM Add. MSS. 6862:108.

18. CL Shelburne MSS. XXII:1–3; *N.Y. Col. Docs.,* X, 388.

19. Waddington, *Louis XV,* pp. 194–221.

tween France and Austria which looked to a *rapprochement* between those two powers.[20] For the present France could not fight; Great Britain must be "entretenue" a little longer. To this end, once more negotiations must be undertaken. Through Frederick a suitable opening was offered, because he had voiced his desire to play the mediator;[21] and, early in February, on his own initiative, he broached the subject to Holdernesse (now Secretary of State for the Northern Department), using as a basis for conversations the French note of December 21.[22] Holdernesse replied that it had been France who had broken off the negotiations of the preceding year, but that, if His Prussian Majesty could find some means of renewing them, Great Britain would weigh with great consideration anything that France might have to say. England would even go so far as to make certain modifications in the counterproposals of March 7, 1755. That is, she would do this: she would grant to France a passage overland from Quebec to a point on the Gulf of St. Lawrence opposite Ile St. Jean (Prince Edward Island), and a *lisière* along the south side of the St. Lawrence River. But she would insist upon the possession of both the peninsula and isthmus of Acadia, and of the entire shore line of the Bay of Fundy. As for the prizes, Great Britain would consent to a reciprocal return of all vessels taken or detained by either side. On the other American questions, the British note was silent.[23]

This was, indeed, a considerable last-minute modification of the former British position on Nova Scotia. France answered by sending Frederick copies of the correspondence between Mirepoix and Robinson in the spring of 1755,[24] and by a review of the concessions she had already made in the face of British shiftiness. The French reply accepted Prussian mediation; but it declared that no accommodation was possible until positive orders were given by George II for the restitution of the French prizes taken by British ships; once those orders were given, France, "*par l'amour de la paix*," would enter into negotiations.[25] The French reply made note of the fact that the same answer had been made to Spain, who had offered her good offices in the Anglo-French dispute. Frederick, in transmitting the French communication, placed the chief emphasis upon the question whether Great Britain would accept the concessions that France had to offer in America, and suggested that all other issues between them might be settled by an international congress.[26] But Great

20. *Ibid.*, pp. 196, 243, 250, 333 ff.   21. *Ibid.*, p. 250.

22. *Politische Correspondenz Friedrich's des Grossen* (Berlin, 1879–1900), XIII, 35–36, 37; BM Add. MSS. 6811:55–60.

23. BM Add. MSS. 6811:55–60.   24. AN K-1351:113–118.

25. CAO AE CP Ang. 440:126–128.   26. BM Add. MSS. 6811:67, 68.

Britain professed ignorance of the concessions offered by France, unless, perhaps, they consisted only of the French willingness to restore the American scene to its *status quo* at the time of the Treaty of Utrecht; even there, the British complained, the French persisted in distorting the meaning of the treaty. Great Britain therefore, in reply to the French letter, asked Frederick to state specifically the concessions offered.[27]

This request having been made, France admitted that the concessions offered were covered by the proposed restoration of conditions in America to those of 1713. Then, replying to the British offer of a passage across Nova Scotia, the French ministry declared that France could never accept anything less in Acadia than the free navigation of the St. John River; nor would she cede to Great Britain the shore of the Bay of Fundy between the St. John and Beaubassin on the isthmus.[28]

This reply finally placed France in the position of refusing to accept the concessions of the British ministry, who had consented both to restore the prizes taken and to assure to France a land passage from Quebec to the Gulf of St. Lawrence. But the French alliance with Austria was now consummated; there was no good reason to postpone the war any longer. If the final negotiations with Great Britain had been undertaken by France to win the sympathy of the European courts, they certainly had failed to demonstrate any genuine desire for peace on the part of France; on the other hand, the two concessions offered by Great Britain demonstrate either that her ministers were sincerely desirous of a last-minute accommodation or that they were possessed by a political finesse not usually attributed to them.

On May 11, 1756, Holdernesse handed to the Prussian minister in London a letter notifying Frederick that His Britannic Majesty had abandoned all hope of a peaceful settlement, and must, therefore, declare war on France.[29] The declaration itself, published on May 17, cited the "unwarrantable proceedings" of the French in the West Indies and North America, "particularly in Our Province of Nova Scotia" as showing a "formed Design and Resolution of that Court" to usurp the British possessions in those parts. It pointed, also, to the failure of France to evacuate the "neutral islands," as agreed, and to the seizure of a British fort in April, 1754;[30] Great Britain had taken only defensive measures, in the hope that France would live up to her assurances of her desire for a peaceful settlement; but an attack upon Minorca, which had already taken

27. BM Add. MSS. 6811:69–70; AN K-1351:119.
28. BM Add. MSS. 6871:95–96; AN K-1351:120; CAO AE CP Ang. 440:167–169.
29. BM Add. MSS. 6811:71–72.
30. The reference is to William Trent's unfinished fort at the forks of the Ohio.

place, made it impossible to delay longer, and Great Britain now declared war against the French King, "who so unjustly began it."[31]

Throughout almost the entire year that had elapsed between Mirepoix's departure from London and the declaration of war, each of the two great colonial rivals had made strenuous efforts to win the sympathy if not the active support of the other courts of Europe, potential neutrals as well as potential allies. The initial failure of the negotiations between Robinson and Mirepoix, after the British counterproposals of March, 1755, had been the signal for appeals by both litigants at the bar of European public opinion. The appeals in both cases also took a twofold form while both sides rushed into print to present their cases. This popular propaganda was supplemented by diplomatic representations at the courts of the other European powers. The idea of publishing the claims of the two countries to the disputed territory in America had occurred to William Shirley as early as September, 1750, when the French commissioners insisted upon exchanging their respective arguments in writing.[32] And, apparently, the idea had also occurred to the French, for Mirepoix surprised Albemarle, in August, 1752, by presenting him with a printed copy of the British memorial on Acadia of January 11, 1751, together with the French reply of October 4. What amazed the British ambassador and commissioners most was the fact that the French court had also printed arguments and notes on the British memorial which the French commissioners had not presented to the British at all. As this procedure was manifestly unfair, Holdernesse prevailed upon the French court to suppress the publication of these documents while the negotiations were still going on.[33]

In the spring of 1755 the French broke into print again. On Saturday, May 17, La Galissonnière called on Ruvigny de Cosné[34] and left with him three quarto volumes containing the memorials[35] that had been exchanged between the French and British commissioners. The British ministry promptly retaliated by publishing an English edition of the memorials

31. HL RB-71446. The Duke de Richelieu, with a strong French force, had landed in Minorca on April 18. (Corbett, *op. cit.*, I, 105 ff.)

32. CAO PRO FO 90 (France) 238:178.

33. Mildmay and De Cosné to Holdernesse, August 30, 1752, CL Mildmay Papers— "Letters from Paris," pp. 88–89.

34. He had taken Shirley's place on the commission.

35. De Cosné to Robinson, May 21, 1755, CL Mildmay Papers—"Letters from Paris," pp. 119–210. *Mémoires des Commissaires du Roi et de ceux de Sa Majesté Britannique, sur les Possessions et les Droits respectifs des deux Couronnes en Amérique; avec les Actes publics et Pièces justificatives* (Paris, 1755). A fourth volume, containing memorials restating the French claim to Acadia and setting forth the French title to Tobago, which had not been presented because of the rupture of diplomatic negotiations, was added in 1757. A second edition of the three-volume collection was printed in six volumes in 1756.

that had been exchanged.[36] This was followed, after the French attempt to renew the negotiations in December, 1755, by a series of British "Observations" on the French note of December 21, to which the French replied with a history of the entire negotiations, from 1749 to 1755.[37]

This last document is interesting. Carefully and logically written, it is built upon the thesis that, although at the time of the Treaty of Utrecht the British did not dream of expanding outside the peninsula "where Acadia is," or beyond the Allegheny watershed in the interior, immediately after the Treaty of Aix-la-Chapelle the British government had formed a plan, or series of plans, to push the frontiers of their colonies farther into the continent at the expense of the French.[38] As evidence of all this, the *précis* cited the military activities of Cornwallis, the seizure of French ships in the Bay of Fundy, and the testimony of the British traders seized on the Ohio. The most damning pieces of evidence were the journal of George Washington and the instructions to Braddock, which were printed. The evidence presented in this *précis* proved, in the minds of those who made it public, that the British were the aggressors all along the line, and that the French, in Acadia, on the lakes, on the Ohio, and in the lands of the Chickasaws, were on the defensive for the preservation of their just rights.[39] The *précis* reviewed the negotiations of 1755, and published the proposals and counterproposals exchanged in the course of those negotiations, to demonstrate the shifty inconstancy of the British and to prove that Great Britain had never really desired to settle the American boundary controversies on the basis of justice, but had consented to negotiate with the intention merely of gaining time to intrench herself in her ill-gotten territorial gains before France could act.[40]

Formal warfare had now begun, following a long series of more or less sincere but uniformly ineffective attempts to avoid it by a peaceful settlement of the disputes at issue. Both sides protested, with a certain amount of justification, their genuine desire for peace, and claimed that they were acting purely in defense of their just and established rights. Yet, almost without realizing it, Great Britain was expanding her colonial possessions in North America, and France, rather more consciously, indeed, was intrenched and fighting to prevent that expansion.

36. *The Memorials of the English and French Commissaries concerning the Limits of Nova Scotia or Acadia* (Vol. I, London, 1755); *The Memorials of the English and French Commissaries concerning St. Lucia* (Vol. II, London, 1755).

37. Jacob Nicolas Moreau, comp., *Mémoire contenant le précis des faits, avec leurs pièces justificatives, Pour servir de Réponse aux Observations envoyées par les Ministres d'Angleterre, dans les Cours de l'Europe* (Paris, 1756).

38. *Ibid.*, pp. 1–36.   39. *Ibid.*, pp. 1–36, 49–167, *et passim*.

40. *Ibid.*, pp. 37–46, 167–198.

CHAPTER VI

COLONIAL DIPLOMACY IN WAR TIME

FOR Great Britain and France, the war that began in 1756 was almost purely a colonial war; Anglo-French diplomacy, and now Anglo-French military conflict, had been set in motion by events in America. The colonies were no longer pawns on a European diplomatic chessboard. European diplomats danced, and European armies marched, as colonial issues piped the tune. And as a part of their *danse macabre*, the English and French diplomats again sought most eagerly to attract the favorable attention of Spain, the neutral nation that was most directly concerned.

The French reference to possible Spanish mediation, early in 1756, had been based upon nothing more substantial than a vague insinuation made to France at about the time when Frederick II offered his services to his two "friends."[1] Spain's "offer" was not accepted, but the Spanish court was fully informed of the Prussian effort.[2] It did serve, however, as a useful precedent and lever, later on, for the French minister in Madrid. For the moment, French influence in Madrid was at a low ebb. Rouillé and Duras had hoped to make much of Boscawen's seizure of the *Alcide* and the *Lys*, in the summer of 1755, and for a time there had, indeed, been a wave of sympathy for France. But the uncanny personal influence of Sir Benjamin Keene, coupled with the disagreeable importunities of Duras for Spanish aid against Great Britain, had made the Frenchman almost *persona non grata* at the Spanish court, and he had been compelled to report, early in August, that Wall not only had refused to assist France, but had been convinced by Keene that the Spanish differences with Great Britain would be settled peaceably.[3] Whereupon Rouillé instructed Duras to return home, which he did early in October.[4]

Thereafter, France had no fully accredited minister at Madrid until April 14, 1757.[5] This did not mean, however, that Keene had the field entirely to himself; for Wall, despite his friendship for Great Britain and the British minister, had no intention of being caught in the British net. Wall knew, as did all Europe, that Spain, as the most important neutral

1. BM Add. MSS. 6811:67; *Recueil des Instructions*, XII *bis*, *Espagne*, p. 334; Lodge, *op. cit.*, p. 460.
2. Lodge, *op. cit.*, p. 460.
3. AE CP Espagne 518:85–89, 98–103, 112–115.
4. AE CP Espagne 518:121–122, 198–212.
5. *Recueil des Instructions*, XII *bis*, *Espagne*, pp. 309–310. An ambassador was finally appointed in the person of Joseph Henri Bouchard d'Esparbès, Marquis d'Aubeterre.

colonial power, was in a strong strategic position to exert a powerful influence upon the course of events, and he did not propose to squander his country's advantages. As a matter of fact, the failure of Duras was Keene's last triumph, and his negotiations during 1756 and 1757, which had as their objective the preservation of Spanish neutrality, became increasingly difficult.[6]

The British government realized that Spain would be invited to join the Franco-Austrian alliance, which had been cemented by the Treaty of Versailles, on May 1, 1756, and it became a cardinal point in British diplomacy to prevent His Most Catholic Majesty from doing so. Fox had anticipated that France would offer Spain Minorca as an inducement, and had written Keene to call upon Wall to refuse the offer, when made, as a mark of friendship for England.[7] The invitation had been extended early in 1756, as anticipated, and Spain had been urged to join a combination of France, Austria, and Russia, which would "give the law to the world," and enable Spain to recover "the ancient Possession in the Mediterranean." Keene reported that though a large body of Spanish opinion supported the idea, Wall was steadfast in his refusal to be moved by it. The Spanish minister was disturbed, however, by reports of fresh trouble with English logwood cutters in the Río Tinto country, on the Mosquito shore.[8]

From this time on, Wall gradually lost faith in British promises to adjust the Anglo-Spanish disputes amicably, and his distrust was increased by new difficulties arising out of the seizures of Spanish ships and the British interpretation of Spanish neutrality and international prize law.[9] The Spanish situation became so difficult, indeed, that the British ministry was forced to order its commanders to let Spanish ships alone.[10]

This eased the situation somewhat,[11] but in the autumn of 1756 and through the year 1757, when the British fortunes of war seemed most desperate as a result of the seizure of Oswego and a series of defeats by the French in America, England felt constrained to do everything possible to hold Spain's friendship. Thus William Pitt, upon his accession to office in the fall of 1756, hastened to send an obsequious personal communication to Wall, assuring the Spanish minister of his friendship and of his

6. Lodge, *op. cit.*, pp. xxi, xxii. Keene died in Madrid, December 15, 1757. He was succeeded by the Earl of Bristol.

7. CL Shelburne MSS. XXII:235–240.

8. BM Add. MSS. 6812:140–149, 6813:137–140; CL Shelburne MSS. XXII:365–374.

9. CL Shelburne MSS. XXII:255–264, 311–324, 357–361; BM Stowe MSS. fols. 292–304; AE CP Espagne 522:508–513.

10. "Additional Instructions," October 5, 1756, PRO Chatham MSS. XCII; CL Shelburne MSS. XXII:381–391.

11. BM Add. MSS. 6813:133–136.

desire to adjust amicably all points at issue between the two governments.[12] As British fortunes sank ever lower and lower, and as France and
Austria continued to importune Spain to accede to the Treaty of Versailles, the British cabinet arrived at the desperate decision to offer Spain
Gibraltar and the evacuation of all British establishments in Honduras,
in return for an alliance that would bring that country into the war on
their side.[13]

But Spain was no more willing to be the ally of Great Britain than to
be the satellite of France. Wall received this significant British offer with
the consideration it deserved, but he was not disposed to push the matter:
Spain did not desire war with either Great Britain or France. Furthermore, the Spanish minister was now clearly distrustful of Great Britain.
He reminded Keene of the obstinate failure of the British government,
since 1754, to reciprocate friendly Spanish gestures. If the British offered
Spain so little satisfaction on old and less important points, he asked,
how could Spain join them in such an important enterprise as war?[14]
After this cool reception, the matter was quietly allowed to drop and
Spain continued to maintain her position of neutrality.

Aubeterre, succeeding Duras in Madrid, played a cautious, waiting
game, and took advantage of every fresh instance of British obstinacy,
and every British violation of Spanish neutrality, to strengthen French
influence. Then, when the tide of war began to change as a result of Pitt's
vigorous administration, France used Ferdinand VI's earlier offer of mediation as a pretext for again urging him to join the Franco-Austrian
alliance. This time, in May, 1758, France offered Spain the island of
Minorca; and in June Louis XV wrote his royal cousin a personal letter
explaining the critical position of France and appealing to Ferdinand
for aid. The siege of Louisbourg, he said, placed France in a critical position, and he urged Ferdinand to intervene, if not in aid of France, at least
with an offer of mediation.[15] Ferdinand replied that the best he could do
would be to offer his mediation.[16] Nevertheless, the Spanish attitude
toward Great Britain perceptibly stiffened; the Earl of Bristol, Keene's

12. William Stanhope Taylor and Capt. John Henry Pringle, eds., *Correspondence
of William Pitt, Earl of Chatham* (London, 1838–1840), I, 209–211, 212–213. Hereafter cited as *Chatham Correspondence*.
13. Minutes of Council, August 18, 1757, PRO Chatham MSS. XCII; *Chatham Correspondence*, I, 247–256; Pitt to Abreu, September 9, 1757, PRO Chatham MSS. XCII.
14. BM Stowe MSS. 292–304.
15. AE CP Espagne 523:178–183, 186–187, 275–279; *Recueil des Instructions*, XII
bis, Espagne, pp. 323–324.
16. AE CP Espagne 523:310–312. Aubeterre called up the ghost of the religious
wars to aid him in his attempts to get the Spanish court to aid France. He also tried
the Jacobite cause (AE CP Espagne 523:270–272), without avail. Finally, referring
to the loss of Louisbourg as cutting off supplies for Quebec, and apparently with the

successor, reported an increasing heat, and even menace, in Wall's protests at British violations of Spanish neutral rights.[17] This tone was reflected, also, in the parallel negotiations of Abreu, the Spanish ambassador, with Pitt in London.[18]

The position of Spain as the most important neutral colonial power had made her the object of the ardent attentions of both sides, and the success with which the Spanish ministry had avoided entanglements with either placed Spain in a position, a little later, again to offer her services as mediator in the colonial dispute. The year 1758 saw a distinct cooling of her friendship for Great Britain, and a corresponding increase in the attention she gave to French overtures. This swing of the Spanish pendulum was carried still farther toward the side of France by the death of Ferdinand VI in August, 1759, and the accession to the throne of his francophile brother, Don Carlos, King of Naples.

Meanwhile, other attempts were being made to arrange a settlement of the Anglo-French colonial quarrel. In the autumn of 1757, Frederick II engaged in secret negotiations with Louis XV on his own account, but the only apparent result was to arouse Austrian suspicions of France.[19] Earlier in the same year, Rouillé, through Louis-Auguste-Augustin d'Affry, French minister to Holland, had sounded out Joseph Yorke, British minister to The Hague, on the prospects of a separate treaty. But Great Britain quickly responded that a peace without the concurrence of Prussia was unthinkable, whereupon these negotiations came to an abrupt end.[20] In June, 1757, Rouillé was succeeded as French minister of foreign affairs by the Abbé de Bernis, who constantly toyed with the idea of peace. Partly because of French losses at Klosterseven and Rossbach, and partly because of a desire to separate England from Prussia, he revived the Affry-Yorke negotiations at The Hague in January, 1758. But Great Britain again refused to be interested.[21] A similar overture was made in Copenhagen, with the same result.[22] As the fortunes of war turned increasingly against France, particularly in the colonies, Bernis became more and more disposed to bring the war to an end. But he did not have the confidence of Louis XV and Madame de

idea of entangling Spain, he asked permission to provision Canada by way of Florida. "Why," Wall replied, "the greater part of the necessary provisioning of that colony is done by the English themselves!" He referred, of course, to the war-time trade with the British colonies. (AE CP Espagne 524:68–73.)

17. Francis Thackeray, *William Pitt* (London, 1827), I, 386–387.
18. José-Antonio d'Abreu y Bertodano; PRO Chatham MSS. XCII, *passim*.
19. Richard Waddington, *La Guerre de sept ans* (Paris, 1899), I, 584–590.
20. CL Shelburne MSS. XXII:447–449, 459–464; BM Add. MSS. 6814:26–27, 59–62.
21. Waddington, *La Guerre de sept ans*, I, 732–735.
22. *Ibid.*, II, 475.

Pompadour, and was replaced in December, 1758, by the Duke de Choiseul.[23]

Choiseul was committed to a continuation of the war. Peace, to be made at all, would have had to be made without Austria, and this would mean abandoning the Franco-Austrian alliance. Choiseul recognized that France was but little interested in the war that was being carried on in Europe, and that the interests of his country did demand a successful conclusion of the colonial struggle with Great Britain. But he realized that if he broke away from the Austrian alliance France would be isolated, with little chance of winning the sort of peace he hoped Great Britain would be forced to make. He renewed the Austrian alliance, therefore, on December 30, 1758. But it was renewed in terms that left no doubt of the distinction in his mind between the colonial war, in which France had a direct, vital interest, and the European struggle, in which France was engaged chiefly as an auxiliary of her ally, Austria, in opposing the ambitions of Frederick.[24]

Choiseul had criticized Bernis for permitting the colonial war to be obscured by the European conflict, and his chief attention was now devoted to the campaign of 1759. While preparing fleets at Brest and Toulon, he sought to win the good will of Holland. But the Toulon and Brest fleets were beaten back, the French were defeated at Minden, and Quebec was taken by the expedition of General Wolfe. These events made hopeless Choiseul's efforts with the Dutch, and he next turned for aid to Russia. But, meanwhile, he had soon come to realize that France greatly needed peace, if it could be had without abandoning Austria, and he began to seek the latter's consent to an attempt to obtain it. Austria was at first utterly opposed to the idea, but the disasters of 1759 forced Maria Theresa seriously to consider it. Austria had little to lose and much to gain by a continuation of the war, and the most that Choiseul could obtain was a reluctant consent to the opening of negotiations between France and England looking toward a separate Anglo-French peace.[25]

Choiseul's enemies were almost as anxious for peace as he was. As early as June 10, 1759, Frederick, despairing of decisive ultimate victory, wrote a personal letter to George II, suggesting the advisability, at the first "favorable events" of the campaign, of calling a general con-

---

23. *Ibid.*, II, 433–465. Etienne-François de Choiseul, Count de Stainville, Duke de Choiseul, was minister of foreign affairs from December 3, 1758, until October 15, 1761, when he surrendered his portfolio to his cousin, César-Gabriel de Choiseul, Count de Choiseul, Duke de Praslin. The Duke de Choiseul continued to direct French relations with Spain, however, until his retirement in 1770.

24. Roger H. Soltau, *The Duke de Choiseul* (Oxford, 1909), pp. 26–32.

25. *Ibid.*, pp. 32–44.

gress of the belligerent powers for the purpose of making an "honorable and useful" peace.[26] But the campaign of the year 1759 was more than "favorable." For England this was "the wonderful year," the "annus mirabilis." But for France it was a year of many woes. From America first came the news that the English had taken Guadeloupe, Basse-Terre, and Marie-Galante; and then followed the victories at Ticonderoga and Niagara, and the fall of Quebec. In Africa the English seized Goree, and with it the valuable trade in slaves and rubber. From India came tidings that they had successfully defended Madras and taken Surat; while "the Marathon of Minden" saved Hanover for the English King. Frederick could say, in his enthusiasm, "England has been long in labor, and has suffered much to produce Mr. Pitt; but at last she has delivered herself of a man!"[27]

The idea of a congress, meanwhile, had not been dropped. On the contrary, the successes of the year placed the Anglo-Prussian allies in a position to hope that such a proposition might be successful and to their advantage. They therefore prepared a declaration to this purpose, and sent it to Duke Louis Ernest of Brunswick for transmission to the representatives of the belligerents at The Hague. At the same time, full information as to this step was transmitted to the new King of Spain, Charles III, now on his way from Naples to Madrid.[28]

The determination to propose a peace congress, as a matter of fact, was hastened by Great Britain's desire politely to avoid offers of mediation between herself and France by the importunate Charles. As King of Naples, even before his brother's death, this prince had indicated his sympathy for the French cause, and Choiseul took advantage of his benevolence to set on foot a move which he calculated would either force mediation or bring Spain into the war on the side of France. Early in the summer of 1759, the Prince of Sanseverino, Neapolitan ambassador to London, approached Pitt with the suggestion that his master would like to mediate the Anglo-French dispute. Pitt delayed making a definite reply, on the ground that the campaign then under way must be terminated, for better or for worse, before he could commit himself. The day after the arrival of news of Ferdinand's death, Sanseverino again tendered Charles' good offices, and received much the same answer as before.[29]

Choiseul, however, instructed the Marquis d'Ossun,[30] French minister

26. *Chatham Correspondence*, I, 413–414.
27. *Ibid.*, I, 444–445.
28. BM Add. MSS. 6813:113–114, 124; *Chatham Correspondence*, I, 460–461, 461 n.
29. BM Add. MSS. 6813:144–146.
30. Pierre Paul d'Ossun, Marquis d'Ossun.

at Naples, to accept Charles' good offices. The repeated defeats of France made peace almost imperative, he said, but he professed to be convinced that the balance of power in Europe now depended upon the balance of power in the colonies. France could not give up her possessions to Great Britain without greatly fearing that the resultant increase in British power would threaten the Spanish empire in America, and reduce both France and Spain to the position of second-rate states in Europe. He therefore reëmphasized the desirability of a strong union between them and, while accepting the mediation of His Catholic Majesty, he expressed the hope that it would be an armed mediation, with the clear warning to both belligerents that, for the preservation of the balance of power in America, Spain would take up arms against either nation that refused her good offices.[31]

Choiseul probably would have preferred Spanish interference in the war on the side of France to a successful Spanish mediation. But to give the color of sincerity to his acceptance of Charles' offer, he outlined to the new Spanish monarch the bases of his own terms for peace. The conflict between England and France had begun, he wrote, as a quarrel over their colonial boundaries in the regions of Acadia and the Ohio River under the provisions of the Treaty of Utrecht. This conflict, with its potential effect upon the balance of power in the world, was the chief issue in the war. Now, to show her desire for fairness and justice, France proposed to leave the interpretation of the Treaty of Utrecht entirely to the impartial judgment of the King of Spain. France proposed, moreover, to restore Minorca to Great Britain in return for permission to fortify Dunkirk, and would consent to raze Louisbourg and to agree never to rebuild it. The prizes taken by Great Britain prior to the declaration of war would be forgotten. Finally, France was willing to withdraw her troops from Germany on the condition that the army of Hanover be disbanded; but both Great Britain and France might continue to support their respective allies with subsidies.[32]

The French line of argument apparently impressed Charles, for in October Sanseverino again approached Pitt on the subject of mediation, using his master's interest in the balance of power in America to justify him in insisting. Pitt, apparently now seeing this phase of the situation for the first time, immediately softened the tone of his refusal and urbanely explained to the Neapolitan envoy that England had no idea of retaining all her conquests in America. He compared the American situation with that in Italy, and hinted that Great Britain would re-

31. *Recueil des Instructions*, XII *bis, Espagne*, pp. 349–350, 352–359.
32. *Ibid.*, pp. 351–352; cf. Waddington, *La Guerre de sept ans*, III, 433–434.

joice with Spain over any increase in the latter's power in America at
the expense of France. Meanwhile, he promised that Bristol would be
instructed to negotiate with Charles' ministers at Madrid.[33]

It was at this juncture that news of the fall of Quebec had arrived,
and in the midst of the rejoicing Great Britain and Prussia launched
their proposal for a peace congress. Pitt wrote Bristol of Sanseverino's
overtures, and instructed him to assure the new Spanish monarch that
the British unwillingness to accept his mediation was not due to any
want of confidence. On the contrary, Bristol was to express great appreciation of the Spanish effort, and to say that His Catholic Majesty's
good offices were certainly not precluded by the Anglo-Prussian proposal for a peace congress, of which he was now "in great secrecy" to
inform the Spanish King.[34]

Thus softly did the British minister turn aside the embarrassing attentions of Charles III, even while Choiseul was desperately endeavoring
to win that king's commitment to a policy of war. The internal condition of France was one of great disorder, and French reverses every-
where were forcing her to contemplate great sacrifices for the cause of
peace. Choiseul professed to see in the proposed Spanish mediation the
only means to obtain a peace that would be just and honorable. He did
not see how Spain could compel England to agree; but just in case the
English should accept Spanish mediation, he sent Ossun a note on the
colonial issues in the war which outlined the possible compromises that
France was prepared to accept.[35] This document surveyed the regional
colonial conflicts that had brought on the war, in North America, the
West Indies, Africa, and Asia. The conflict in North America, it said,
resolved itself into two questions, that of Acadia and that of the frontiers
of Canada. After a review of the dispute over Acadia, the French note
proposed the arbitration of that question; failing that, it would become
a question of choosing "the lesser evil." Whatever happened, France
ought to preserve her communications between Quebec and the sea by way
of the St. John River, perhaps by neutralizing it. But if England should
now find herself in a position successfully to insist upon the cession of an
Acadia which would include the south bank of the St. Lawrence, it would
be better for France to abandon Canada altogether, and transport its
inhabitants to Louisiana. France must also insist, in the proposed negotiation, upon the restitution of Cape Breton, for its loss would make it
impossible to defend Canada. As to the frontiers of Canada, nothing
short of complete defeat should be allowed to force the French to concede

33. LC Add. MSS. 32897:285–287; Waddington, *La Guerre de sept ans*, III, 435.
34. Thackeray, *op. cit.*, I, 458–461.
35. AE CP Espagne 525:325–329; LC AE Méms. et Docs. Amérique 21:27–37.

the Great Lakes to England. For this, too, would make Canada useless
and untenable, because it would block communications between Canada
and Louisiana, and place the British in a position to seize both. As for the
frontier in the Ohio region, it ought to follow the watershed, and no
means should be spared to avoid the hard necessity of surrendering
more, especially because a foothold in the Ohio Valley would make it
easy to attack Louisiana. But the English would surely demand more;
in which case the French must try to confine the cession to the right
bank of the river as far as the Wabash. It was to be feared that the
English might demand the territory as far as the confluence of the
Cherakee (Tennessee) River and the Ohio, which would place them in
dangerous proximity to the Mississippi.[36]

Thus Choiseul outlined the terms of a possible American peace. In his
desire to establish the Appalachian watershed as the boundary, he followed the ideas of La Galissonnière. France was still in dread of the ir-
resistible expansion of the westward-moving English. The concessions
envisaged here were still inspired by a hope for the security of New
France; but by their very nature they were almost a confession of the
futility of that hope and an acknowledgment that the war in America
was being fought in vain. Whether or not this was true, the French plea
fell on receptive Spanish ears, and until his arrival in Madrid, Charles'
tone, under the pressure from Ossun, became increasingly belligerent.
Soon after he landed at Barcelona he confessed his desire to join the
French as soon as his forces might be made ready. Moreover, Charles
was not happy over the way Pitt had put aside his proposed mediation;
and he ordered Abreu to renew his offer.[37]

Abreu, conformably with his orders, expressed to Pitt his master's
extreme desire to bring about peace, and his concern over the status of
the balance of power in America established by the Peace of Utrecht,
which His Catholic Majesty considered as already seriously disturbed
by the extent of the British successes.[38] Pitt replied by again pointing
to the Anglo-Prussian call for a peace congress as a step which precluded Spanish mediation. As for the American balance of power, said
to have been established by the Peace of Utrecht, he declared there was
no such thing.[39] Abreu's orders had been written by Squillace, the finance
minister, from Saragossa, before the King had talked to Wall, and apparently without Wall's knowledge. This fact gave Pitt an opportunity

36. LC AE Méms. et Docs. Amérique 21:27–32.
37. *Recueil des Instructions*, XII *bis, Espagne*, p. 338; AE CP Espagne 526:144–
149, 181–188; Waddington, *La Guerre de sept ans*, III, 436–437.
38. BM Add. MSS. 6813:137–139; LC Add. MSS. 32899:303.
39. BM Add. MSS. 6813:140–143.

to complain about the irregularities involved in communicating with the Spanish government, and to insinuate that Spain's concern over the pretended "balance of power" in America was due to the influence of the French ambassador.[40]

It was true that Ossun was attempting to force the Spanish King's hand. He expressed to Charles his opinion that the Anglo-Prussian declaration was only an effort to avoid Spanish mediation, and even advised the King to insist that Great Britain lay before him the British terms of peace. His Catholic Majesty was completely convinced, and agreed to demand that both belligerents submit their peace terms. "They [the British] will have to make peace," he cried. "If not, they will force me, against my will, to make war; but, in one way or another, I will not suffer them to remain the masters of Europe and America."[41]

The new ruler arrived in Madrid about the middle of December, and there he met Wall. That minister soon brought him to his diplomatic senses by pointing out that Great Britain would not negotiate a separate peace, and that Spain could do nothing to force her to. Spain, in any case, was certainly in no condition to undertake a war. More than that, the British conquest of Canada affected her little, if at all. The only alternative to accepting Britain's refusal of Spanish mediation was war, and Spain had so little at stake in the conflict that war in support of France would be ridiculous.[42] At the same time, Wall met Bristol's complaints with soft words. Although obviously embarrassed by his sovereign's precipitate action, he insisted that Spain could not see the extensive British conquests in America without concern; but he was careful to point out that "good offices" had been extended to both France and Great Britain in the same terms.[43]

France promptly accepted the Spanish offer of mediation, and replied to Charles' demand for a statement of terms by proposals for a preliminary convention, the terms of which, with regard to the three essential problems in North America—Acadia, the Canadian boundary, and the Ohio—were to be identical with those proposed in the British counter-proposals of March 7, 1755. If this was not acceptable to Great Britain, France would submit the entire question to the arbitration of the King of Spain.[44]

Nothing came of this for the time being, because the British could

40. BM Add. MSS. 6813:140–143, 147–149; cf. Waddington, *La Guerre de sept ans*, III, 439; Thackeray, *op. cit.*, I, 461–463.
41. AE CP Espagne 526:175, 176–179, 181–188.
42. AE CP Espagne 526:203–214; Waddington, *La Guerre de sept ans*, III, 439.
43. BM Add. MSS. 6818:70–71, 80–81, 82–83.
44. CAO AE CP Ang. 442:275–277.

now evade the Spanish proposals by referring to the congress at The Hague, while Anglo-Spanish relations took a momentary turn for the better. In February, 1760, Abreu was replaced as ambassador in London, by the Count de Fuentes, probably at the suggestion of Great Britain,[45] and he came instructed to seek to temper the attitude of the British government. He was to take a firm stand, nevertheless, on the desire of Spain to see her good offices accepted, and on the Anglo-Spanish disputes over the contraband trade and the British logwood cutters on the Mosquito coast.[46] Fuentes was well received in England, and it began to look as though the Anglo-Spanish quarrel might be patched up. It was even suggested that some sort of entente cordiale might be arranged between the two countries.[47] As a matter of fact, however, the quiet of apparently good relations was only the lull before the storm.

The Anglo-Prussian declaration of November 25, 1759, was now bearing fruit. Choiseul recognized in the declaration a move to obviate the proposed Spanish mediation for a separate peace between Great Britain and France. But he saw in it also an evidence of distrust between Great Britain and her ally, Prussia, and he accepted the plan for a congress with the twofold hope that it might result in a split between them and throw Great Britain back upon the choice between either accepting the Spanish mediation or forcing Spain into the war on the side of France.[48] Great Britain, on the other hand, took her peace-making seriously, and the British ministers began to take thought as to just what they should demand of France as the price of peace. The victories of the year had lifted British spirits high. The King was for keeping all conquests, as was also popular opinion.[49] But the ministers were more cautious. "The Nonsense of ye Populace, and ye printed Papers, about holding and keeping everything, and reducing France to Nothing, should be batter'd down, and discountenanced," wrote Hardwicke to Newcastle. "If you keep Quebec, you must keep all Canada, and Louisbourg as the Key to it, and is That possible without fighting on for ever?"[50] The basic principle of the peace, as of the prewar negotiations, and, indeed, the chief

45. *Chatham Correspondence*, II, 22–23. Joaquín Atanasio Pignatelli de Aragón y Moncayo, Count de Fuentes.

46. *Recueil des Instructions*, XII *bis, Espagne*, pp. 338–339; AE CP Espagne 527: 140–151, 528:38–48.

47. AE CP Espagne 528:65–67; LC Add. MSS. 32908:34–38; Corbett, *op. cit.*, II, 85; *Chatham Correspondence*, II, 46–47.

48. AE CP Espagne 528:20–24; cf. Corbett, *op. cit.*, II, 75–76.

49. LC Add. MSS. 32897:512–520.

50. LC Add. MSS. 32897:138–140. Many suggestions were made to the British ministry as to what the terms of peace ought to be. The Earl of Kinnoull, ambassador to Lisbon, an expert on American affairs, and one of Newcastle's confidants, suggested that Great Britain must demand Lake Ontario as a boundary, and Crown Point as a

objective of the war, he thought, was the security of the British possessions in America, and British demands must be based on that.[51] Pitt,
however, was not ready to commit himself. He desired peace. But he
ridiculed the King's exorbitant expectations, and indicated to Newcastle
a desire to keep Goree and Senegal, in Africa, and the Bay of Fundy,
Crown Point, Niagara, and the lakes in North America. But with regard to Quebec, Louisbourg, and Montreal, he was disposed to negotiate, and indicated a willingness to surrender them, for a consideration.[52]
Negotiations never reached a point where he felt called upon to express
himself definitely; but his cautious position in the autumn of 1759 was
in distinct contrast with his exorbitant demands a little more than a
year later.[53]

Negotiations at The Hague began in December, 1759. Affry, for

bulwark against possible French aggression from Canada. Louisbourg must now be
taken, to control both the navigation of the St. Lawrence and the fishery, and Nova
Scotia must be carefully delimited for the security of all the colonies. (LC Add. MSS.
32897:178–180.) One anonymous adviser of the government proposed that the "neutral
islands" be divided between France and Great Britain. The British islands should be
peopled with emigrants from Georgia, which would be assigned to France—though
for what reason is not stated. (LC Add. MSS. 32897:390–391.) Still another pointed
out the desirability of leaving the French in Canada as a check upon the "Sturdiness
. . . of our American Colonists towards his Majesty's Governours and Measures."
(LC Add. MSS. 32900:374.)

51. LC Add. MSS. 32897:178–180.   52. LC Add. MSS. 32897:512–520.

53. *Infra,* Chapter VII. The most thoroughgoing terms suggested for the anticipated treaty were submitted to Pitt by William Patterson, on December 20, 1759.
Patterson's memorandum, dated October 30, has sometimes been attributed to Pitt
himself, because signed "W.P." (Cf. Waddington, *La Guerre de sept ans,* III, 540,
and Pease, *op. cit.,* p. lxxviii n.) A postscript, dated December 4, indicates that it was
not delivered until after that date, and the presence of a copy in the Newcastle Papers (LC Add. MSS. 32897:484–491) indicates that it may have been submitted to
Newcastle first, and then, at his encouragement, sent to Pitt. The covering letter to
Pitt, together with a copy of the memorandum, is in PRO Chatham MSS. XCVI.

Patterson's memorandum proposed that Great Britain keep all conquests in
America; thus Great Britain would have no more troublesome boundary questions
with France, and would have a monopoly of the fur trade, the fisheries, the lumber
and naval stores of North America. The retention of Senegal and Goree would give
her control of the slave and rubber trades. If other nations should take umbrage at
Britain's increased empire, let them come on; Great Britain was never so well prepared to receive them.

As for the rest of North America, Patterson proposed that the boundary of Acadia
be the St. Lawrence, which would, indeed, become the boundary between Canada and
the British colonies as far as Montreal; the navigation of the river he would leave
open to both French and British. Beyond Montreal, he proposed that the boundary
follow the Ottawa and the forty-seventh degree of latitude to the eighty-third degree
of longitude and the north shore of Lake Huron, through the middle of Lake Michigan, the Illinois River and the Mississippi to the Gulf of Mexico. And thus, he says,
"by settling our Boundaries, the great Point in Dispute, in North America, [our possessions there would be] extensive enough, as above run out, for all the British who
shall resort thither or be born there for a thousand years to come."

France, informed Duke Louis Ernest of Brunswick that France and her allies would prepare a joint response to the Anglo-Prussian statement,[54] but he began secretly to propose that the Anglo-French dispute over American boundaries be separated from the European disputes.[55] Yorke parried the proposal, and he was promptly instructed to say to Affry that Great Britain would hear of no negotiations save as an ally of Prussia.[56] On the other hand, if France, separating herself from her allies— Austria, for example—was willing to negotiate with Prussia alone, he was to listen to what Affry had to propose.[57] Affry pointed out the difficulty of settling the Anglo-French disputes by a general congress, and the corresponding impossibility of ending the European war before the Anglo-French quarrel was cleared away; and he intimated that the best way to avoid Spanish mediation would be by direct negotiations between Great Britain and France.[58] A few days later, in a dramatic secret meeting in a carriage on the road near the castle of Ryswick, Affry explained to Yorke that France, having accepted the Spanish offer of mediation, could not take matters out of Spain's hands without knowing how things stood between Spain and Great Britain; but that the Duke de Choiseul was ready to negotiate in any way Great Britain might suggest; provided he might transmit copies of the transactions to Spain, for that country's satisfaction. He intimated, further, that France was tired of the Austrian alliance, and that, could the American disputes only be settled, France would gladly get out of Germany and leave the balance of power there undisturbed.[59] Choiseul similarly proposed to Frederick, who had sounded him out, that the Franco-Prussian disputes be settled separately.[60]

Obviously, it was Choiseul's desire to separate the Anglo-French colonial quarrel from the war in the Germanies, whether because he genuinely believed this to be the most effective means to peace, or whether he hoped thereby to weaken the Anglo-Prussian alliance. For whatever motive, he succeeded in injecting the principle of separation into the counterdeclaration of France and her allies that was made early in April, 1760. That document proposed, for the purpose of peace-making, the separation of the Anglo-French conflict and the continental war; for the former, it suggested the acceptance of the Spanish offer of mediation; for the lat-

54. BM Add. MSS. 6813:150, 152.   55. BM Add. MSS. 6818:5, 9, 11–12.
56. BM Add. MSS. 6818:13.   57. BM Add. MSS. 6818:15, 17–18.
58. BM Add. MSS. 6818:28.
59. BM Add. MSS. 6818:64–67; cf. *Recueil des Instructions*, XII *bis, Espagne*, pp. 338–339, and Corbett, *op. cit.*, II, 72–73.
60. Frederick to Chevalier de Froulay [February 14, 1760]; Froulay to Frederick, March 19, 1760; "Choiseul's articles toward peace" [March 17, 1760]; all in PRO Chatham MSS. LXXXV.

ter, it proposed a congress to settle the issues in Germany and elsewhere in Europe.[61] At the time the counterdeclaration was made, however, Affry, under instructions from Choiseul, assured Yorke that these articles in no way precluded a direct settlement between England and France, if England preferred it that way.[62] Choiseul later agreed to include in the Anglo-French negotiations the questions of Hanover, Hesse, and Brunswick, as being essentially parts of the Anglo-French war. But the war between Austria, Russia, and Prussia, he said, must be settled separately, by a congress. If England could not agree to this, France would break off negotiations.[63]

Yorke's suspicions were aroused by the repeated insistence by France that Spain be informed, and by the close association of Affry with the Marquis de Grimaldi,[64] Spanish minister at The Hague. Further, the French proposals for separate, secret, and direct negotiations convinced Holdernesse that the whole French maneuver was an attempt to exclude Prussia, and Yorke was told to say plainly that Prussia must be included in any settlement made between England and France. Upon the delivery of this message, Affry abruptly brought negotiations to an end.[65]

These abortive negotiations failed to produce peace, or to do more for England and Prussia than strengthen their confidence in each other. But for Choiseul, while negotiations failed to bring the belligerents to a settlement, they left Pitt under the embarrassing necessity of again facing Spain for war or for peace. Pitt tried to evade the issue, blaming Yorke and Holdernesse for having misunderstood Choiseul's assurances with regard to Prussia, and intimated that the negotiations at The Hague might be reopened.[66] Affry did, indeed, go back to The Hague to learn whether Yorke had been instructed to try again, but the gesture was without result.[67]

Neither side had any real intention of reopening the discussion, apparently, and Spain now took those first steps toward a rapprochement with France that eventually culminated in the renewal of the Family Compact. Ricardo Wall, long the friend of Great Britain, hitherto convinced both of Britain's good faith and that the Anglo-Spanish disputes in America would be settled peaceably, at last began to lose his patience.

61. BM Add. MSS. 6818:142–143.
62. BM Add. MSS. 6818:137–139, 148–149; note on dispatch from Choiseul to Affry, 31 March, 1760, PRO Chatham MSS. LXXXV.
63. BM Add. MSS. 6818:172–173.
64. Jeronimo Grimaldi, Marquis de Grimaldi.
65. BM Add. MSS. 6818:168–171, 178–180; AE CP Espagne 528:232–235.
66. AE CP Espagne 529:22–24.
67. LC Add. MSS. 32908:69; AE CP Espagne 529:73–75.

He was still convinced that Great Britain desired peace; but he was also coming to believe that she had no intention of giving any adequate consideration to Spanish complaints of British misconduct in America. On the contrary, it now appeared to him that, once Great Britain had disposed of France, she would turn upon Spain, and dictate a settlement upon her own terms.[68] It was for this reason that, while genuinely desiring a speedy end to the struggle between France and Great Britain, Wall and his master could not permit such a settlement to be too much of a defeat for France.[69] After peace was made, he thought, France and Spain might reorganize their fleets, their finances, and their armies, and join forces to bring the British to reason. But Spain must have time to prepare. Wall may have taken this line of argument as a compromise between the belligerent emotions of his master and his own conviction that, despite everything, Spain's best course with Great Britain was neutrality and friendly argument. In any case, he convinced the French ambassador that Spain did not wish to become involved in the present war.[70] Nevertheless, both he and the King now felt that Spain was in a position to take a more determined attitude toward Great Britain, and the instructions to Fuentes, in London, clearly reflect this feeling, especially since word had come that in April, 1760, the French army under Lévis had laid siege to Quebec.[71] Incidentally, Charles III intimated to France that Spain would like to receive Louisiana in return for any aid furnished France—an idea that Choiseul promptly and decisively overruled, only to have it emerge again later on.[72]

Fuentes began his negotiations with the British government on a plane of moderation as regarded the British establishments on the Bay of Honduras, the logwood cutters, and the Spanish right to fish on the banks of Newfoundland; and he took care to "renounce any Intention in His Court to insist upon their Mediation or *Good Offices*."[73] He found the ministry divided and Pitt undecided and difficult as to ways of compromise, but quite unwilling to concede any of the Spanish demands.[74] The inflexibility of the British minister resulted only in deciding the Spanish government to take another step in the direction of war. Fuentes was instructed to stiffen his demands.[75]

On September 9, 1760, the Spanish ambassador presented to the British secretary of state two "extraordinary" notes, one dealing with

68. AE CP Espagne 528:187–193.
69. AE CP Espagne 528:172–180, 187–193.
70. AE CP Espagne 528:187–193.   71. AE CP Espagne 529:22–34.
72. AE CP Espagne 529:22–34, 73–75.   73. LC Add. MSS. 32908:34–38.
74. LC Add. MSS. 32908:80, 307; AE CP Espagne 529:123–137.
75. AE CP Espagne 529:243–249; *Recueil des Instructions*, XII *bis, Espagne*, p. 339.

the British logwood establishments, the other with Spain's claim to fishing rights on the banks of Newfoundland. The tone of both was forceful, even peremptory; but the point that attracted most attention was the statement in the note on fishing rights that a copy of that note had been sent to the court of France.[76] This was regarded by the British ministers as a clear threat that Spain might join France; and it was agreed that peace or war with Spain probably depended upon the answer.[77] Pitt took immediate and vigorous verbal exception to this extraordinary procedure;[78] but he had no intention, as yet, of precipitating a war. On the contrary, the Spanish appeal to France was rather welcomed as an excuse to delay the British answer to the notes until the end of that year's campaign,[79] and Pitt's instructions to Bristol, for communication to Wall, were distinctly conciliatory in tone.[80]

But Wall's influence in the Spanish court was no longer what it had been. The Marquis de Enseñada, expelled from the court in 1754 for his unfriendliness to Great Britain, had now returned and was making his influence felt.[81] Montreal fell to the British in the autumn of 1760, and even Wall now began to admit the possibility of Mexico's being exposed to a British menace by way of Louisiana. The French ambassador lost no time in playing up the danger to Spain's colonies, while informing the Spanish court that at the end of the year's campaign France must certainly make peace.[82] Charles was already piqued at Pitt's treatment of Fuentes; now he became panic-stricken, and in his desire to prevent a peace that might bring the British to the borders of Mexico, he offered to join France as soon as his forces could be made ready.[83] This was exactly what Choiseul had wished, and on March 3, 1761, he instructed Ossun to propose an offensive and defensive alliance.[84] Three weeks later, using his Spanish negotiations as a club, he entered upon direct peace negotiations with Great Britain.

Choiseul's various and skilful diplomatic maneuvers were hardly more than jockeyings for position. They had not brought peace to France; but they had strengthened the Austrian alliance and now placed in

76. The two notes of Fuentes to Pitt, September 9, 1760, PRO Chatham MSS. XCII.

77. LC Add. MSS. 32911:269, 285.

78. "Réponse verbale, faite a Mons[r.] le Comte de Fuentes par Mons[r.] Pitt, ce 16[e.] Sep[re.] 1760," PRO Chatham MSS. XCIII; CL Shelburne MSS. XXII:541-542; LC Add. MSS. 32911:367.

79. LC Add. MSS. 32911:285-288, 361-362.

80. Pitt to Bristol, September 26, 1760, PRO Chatham MSS. XCIII.

81. AE CP Espagne 529:243-249; Chatham Correspondence, II, 68-72.

82. AE CP Espagne 530:136-147, 242-254, 274-278.

83. AE CP Espagne 530:49-63, 64-82, 136-147, 242-254, 531:226-228.

84. AE CP Espagne 531:280-281.

Choiseul's hands a powerful instrument of coercion for possible use in his approaching negotiations with Great Britain. He had reason to believe that his overtures for peace might now be successful. But he reckoned without the character of his most formidable opponent, William Pitt.

CHAPTER VII

PITT'S NEGOTIATIONS, MARCH–SEPTEMBER 1761

THE Duke de Choiseul was now playing a three-cornered game. He desired peace with England, but his engagements to Vienna forestalled his impulse to make a separate peace that might involve the prerequisite evacuation of the lands of England's ally, Frederick. He saw in Spanish mediation a way to peace, or, failing that, the entrance of Spain into the war on the side of France; but his chief desire was peace, and he would use the Spanish menace only in case everything else failed. Meanwhile he would keep the Spanish negotiations alive. Because he was absolutely convinced of the futility of the idea of a general congress for the settlement of the colonial and maritime conflict with England, he must negotiate for Austria's permission to settle the English quarrel separately; for peace, to be made at all, must first be made with England. Thus it was, that, early in 1761, while continuing his negotiations with Spain, Choiseul entered upon negotiations with Austria and Russia looking toward a joint move for peace, a necessary part of which would be a preliminary arrangement between the two chief protagonists, France and England.

For France, peace was a dire necessity. The country was in desperate financial straits, and the year 1760 had added to the number of colonial disasters: a series of victories in India all but completed the English conquest there; the fall of Montreal in September gave England all of Canada; while the tide of war in Germany had turned—at Warburg, Liegnitz, and Torgau. Nevertheless, France would not negotiate as a completely beaten country, but as one which had a strong potential ally in Spain. France's allies, too, were opposed to peace: Maria Theresa was determined that Frederick must be completely and forever crushed. Choiseul's negotiations with Vienna and St. Petersburg were of the stormiest, therefore, and it was only with the greatest difficulty and by the threat of abandoning them altogether that he won their collaboration in a joint declaration for peace—a sort of belated acceptance of the Anglo-Prussian declaration of November 25, 1759.[1]

The allied move for peace found Great Britain and Prussia in a mood to welcome it. Frederick now doubted the effectiveness of a congress,

1. Waddington, *La Guerre de sept ans*, IV, 481–496; cf. Arthur Frederick Basil Williams, *The Life of William Pitt, Earl of Chatham* (London, 1913), II, 80.

and encouraged Great Britain to make some secret and direct contact
with France. He suggested that, in a separate Anglo-French treaty,
France be required to evacuate Westphalia and to promise to give no
aid to Austria other than the 24,000 men stipulated in the Treaty of
Versailles.[2] The British ministers, with the exception of Pitt and his
friends, were wholly desirous of peace, and welcomed the secret negotiations that opened, first, in The Hague in February, 1761.[3]

The joint declaration of the Allies, dated March 26, 1761, was presented to the British ministry by Prince Galitzin, Russian ambassador
at London. The declaration proposed that all the belligerents send
plenipotentiaries to a congress to be held at Augsburg, for the purpose
of making peace.[4] But with the tacit recognition of all the belligerents
that the success of the congress must depend upon a preliminary agreement between France and Great Britain, Choiseul sent with the declaration a note and a personal letter to Pitt, proposing that the two countries proceed directly to a settlement of their private disputes before
the opening of the congress. As a basis for the negotiations, Choiseul
proposed the principle of *uti possidetis*, to be applied as of May 1 in
Europe, July 1 in America and Africa, and September 1 in the East
Indies.[5]

Great Britain accepted the proposal for a congress for herself and
Prussia on April 3,[6] and proceeded to name plenipotentiaries.[7] But
Choiseul's plan for an Anglo-French peace had to be debated by the
cabinet before the negotiations could proceed. To begin with, the British cabinet was divided within itself, and its members were in a sensitive
mood over a recent shake-up that had placed the Earl of Bute in the
office of the Secretary of State for the Northern Department as a team-
mate of the fractious Pitt.[8] Most of the ministers, and particularly
Newcastle, favored peace and were disposed to proceed; but Pitt was
hesitant. While in a sense desirous of peace, he had on foot plans for
several campaigns which he apparently hoped to push to a successful
conclusion, and, in March, he had intercepted several letters exchanged
by the Spanish ambassadors in London and Paris that informed him of
Choiseul's negotiations for an alliance with Spain.[9] To accept the dates

2. BM Add. MSS. 6808:162–164.
3. Waddington, *La Guerre de sept ans*, IV, 494; Corbett, *op. cit.*, II, 148–149.
4. BM Add. MSS. 32921:76–77.   5. BM Add. MSS. 6819:37, 39–40.
6. BM Add. MSS. 6819:33–34.
7. Thackeray, *op. cit.*, I, 505, II, 516–517.
8. *Cambridge Hist. Brit. Empire*, I, 488–489. John Stuart, third Earl of Bute, the
favorite of George III, had succeeded Holdernesse as Secretary of State for the
Northern Department on March 25.
9. PRO Chatham MSS. XCIII; *Chatham Correspondence*, II, 92–93.

suggested by Choiseul for the application of the *uti possidetis* principle would rob him of the fruits of his expected military successes, and his knowledge of Choiseul's parallel negotiations with Spain apparently made him suspicious of that minister's good faith, a suspicion that probably was chiefly responsible for the eventual failure of the negotiations.[10] But the sentiment for peace was too strong to be opposed, and Pitt himself believed Choiseul to be more disposed to make peace than to continue the war.[11] His reply to the French minister was therefore couched in friendly terms. He accepted the principle of *uti possidetis;* but because of the possibility of delays in the negotiations, and, probably, with one eye on his projected campaigns, he declined the dates suggested by Choiseul for the application of the principle, and proposed that it be applied only with reference to the date of the anticipated treaty. He agreed to Choiseul's proposed exchange of agents, for the further conduct of the negotiations, and named Hans Stanley as British representative in Paris. He made it perfectly clear, however, that the interests of his Prussian ally would be considered at every stage of the discussions.[12]

The negotiations were now assured. Most of the British ministers were optimistic as to the outcome, and set about clarifying their ideas as to what the peace should include. Pitt was apparently determined to retain Canada and to exclude France from the Newfoundland fisheries. Beyond this, his ideas seem to have been vague.[13] In true mercantilistic fashion he thought of North America as a source of raw materials for Great Britain and a market for her products, and the fishery as the foundation of British naval power. Thus his long-range view of the national interest impelled him to demand a settlement that would guarantee to Great Britain not only all Canada, both for its economic value and for the security of British North America, but also a monopoly of the fishery as a nursery for the British marine.[14] On both these points he was opposed by the peace advocates among the followers of Newcastle and the Duke of Bedford, who argued that it would be a mistake to ask so much of France. The removal of the French from Canada, they said, would tend to encourage the old colonies in their growing mood of "independency"; and the claim of Britain to a monopoly of the fishery in the open sea was both untenable under international law and certain to

10. Cf. Corbett, *op. cit.,* II, 142–143, 155; cf. also Albert von Ruville, *William Pitt, Earl of Chatham* (London, 1907), II, 365.

11. LC Add. MSS. 32921:272.

12. Pitt to Choiseul, April 8, 1761, and accompanying note, PRO Chatham MSS. LXXXV; *Chatham Correspondence,* II, 116–119.

13. LC Add. MSS. 32921:272.

14. LC Add. MSS. 32921:340, 381, 32922:15–21; cf. Williams, *op. cit.,* II, 82–83.

arouse the combined opposition of the other maritime nations, particularly Spain.[15]

The Board of Trade, which was asked to draw up recommendations for the peace, submitted specific suggestions: Canada should be retained in its entirety "as a security to our other dominions in America, and as a means of wealth and power to Great Britain." Because of the difficulty already encountered in the definition of boundaries, the cession of Louisiana ought also to be demanded by Great Britain; for if not, the Board thought the French in Louisiana would soon begin encroaching upon the frontiers of Georgia and Carolina, as they had formerly done in the north. The Newfoundland fishery was thought to be "of more worth than both the forementioned provinces," and the entire exclusion of the French therefrom was "extremely to be wished." But the Board of Trade recognized that the fishery had not been one of the objectives of the war, and, more important still, that Great Britain's assumption of a monopoly of the open-sea fishery could only be made as an act of force, feasible, perhaps, because of Britain's supremacy on the sea, but certain to excite the resentment of the other maritime powers. The Board concluded that if the French were confined to drying their fish on the northern and western shores of Newfoundland, as provided by the Treaty of Utrecht, their fishery would soon decline anyway, and the international dangers inherent in a monopoly would be avoided. Nevertheless, if practicable, an attempt should be made to exclude them "from even a pretence of Navigating in North American Seas." The "neutral islands" in the West Indies should be recognized as British; if anything were to be returned to France, said the Board, let it be Guadeloupe.[16]

Choiseul, on his side, was the recipient of suggestions for the peace, the most notable of which was given in a note submitted by Jean-Daniel Dumas on April 5.[17] Dumas was a logical successor of La Galissonnière, and his arguments were based, like those of La Galissonnière, upon considerations for the security of Canada. For him the only secure boundary between the English and the French in North America was the watershed; and, should this not be possible, it was wiser to cede all of Canada and all of Louisiana, as the latter could not be defended without the former.[18] If France should retain Canada, then the Penobscot and the St. John rivers should be the boundaries in Acadia, with the intervening territory left neutral. The lakes, he wrote, should be retained by France, together with the title to the land as far as the watershed; but the British should be allowed a trading post at Oswego. On

15. LC Add. MSS. 32921:340, 381, 32922:449–451.
16. BM Add. MSS. 35913:73–74.   17. *N.Y. Col. Docs.*, X, 1134–1138.
18. *Ibid.*, X, 1135.

the Ohio side, the mountains should be made the boundary; otherwise, the movement of the British population westward would soon clear the mountains and irresistibly flow down the river valleys into the heart of Louisiana. To compensate for the return of Canada, Dumas proposed to give the British more territory in the region of Hudson Bay, perhaps even the whole of Lake Superior, as being a much less dangerous cession than even one inch of the territory west of the Alleghenies. But the most remarkable proposal of all was his suggestion that the Canadian boundary be disarmed; forts along the frontier, said Dumas, are useless, and "are adapted only to create difficulties, to afford umbrage and sometimes furnish pretexts for a rupture."[19] As Choiseul was faced with the cession of Canada as a foregone conclusion, and as he hoped to save Louisiana, he did not adopt the suggestions in this note, although he did claim the watershed as the boundary of Canada in the direction of the Ohio.[20]

Choiseul's reply to Pitt, on April 19, accepted the British reservation as regarded Prussia, but reiterated the French desire for putting the "given periods" for the application of *uti possidetis* at the dates already suggested. Meanwhile, however, he notified Pitt of the appointment of François de Bussy as French agent for the negotiations, and invited the British minister to reciprocate.[21] Pitt, in his turn, then notified Choiseul of the appointment of Hans Stanley, and proposed that the question of the given periods be made a matter of negotiation, along with the question of the compensation, if any, for the conquered territories to be ceded by the respective belligerents.[22] There remained only the business of exchanging agents, which was accomplished about the middle of May.

Thus the negotiations got under way; but it was not without the attendance of evil omens. Austria and Russia were skeptical and critical,[23] and Spain was becoming increasingly interested. Choiseul, conscious of the difficulties surrounding him, and rendered suspicious of British intentions by the vagueness of Pitt's replies,[24] pursued his Spanish negotiations with as much avidity as though that were his sole diplomatic objective. On January 27, 1761, he had suggested to Spain a treaty of commerce and mutual defense;[25] Spain even wished to make an alliance that would be offensive as well, in the hope, as Choiseul supposed, of winning French aid for the forcible settlement of the Spanish colonial

19. *Ibid.*, X, 1135–1138.
20. Pease, *op. cit.*, p. 298; Stanley's Memorandum, June 17, 1761, PRO Chatham MSS. LXXXV.
21. Thackeray, *op. cit.*, II, 514–516.   22. *Ibid.*, II, 514–515, 517–518.
23. AE CP Espagne 532:221; CAO AE CP Ang. 443:99; Waddington, *La Guerre de sept ans*, IV, 555 ff.
24. AE CP Espagne 532:221.   25. AE CP Espagne 531:95–97.

dispute and of writing the settlement into the proposed treaty between Great Britain and France.[26] Fuentes, the Spanish ambassador in London, believed that a postponement of the peace would precipitate a civil war in England, which would improve France's prospects and provide Spain with a profitable opportunity to fish in the troubled waters of the new peace negotiation that would result. He therefore agreed with Grimaldi that Spain's best game was to try to prevent France from making peace.[27]

Choiseul humored Spain, hoping to use her as a makeweight in the rectification of France's balance with England. He suggested that if England refused the overtures which were to be made, Spain might bring about the making of an advantageous settlement by threatening to join forces against that country which refused to accept reasonable terms.[28] On March 3 he went beyond his suggestion of January 27, and proposed an offensive and defensive alliance.[29] But with the announcement of the English negotiations, His Catholic Majesty thought it prudent to make the proposed alliance defensive only, as France would need several years of rest and recuperation before undertaking a new struggle with England.[30]

Thus far had Choiseul's game with Spain proceeded when Bussy went to London. Copies of the documents connected with the negotiations had been sent to the Spanish court promptly,[31] and Bussy was instructed to keep the Spanish ambassador in London informed of every step in the negotiations, and to ask his counsel on all important questions. Choiseul doubted whether Pitt would really make peace, and, while he was willing to limit the proposed Family Compact to one of defensive purposes, he had no intention of throwing away his Spanish trump just on the chance that he might be wrong about the British minister. To Bussy he said that, if Great Britain were really disposed to make peace, France would make no offensive alliance against her; and he probably meant what he said.[32] But he directed Ossun to ask Wall directly whether, should England not make peace by May 1, 1762, Spain would declare war on the side of France.[33] Should the Spanish answer be in the affirmative, France would be prepared for eventualities, whether British action directed the course of events toward peace or war.

26. AE CP Espagne 531:125–126; *Chatham Correspondence,* II, 95–97.
27. *Chatham Correspondence,* II, 100–101; Grimaldi to Fuentes, March 28, 1761, PRO Chatham MSS. XCIII.
28. AE CP Espagne 531:226–228.   29. AE CP Espagne 531:325.
30. AE CP Espagne 532:7–18.
31. AE CP Espagne 531:392–393; Waddington, *La Guerre de sept ans,* IV, 514.
32. Waddington, *La Guerre de sept ans,* IV, 514–515.
33. AE CP Espagne 532:221, 334–338.

Pitt, on his side, was trying to forestall Choiseul's game and soften the warlike tone of Spain by offering to abandon the British military establishments on the coast of Central America. He made the offer, however, on condition that Spain should guarantee to find some other way of meeting the British demand for dyewoods.[34] Perhaps because of this concession, perhaps because the projected Family Compact had been shorn, for the moment, of its offensive provisions, Wall's belligerent tone toward Great Britain did soften. But he stuck to the point of national honor involved in the Spanish demand for evacuation first and a guaranty of the dyewoods supply afterwards.[35] Pitt was suspicious of both Wall and Choiseul, and refused to concede the prior evacuation demanded by Spain, thus throwing that country back into the arms of Choiseul at the beginning of July.[36]

Meanwhile, Bussy and Stanley had gone to their posts late in May. As it was expected that the major part of the negotiations would take place in London, the British agent's instructions, dated May 18, 1761, were brief and noncommittal. He was told to listen to any proposals France might present for making effective the principle of *uti possidetis;* he might negotiate as to the dates to be set for the application of this principle. He was to say that Great Britain agreed to a separate peace; but he was to inform the French minister plainly that Great Britain would continue to support Prussia in the German war.[37]

Bussy, on the other hand, coming as he did from the nation which had proposed the negotiations, was more particularly instructed as to the definite proposals he should make. Recognizing that France had little with which to bargain, Choiseul offered to give up Minorca in return for Guadeloupe, St. Lucia, Tobago, Marie-Galante, and the island of Goree off the coast of Africa. The influence of the Spanish game could be seen in Choiseul's demand that Great Britain secure the acquiescence of Spain —who had, herself, always claimed these West Indian islands—in the recognition of France's title to them. Acadia, "in its entirety," was to be ceded to England; but Canada, entirely or in part, and Cape Breton were to be restored to France in consideration for the restoration of other territory won by French armies from Hanover and Prussia.[38] Bussy was instructed to keep in close touch with the Spanish ambassador, and to urge upon the British minister, if necessary, the threat of a war with Spain; but if Pitt should prove to be reasonable Bussy was not to forget that the first object of his mission was peace, and that "it

34. Thackeray, *op. cit.,* I, 499–500.   35. *Ibid.,* I, 501–504.
36. *Ibid.,* I, 560–562.   37. *Ibid.,* I, 506–508.
38. CAO AE CP Ang. 443:119.

can only be when we lose hope [of success in the negotiations], that we shall be obliged to give ourselves up to the ideas of Spain."[39]

The conversations in London and Paris began early in June. Stanley was well received, generously entertained, and convinced of Choiseul's determination to make peace. Bussy was not so devoted to peace as his master, and adopted an almost peremptory tone, despite his mortal terror of Pitt. Early exchanges turned upon the "given periods" for the application of the principle of *uti possidetis*, and the relations to be maintained between Great Britain and France and their respective allies.[40] On June 17, after news had arrived that Belle Isle had fallen to Commodore Keppel, Choiseul submitted to Stanley a memorandum expressing the minister's ideas as to the colonial settlement.[41] In it he now proposed that Guadeloupe, Marie-Galante, and Goree be returned to France in exchange for Minorca. The islands of St. Lucia and Tobago, which, according to Bussy's instructions were to have been included in the cluster of islands to be given for Minorca, were not mentioned. Choiseul now proposed, also, to cede all Canada to Great Britain, with its southern limits to be fixed at the watershed between the lakes and the Ohio. He asked, however, that the island of Cape Breton be left to France. He would agree never to fortify it; but, although Stanley discouraged him, he persisted in demanding the island for French fishermen.[42] As a consideration for the cession of Canada, he demanded a continuation of the French right to the codfishery as established by the Treaty of Utrecht. France would evacuate the territories of Great Britain's allies in Germany. But nothing was said about Spain's title to the islands in the West Indies.[43]

This set of proposals, which Choiseul hoped would be "the foundation of a treaty,"[44] split the British cabinet wide open. All the ministers were agreed that the island of Cape Breton could not again be returned to France, and that "all Canada" must be insisted upon. But on the ques-

---

39. Quoted in Waddington, *La Guerre de sept ans*, IV, 515–516.

40. Thackeray, *op. cit.*, I, 514–537, II, 523, 525; *Chatham Correspondence*, II, 124–128.

41. Memorandum, June 17, 1761, PRO Chatham MSS. LXXXV.

42. Thackeray, *op. cit.*, I, 540–541.

43. Memorandum, June 17, 1761, PRO Chatham MSS. LXXXV. As a matter of fact, the reference to the Spanish title in Bussy's instructions was not intended really to be called to the attention of England. Choiseul confessed to Bussy in a private letter a little later: "I know very well that we are masters of St. Lucia and Tobago; and in your instructions you will see that I spoke of these islands, which have been considered neutral in other countries, only to establish the fact of our possession, and to bind our negotiation to Spain, in case, the peace failing, that liaison should become necessary to us." (CAO AE CP Ang. 443:220.)

44. Thackeray, *op. cit.*, I, 540–541.

tion of the fisheries, Pitt, representing the interests of the British mer-
cantile world, differed widely from his colleagues. He desired never again
to surrender any part of this source of British wealth to France or any
other nation, and was ready to break off negotiations if France insisted upon it. But the majority of his colleagues were against him, and
he was prevailed upon to compromise. He finally agreed to distinguish
between the St. Lawrence fisheries and the Newfoundland fisheries, and
to offer France the latter in return for some important compensation,
such as, perhaps, the demolition of the fortifications at Dunkirk.[45] This
being agreed, Pitt drew up a set of instructions which, in part, amounted
to an ultimatum. The document expressed the desires of the cabinet, but
it was couched in terms which even Pitt's colleagues deprecated as being
offensive and ill-calculated to promote good feeling between the two
courts.[46] In the first place, the territories of Great Britain's German
allies, which belonged to neither nation, were ruled out of the discussion
as subjects for exchanges between England and France. With regard to
the cession of Canada, Pitt rejected Choiseul's "new limits" in the Ohio
country. To accept them, he said, would be "to shorten thereby the extent of Canada, and to lengthen the boundaries of Louisiana," as also
to establish the principle "that all which is not Canada is Louisiana;
whereby all the intermediate nations and countries, the true barrier to
each province would be given up to France."[47] As he explained to Bussy,
the course of the Ohio did not belong to France at all, but was a part
of Virginia; nevertheless, he was willing to leave the territory between
the Ohio and the mountains uninhabited, provided only that the Virginia title were recognized.[48]

Pitt likewise rejected the "mutilation" of Canada by the amputation
of Cape Breton. Acadia, which indeed belonged to England by prior
right, the whole of Canada, and the Gulf of St. Lawrence fishery, one
and all came within the *uti possidetis* arrangement, he maintained, and
must be surrendered on the basis of that principle. As for the Newfoundland fishery, said Pitt, the Treaty of Utrecht was in force no longer;
therefore, the French demand for a restoration of privileges under that
treaty might be granted only in return for some important concession.
Discussion of this proposal he postponed until the renewal of the other
terms of that treaty, and particularly those with regard to the fortifications at Dunkirk, should come to be discussed. For Minorca, instead
of the constellation of islands demanded by Choiseul, Pitt offered Belle

45. LC Add. MSS. 32924:311–322; cf. Williams, *op. cit.*, II, 92–93, and Von Ruville,
op. cit., II, 377.
46. LC Add. MSS. 32924:320.   47. Thackeray, *op. cit.*, I, 545.
48. Pease, *op. cit.*, p. 319.

Isle. Guadeloupe and Marie-Galante he made the price of French evacuation of the territory of England's allies in Germany.[49]

Pitt specified the following points as essential: (1) the cession of Canada "without new limits," Cape Breton, and the other islands in the Gulf of St. Lawrence, together with the St. Lawrence fishery; (2) the cession of Senegal, which had not appeared in Choiseul's memorandum, and the island of Goree; (3) the demolition of the fortifications at Dunkirk; (4) the evacuation of the "neutral islands," or their division between France and England; (5) the restoration of Minorca and Benkulen (on the island of Sumatra); (6) the evacuation of the territories of England's allies in Germany, and, specifically, of Hesse, Brunswick, Wesel, and Hanover, as also those parts of Prussia occupied by French armies. These points expressed what Pitt called the unalterable intention of His Britannic Majesty; others were left for Stanley to negotiate with Choiseul.[50] It is to be noted that the St. Lawrence fishery was reserved, whereas the Newfoundland, or open-sea, fishery might be an object of negotiation. Otherwise, the statement of the irreducible points left little choice for France. They amounted, in effect, to a settlement dictated to the vanquished by their vanquisher, and could not fail to arouse the indignation of the French court.[51]

The tone and vigor of Pitt's reply to Choiseul's offer can hardly be explained unless they had their source in his suspicions of a French liaison with Spain. For his distrust, aroused by the interception of the letters between Fuentes and Grimaldi, had not abated; on the contrary, it had apparently been increased by the differing tone of Bussy and his master, and by Stanley's reports of the adverse pressure being exerted upon Choiseul by the ambassadors of Austria and Spain.[52] In any case, this communication seems to have convinced Choiseul that England was not yet ready to make peace, and to have led him to expose his Spanish cards, in the hope either that Pitt would grow milder in the face of the Spanish threat, or that France, with a new ally at sea, might be able to recoup some of her losses. In this he shared the revulsion of feeling that was now general in the French court,[53] and he wrote to Bussy that, henceforth, his policy would be to cultivate the Spanish alliance and delay peace negotiations long enough to prevent further military action that summer and to give Spain time to prepare. "It will be August," he said, "before they can answer my note: to their answer I shall have to reply in my turn, and I shall do so in such a way as to provoke another

49. Thackeray, op. cit., I, 543–547.   50. Ibid., I, 547–549.

51. Cf. Von Ruville, op. cit., II, 378–379.

52. Thackeray, op. cit., I, 500, 540, 560–562; II, 525, 526; cf. Corbett, op. cit., II, 173.

53. Von Ruville, op. cit., II, 382.

answer from England. This will bring us to September, when it will be too late for attempts on our coast."[54]

Choiseul's reply to Stanley was therefore of a temporizing nature. In conference he told Stanley he could turn the German territories to good advantage elsewhere, should Pitt persist in refusing to consider them legitimate material for exchanges; and this statement was of such good effect that Stanley was convinced that Austria, and perhaps Spain, had made some new effort to induce France to continue the war. Nevertheless, Choiseul apparently took Pitt's equivocal suggestion of a restitution of Guadeloupe as an offer of that island as compensation for the French evacuation of the Germanies, and indicated that he might agree on that basis. Canada, Choiseul agreed, should be ceded "undismembered"; but because he believed strongly in the value of the codfishery to France, he fought hard for Cape Breton, almost to the point, as Stanley thought, of breaking off the negotiations; and he finally suggested that England might name some port which would take the place of Louisbourg as a shelter for French vessels engaged in the open-sea fishery.[55] Choiseul accepted the disposition of the "neutral islands" proposed by Pitt, giving preference to a division between France and England. With regard to India, Stanley thought Choiseul would make no trouble, if the other questions were successfully adjusted, and reported that the minister agreed to the restitution of Minorca and Senegal. But Choiseul also insisted upon the return of Goree, and displayed anger at Pitt's demand for it. Both the French slave trade, and the "sugar islands" dependent upon that trade, he said, would suffer if the French were left with only that one small slave-trading station which would then remain to them on the African coast. He hinted, however, that, if given a slave station elsewhere, France would not insist upon retaining Goree.[56]

The conversations reported in these dispatches of July 1 and July 5 were of an informal nature, and did not constitute an official reply to Pitt's instructions to Stanley. They did indicate, however, that Choiseul

54. Quoted in Williams, *op. cit.,* II, 93.

55. Choiseul thought little of the old La Galissonnière assumption that Canada and Louisiana would be lost if the English were allowed to go beyond the mountains. "Even though one were to admit," he wrote, "as I do not admit, that Canada is the highroad to Louisiana, which pays no profit to France; and even though one admits that a highroad might be eight hundred leagues long, and that a maritime power like England would attack Louisiana by land and by traversing these eight hundred leagues, I would still wager that the codfishery in the Gulf of St. Lawrence is worth infinitely more for the realm of France than Canada and Louisiana." (Pease, *op. cit.,* p. 338.) This explains why Choiseul gave up Canada and the interior so easily and struggled so persistently to preserve a foothold for French fishermen in the Gulf of St. Lawrence.

56. BM Add. MSS. 36798:112–123.

was far from accepting the *sine qua non* points in Pitt's demands. Without definitely rejecting those demands, Choiseul had parried them so skilfully as to make further discussion necessary. Meanwhile, he clearly intimated to Stanley that if England remained inflexible in her demands, France would continue the war, and, in that case, would have the aid of Spain. Stanley rejected Choiseul's suggestion that Spain be asked to guarantee the peace and his hint of Spanish aid to France, as an empty threat, made to force England to soften her demands. He admitted the possibility that Spain might come to France's aid; but he scoffed at the idea of France fighting to settle Spain's quarrel. "She who acquiesces in the loss of Canada, will not soon enter into a war for the logwood of Honduras."[57]

But Choiseul's warning was no idle threat. As he explained to Bussy, there were three points with regard to which France would rather continue the war than surrender. The first was the question of an island or port in the Gulf of St. Lawrence to serve as a haven, or *abri*, for French fishing ships. Even if Great Britain ceded Cape Breton, Ile St. Jean (Prince Edward Island), the Island of Canso, or the port of Canso on the Acadian Peninsula, and even if she were willing to cede Newfoundland in exchange for French Guiana and its port of Cayenne, in no case would France make peace without some provision being made for such a haven. Choiseul's second point was his demand for Goree or some other slave station on the coast of Africa, and the third was his refusal to agree to the demolition of the fortifications at Dunkirk. He was willing to negotiate as to terms on these last two points, but he was adamant upon the general principles involved.[58] The "neutral islands," Choiseul indicated to Bussy, constituted another point which made for trouble. Spain claimed these islands, and France could not make any agreement as to their final disposition unless Spain concurred in it.[59]

Bussy told Pitt of the three points on which his master would never

57. Thackeray, *op. cit.*, II, 544; BM Add. MSS. 36798:119, 122, 127.

58. CAO AE CP Ang. 443:324–327.

59. CAO AE CP Ang. 443:327. As a matter of fact, Choiseul, in his negotiation of the Family Compact, was at this moment proposing that an article ceding these islands to France be included in the proposed treaty. (AE CP Espagne 533:34–37.) When this idea was presented to Wall by Ossun, the Spanish minister indicated a willingness to acknowledge France's title both to the islands and to Louisiana, but he suggested, in his turn, that the proposed treaty ought also to contain a provision that the boundary between Louisiana and Mexico should be definitely settled by a joint commission. (AE CP Espagne 533:122–128.) Shortly afterwards, Wall informed the English ambassador that His Catholic Majesty, at last despairing of obtaining justice at the hands of Great Britain, had placed his interests in the hands of France. (LC Add. MSS. 32926:4; AE CP Espagne 533:137–141.)

consent to yield, only to find the British minister obstinately intransigent on every one of them. Pitt disavowed Stanley's expressed concession of the St. Lawrence and Newfoundland fisheries as due to Stanley's misunderstanding of his instructions, and frankly gave Bussy to understand that his own personal conviction was that France should be excluded from the fishery entirely. Bussy's hint that France would cede Guiana for Newfoundland he dismissed with the remark that the British were a northern people, and would not desire establishments so far south. Pitt was equally immovable on the cession of Goree and the demolition of Dunkirk. But when Bussy spoke of the Spanish title, and of his master's feeling that he must conduct the negotiations relative to the "neutral islands" with Spain as a fellow negotiator, Pitt exploded. "Oh, my God," he cried, "I certainly hope that will not happen. Spain has nothing to do with the negotiations between these two courts, and England will never permit her to be admitted to them!"[60] Bussy would have despaired of the negotiations, then and there, had he not believed Pitt would be overruled on all these points by his cabinet's peace party led by Bute. In this belief he was, as events were to show, largely justified.[61]

These conversations in Paris and London indicate the direction of French policy, and the willingness of France to identify the Spanish cause with her own. Their net effect was to increase the stiffness of Spain toward Great Britain, to strengthen the conviction in Choiseul's mind that Pitt would not make a reasonable peace, and to increase Pitt's suspicions of Choiseul. That minister, indeed, was willing to present the Spanish case, if it became absolutely necessary, for he probably hoped England would accept it. If so, it would increase French prestige at Madrid; if not, it would inevitably draw Spain closer to a defensive union with France. He therefore instructed Bussy to present the Spanish case if it should seem desirable after consultation with the Spanish ambassador.[62]

Choiseul's formal reply to Pitt's demands was presented in a memorial dated July 13, which was delivered by Bussy on July 20. As both Stanley and Bussy had already anticipated, there were three points on which Choiseul refused to budge. He was willing to cede Canada with the boundaries it had had while owned by France, but with four reserva-

---

60. CAO AE CP Ang. 443:334–347.   61. CAO AE CP Ang. 443:343.

62. Ossun reported it to be his conviction that, in view of the ease with which the Anglo-Spanish disputes could be settled, England would not risk a new war with Spain over them, but that their successful conclusion under the auspices of France would tremendously increase French prestige at Madrid. (AE CP Espagne 533:203–209.)

tions, for the protection of the French inhabitants.[63] As a consideration for this cession, France would expect England to renew France's
fishing privileges on the Banks of Newfoundland as provided for in the
Treaty of Utrecht, with Cape Breton as a base and shelter for the
French fishermen. Choiseul offered England her choice of either Senegal
or Goree, but insisted that it be simply one or the other. Dunkirk was
not mentioned. As for the "neutral islands," France was willing to let
Dominica and St. Vincent continue to remain neutral, and divide the
other two by giving Tobago to England and keeping St. Lucia. But
Bussy was instructed to say that this provision could have effect only
upon the prior settlement of His Catholic Majesty's disputes with England. And because Spain's interests were thus so inextricably bound up
with the Anglo-French dispute, Bussy was instructed to present a separate memorial on the Anglo-Spanish disputes, and demand that those
disputes be settled.[64]

At several other points the French memorial showed a stiffening in
Choiseul's attitude. With regard to the Germanies, he tried to escape
the evacuation of Wesel, Gelderland, and Frankfort, which he had formerly agreed to evacuate, on the ground that they were conquered territory, and were now occupied in the name of the Empress-Queen of
Austria; he suggested that Belle Isle be restored as a counterbalance
for the evacuation of Hesse, Hanau, and Hanover. As the situation in
India was unknown, he proposed that conditions there be restored to the
status quo, as fixed by the abortive treaty between Godeheu and Saunders in 1754.

But the thing that infuriated Pitt and his colleagues most was the
presentation of two other memoranda calculated to promote the interests of Austria and Spain. The first of these, purporting to submit Aus-

63. First, the free exercise of the Roman Catholic religion; second, the freedom of
the inhabitants to retire with their possessions to French territory; third, the delimitation of boundaries for Canada which would leave no room for future quibbling;
fourth, the right to dry fish on the shores of Newfoundland. (Thackeray, *op. cit.*, II,
547–548.) With regard to the boundaries between Louisiana and the English territories, old and new, Choiseul sent Bussy a note on the boundaries of Louisiana, which
vaguely defined that province as including Mobile and the valleys of the Alabama and
the Coosa, the valley of the Tennessee up to the Appalachian Mountains, the lower
part of the Ohio Valley, and the territory between the Great Lakes and the Mississippi from the lands of the Miamis to Lake Nipigon. The upper part of the Ohio
Valley was spoken of as a part of Canada. (CAO AE CP Ang. 443:358–359. Cf. the
translation of this text given in Pease, *op. cit.*, pp. 321–324.)

64. Thackeray, *op. cit.*, II, 546–552; [Etienne-François Choiseul, Duke de Choiseul-
Stainville], *Mémoire Historique sur la Négociation de la France et de l'Angleterre,
depuis le 26 Mars 1761, jusqu'au 20 Septembre de la même année* (Paris, 1761),
pp. 25–30.

tria's conditional approval of a separate peace, demanded that France retain possession of the territories belonging to Prussia, and that both England and France refrain from aiding their allies, with troops or otherwise.[65] The second memorandum, which Bussy presented only after considerable hesitation and upon the insistence of the Spanish ambassador,[66] definitely proposed that Spain be invited to guarantee the peace. Its author professed to fear a future disturbance of peace by the Anglo-Spanish disputes; Spain had communicated to France the three points in dispute between Spain and His Britannic Majesty: these were so easy of adjustment that His Most Christian Majesty earnestly desired Great Britain to consent to settle them now, and invite Spain to participate in the general settlement.[67]

Choiseul must have known that Pitt would never accept such an extraneous proposal. Yet he acquiesced in its submission with the thought that Great Britain in her present condition of financial distress would never undertake a war with Spain; that the threat of a Spanish alliance with France would force Britain to moderate her demands; and that, whether successful or not, it could not fail to put Spain squarely on the side of France and bring to the latter the full strength of Spain for the continuance of the war. He played his Spanish trump in the shape of a desperate appeal over the head of William Pitt to the ministers in the cabinet who favored a reasonable peace. But Choiseul realized what sort of reception these memoranda would probably have; and he was forced to agree to present them, against his better judgment, by the insistence of his allies, particularly Charles III and his ambassador in London. If they succeeded, so much the better; if they failed, at least he would gain time while Spain was preparing for war.[68]

Whatever may have been in Choiseul's mind, the reaction of his opponent was immediate, peremptory, and final. Pitt was at his best in the dramatic hours of a crisis; and here was a crisis to satisfy even his histrionic nature. With the full approval of the cabinet, he returned to Bussy the note on the Prussian territories as "totally inadmissible," and "implying an attempt upon the honor of Great Britain."[69] The memorandum on Spanish questions he likewise returned: Great Britain would not permit Spain to inject her quarrel into the negotiations with France, nor would she permit France to meddle in her quarrels with Spain; any

65. Thackeray, *op. cit.*, II, 553. 66. CAO AE CP Ang. 444:59–72.
67. Thackeray, *op. cit.*, II, 552–553.
68. CAO AE CP Ang. 44:59–72; AE CP Espagne 533:122–128, 203–209, *et passim;* Francis Paul Renaut, *Le Pacte de famille et l'Amérique; la politique coloniale franco-espagnole de 1760 à 1792* (Paris, 1922), p. 33. Cf. Williams, *op. cit.*, II, 93–94.
69. BM Add. MSS. 36798:144; Thackeray, *op. cit.*, II, 553–554, 555–556.

further mention of them by France would be considered "an affront to his Majesty's dignity."[70]

Having delivered himself of this blast, which he must have thoroughly enjoyed, Pitt turned to the points in Choiseul's formal reply to his own proposals, and sent to Stanley a note based upon the instructions of June 26 which France was to consider as the British ultimatum, and to which Great Britain demanded a categorical answer.[71] In this ultimatum, Pitt again listed his irreducible minima, practically without change. As for the boundaries between Louisiana and the British colonies, whether in the Canadian areas or in the south, he rejected in advance any idea that all that was not Canada was Louisiana, and injected the principle that the Ohio Valley was a third area, owned by Great Britain, and distinct from both Canada and Louisiana.[72] On one point alone Stanley was authorized to compromise: should the success of the negotiations seem to turn upon it, he was to accept the milder provisions of the Treaty of Aix-la-Chapelle with regard to Dunkirk in place of those of the Treaty of Utrecht.[73]

While he was pouring out the vials of his wrath upon France, Pitt also turned on Spain, and instructed Bristol to protest against "the enormity" of mixing Great Britain's disputes with Spain, a neutral, with her negotiations with France, an enemy. Bristol was to demand a categorical statement of Spain's intentions, as well as an explanation of Spain's warlike preparations and the destination of her fleets. At the same time, he was to keep the door open for a friendly adjustment of the Anglo-Spanish quarrel.[74] All of which Bristol did, only to receive from Wall, who had now ratified the Family Compact, an equivocal reply which successfully threw dust in his eyes and compelled his superior, albeit convinced of Spain's duplicity, to carry the discussions further.[75]

Pitt's conditions had been submitted to Choiseul by Stanley, and Choiseul was angry. He expostulated against Pitt's unbearable language, and against his intransigence on the essential questions of the fishery and the obligations of France to her allies. All he asked, he told Stanley, was "a Rock that would afford shelter to the Barks of their Fishermen, which they were ready to receive on almost any Terms that England would prescribe." As for the evacuation of Wesel, "it would be impossible for France, without incurring the most indelible stain of Per-

70. *Ibid.*
71. Thackeray, *op. cit.,* II, 556–557.
72. LC Add. MSS. 35421:34–37.
73. Thackeray, *op. cit.,* II, 556–557.
74. BM Add. MSS. 36807:89–96.
75. BM Add. MSS. 36807:105–120, 124–129. Pitt had just intercepted another letter from Grimaldi to Fuentes, dated August 31, which spoke of the "Family agreement and the Convention," and said that "both instruments were signed on the 15th." (*Chatham Correspondence,* II, 139–141.)

fidy to consent to any Peace by which the Army under Prince Ferdinand of Brunswick should be let loose upon the Empress-Queen." But this latter point, Stanley believed, would be easily resolved, if some solution could be found to the question of a haven in the Gulf of St. Lawrence for French fishermen. The British agent realized that his attempt to negotiate had failed; and he was convinced that this question of the haven, or *abri*, was the one essential cause of that failure.[76]

In his report to his superior, Stanley made an effort to explain the apparent French inconsistencies, and to soften the imperious minister's attitude.[77] At the same time, Choiseul sent to Bussy a new memorial which was to constitute France's reply to the British ultimatum. France insisted upon the conditions previously attached to the cession of Canada,[78] and the fishery, both in the Gulf of St. Lawrence and off Newfoundland, together with some shelter for French fishermen. As for Louisiana, Choiseul accepted, with some asperity, Pitt's idea of regarding as neutral the "Nations intermediate between Canada and Louisiana, as well as between Virginia and Louisiana."[79] With regard to Africa, if Great Britain insisted on both Senegal and Goree, France would be willing to make some other arrangement to provide for French needs in the slave trade. Pitt's proposal as to Dunkirk, Choiseul was willing to accept on condition that France's demand for an *abri* in the Gulf of St. Lawrence was satisfied. The evacuation of Wesel, Gelderland, and Westphalia he refused, as being extraneous to the Anglo-French war, and part and parcel of the war between Austria and Prussia; this question, he said, must be left to the congress at Augsburg. Pitt's demands as to India he accepted. Spain was not mentioned.[80] In a covering letter to Bussy, Choiseul authorized his agent to delimit, with Pitt, the boundary line in the Mississippi Valley on duplicate maps. On the question of the *abri*, he was to insist, as also on his, Choiseul's, proposal to refer the question of Prussian territories to the congress at Augsburg. If Pitt failed to give a favorable reply within eight days after the presentation of the French ultimatum, Bussy was to return to France.[81]

---

76. BM Add. MSS. 36798:150–173.   77. *Ibid.*

78. The boundaries of Louisiana were now redefined, but hardly more clearly than before. The line now proposed would extend from the River Perdido between the Bay of Mobile and that of Pensacola, passing by Fort Toulouse in the lands of the Alabamas, to the western end of Lake Erie in such a way as to include the Miami River, and through the eastern end of Lake Huron to the height of land between Hudson Bay and the lakes, and thence northward to the Lake of the Abitibis. Such a line was intended to leave Lakes Michigan and Superior in the possession of France. (CAO AE CP Ang. 443:150–159, 182.)

79. Reported in Bussy's letter to Choiseul, July 3. (Pease, *op. cit.*, p. 319.)

80. LC Add. MSS. 35421:40–44.   81. CAO AE CP Ang. 444:114–117.

The negotiations had now to all intents and purposes been reduced to the question whether Great Britain would grant France an island in the Gulf of St. Lawrence. When Pitt saw Choiseul's memorial he expressed the belief that there could be no peace. But the more reasonable members of the British cabinet—Hardwicke, Bedford, Devonshire, Newcastle, and Bute—all were in favor of giving in, both in the matter of making the Gulf of St. Lawrence a *mare clausum*, and that of assigning a shelter for French fishermen in the Gulf. At last, despite much thumping on the table, and Pitt's refusal to have his draft of a reply "cobbled with," the irascible minister was constrained to concede to France the tiny island of St. Pierre, at the entrance to the Gulf, and the "cobbled" reply was sent.[82]

More conciliatory than its predecessors, this note conceded to France the island of St. Pierre, together with a share in the fishery both in the Gulf of St. Lawrence and on the Banks of Newfoundland. Further, it substituted the provisions of the Treaty of Aix-la-Chapelle which dealt with the fortifications at Dunkirk for the more rigorous terms of the Treaty of Utrecht, and went so far as to express a willingness on the part of Great Britain to aid her Prussian ally only with money subsidies; Prussian territory, however, must be evacuated by the French armies.[83] For the first time Pitt now expressed himself in detail on the subject of the boundaries between the British colonies and Louisiana. Rejecting the line proposed by Bussy, he claimed that the western boundary of Canada, as drawn by the Marquis de Vaudreuil at the capitulation of Montreal, was the Wabash River and the height of land from its source to the Mississippi, thus including Lakes Huron, Michigan, and Superior in that province.[84] With regard to the land to the southward, he was not specific upon its boundaries, although he rejected the line of the Perdido River, stating merely that "the King . . . might

82. LC Add. MSS. 35421:50–51, 32926:308–310, 358–359; *Bedford Correspondence*, III, 35–36; Williams, *op. cit.*, II, 97–98.

83. Thackeray, *op. cit.*, II, 591–597. While the terms of the note were conciliatory, the language of Pitt's covering letter to Stanley was insulting and humiliating in the extreme, and doubtless greatly lessened its good effect. (*Ibid.*, II, 604–607.)

84. Vaudreuil himself did not draw the line. Frederick Haldimand, acting for General Amherst, asked Vaudreuil for a map of Canada, and, when told there was none, traced on a map of North America the course of the line, as dictated to him orally by Vaudreuil, while the Marquis looked over his shoulder. (BM Add. MSS. 21661: 257; LC AE Méms. et Docs. Amérique 21:96.) The line drawn follows the Ohio and Wabash rivers from the confluence of the Ohio with the Mississippi to the source of the Wabash, and thence follows the height of land to Lac Rouge, at the headwaters of the Mississippi. Vaudreuil evidently thought of the Wabash as flowing into the Mississippi, and of the Ohio as flowing into the Wabash. The map is reproduced in Pease, *op. cit.*, opposite p. 568.

consent to leave intermediate countries under the protection of Great Britain, and particularly the Cherokees, the Creeks, the Chickasaws, the Choctaws, and other nations situated between the British settlements and the Mississippi"—which modest proposal would have given Great Britain a protectorate over all the lands between the Alleghenies and the Father of Waters! Choiseul's reservations in favor of the French inhabitants Pitt accepted.[85]

Unfortunately, this genuinely conciliatory gesture came too late. "I most ardently wish," wrote Stanley, "that the cession of the Island of St. Peter's [St. Pierre], if now advisable, had been Earlier made. I have secretly seen an Article drawn up between France and Spain, in which the former engages to support the Interests of the latter."[86] Pitt's intransigence had driven Choiseul into the arms of Spain. For the British reply to the French note of July 13 had apparently convinced that minister that France had more to gain by continuing the war with the aid of Spain than by a peace so humiliating and disastrous as that which Pitt now seemed to be seeking to impose. By August 1 he had made up his mind. He was convinced that Pitt would make no reasonable peace, and advised the King to continue the war in close alliance with Spain.[87] He therefore pushed the Spanish negotiations to a conclusion, and the Franco-Spanish alliance was signed on August 15. This alliance, the Third Bourbon Family Compact, provided, in addition to a mutual guaranty of their respective territories, that Spain should declare war on Great Britain if France did not make peace with that country by May 1, 1762. France, in her turn, agreed not to make peace with Great Britain until the Anglo-Spanish disputes had been settled.[88] But Choiseul did not wish to wait until the following spring for Spain to enter the war. He saw great advantages in a surprise move upon Great Britain, and asked His Catholic Majesty to declare war immediately. "At the moment of the declaration," he said, "we will deliver to him, according to the Convention, the island of Minorca, and we will propose to him some arrangement as to Louisiana."[89] He proposed that Spain declare war on Great Britain in the approaching autumn; but Spain demurred, on the ground of unpreparedness and a desire to wait till the treasure fleet from America was safely in port.[90]

85. Thackeray, *op. cit.*, II, 591–597; cf. Pease, *op. cit.*, pp. 383–389.
86. LC Add. MSS. 32927:336.   87. Pease, *op. cit.*, p. 339.
88. AE CP Espagne 533:331–337: Renaut, *op. cit.*, p. 36.
89. Quoted in Waddington, *La Guerre de sept ans*, IV, 571. This arrangement was nothing less than an immediate loan of 3,600,000 piastres, in return for which His Most Christian Majesty was disposed to cede Louisiana to his Spanish cousin. (AE CP Espagne 533:210–212, 240–245, 320–325.)
90. AE CP Espagne 533:231–239.

Pitt's conciliatory reply to the French ultimatum of August 5 therefore arrived at Paris after the alliance between France and Spain had been sealed. The door to peace had not been completely closed by that alliance, because there was nothing in it to prevent an Anglo-French treaty, except, perhaps, France's agreement not to make peace until the Anglo-Spanish disputes were settled. Even that, as Choiseul informed Bussy, could be so arranged as to allow of a treaty between France and England first and, afterwards, a friendly mediation of the Anglo-Spanish matter by France, provided England was so disposed.[91] Choiseul was playing his double game very skilfully, and according to plan; and Stanley, his own suspicions now aroused, doubted whether the volatile Frenchman might not, on some pretext or other, repudiate the treaty now so nearly made, should it suit his convenience to do so.[92]

Choiseul probably still desired, most of all, to make peace with England; in any case, he continued the negotiations in apparent good faith, and framed a response to England's gesture. There was little that remained to be adjusted. On the question of the North American boundary, Choiseul complained to Stanley of the extreme nature of Pitt's claims. The governors of Canada and Louisiana had long disputed, he said, as to what constituted the real boundary between the two provinces. Nevertheless, when Stanley showed him the Vaudreuil-Haldimand map, he agreed that the boundary should be as it had there been drawn. He then proposed that the map should be so divided that it would make clear which Indian nations of the south were to be considered as being, respectively, under the protection of each of the two signatory powers. Pitt's offer of St. Pierre as an *abri* for French fishermen, he tentatively accepted: he had asked for a rock, and he had been given it. He asked for St. Lucia in the proposed division of the "neutral islands," and agreed to cede to England both Senegal and Goree, on condition that England grant some other depot, and proposed, for this purpose, Anamabu and Accra.[93]

This apparent progress was encouraging. But two days later Stanley wrote that Choiseul, after having made inquiry as to the suitability of St. Pierre, and having discussed with the Council the humiliating conditions under which England proposed to cede it,[94] now protested and refused, though not absolutely, to accept it. He insisted upon Anamabu and Accra in exchange for Senegal and Goree. He refused to evacuate

91. LC Add. MSS. 32927:336.   92. LC Add. MSS. 32927:367-376.
93. LC Add. MSS. 32927:339, 367-376.
94. No fortifications, residence of an English commissary, and periodic inspections by the British naval commandant on the Newfoundland station.

Wesel, but said he would welcome any expedient proposed by England that would protect Maria Theresa from the armies of Prince Ferdinand of Brunswick and proposed a new method for regulating British aid to Prussia after peace should have been made.[95] Stanley, however, was convinced that peace was now impossible. He heard reports that Spain had given great sums of money to France and would soon declare war. Choiseul, indeed, again informally mentioned the right of France to sponsor Spain's claims against England. The French minister was being severely criticized at home for the apparent supineness with which he had surrendered Canada, a French possession, and his anxiety to protect Maria Theresa, a foreigner whom the French detested. Choiseul probably desired peace, but the constant pressure from Austria and Spain, along with the criticism at home, were making the chances of peace ever more remote. Still, Pitt's offer of St. Pierre had not been definitely rejected; Pitt's suggested line for the Carolina boundary would probably be accepted; and Choiseul had asked England for a compromise proposal for the adjustment of the German question. Under the circumstances, Stanley did not feel authorized to ask for his passport and go home; on the contrary he asked Pitt for further instructions.[96]

The final French note, the *"ultimatissimum"* of France, was presented by Bussy on September 13. As Choiseul had previously explained to Stanley, France accepted with slight modifications all but one of the British conditions. The note asked for a definition of the word "dependencies" as used by Pitt with regard to Canada, and a clarification of the terms defining the boundary in the south; it accepted St. Pierre as an *abri*, but, because of the inadequacy of that tiny island, asked that Miquelon, which adjoined it, be ceded also; France accepted the British plan for the division of the "neutral islands," provided she was awarded St. Lucia. She merely refused to evacuate the territories held for the Empress-Queen, while at the same time she asked Great Britain to make new proposals of a kind that might free her from her difficult position.[97]

Such was the narrow margin of difference by which the chance of making peace was lost. The French ministry did not expect their note to be accepted; they may not even have wished that it might be. But Choiseul could hardly have sent it had he been unprepared to have it accepted.[98]

95. To the effect that soldiers actually in the pay of England would not be allowed to serve Prussia; he inferred, however, that as soon as their home service had expired, they might be free to enter that of Prussia.

96. BM Add. MSS. 36798:236–249.   97. Thackeray, *op. cit.,* II, 619–623.

98. CAO AE CP Ang. 444:264–265; cf. Pease, *op. cit.,* pp. cxix, cxx.

Certainly it was the last chance England was to have to bring the negotiations to a successful conclusion.[99]

But Pitt regarded this French note as an obstinate failure to meet the final English conditions, and a proof positive that Choiseul was only playing for time. As a matter of fact, it appears that that was exactly what he was doing, in the light of his "plan" for negotiations after his receipt of Pitt's conditions in June, and his present statement that he would never have made such concessions had he expected Pitt to accept them.[100] Technically, France failed to comply with England's conditions. Because of this fact, coupled with Wall's unsatisfactory answer to Bristol's demand for an explanation of Spanish intentions, the cabinet authorized Pitt to recall Stanley from Paris,[101] and on September 20, Stanley demanded his passports.[102]

So ended Mr. Pitt's negotiations—but only to the great regret of many of his colleagues. "We lost l'Heure de Bergier [sic]" wrote Newcastle, sadly,[103] and it is impossible to escape the conclusion that responsibility for the failure of the negotiations rests squarely upon the shoulders of William Pitt. He was a great conqueror. But his ambition to extend the Empire, coupled with his hatred of France, and his extreme suspiciousness, his irascibility, and his intractability made him a poor diplomat. On the other hand, Choiseul, under pressure from Austria and Spain, and compelled as the loser to play as high as possible while still keeping open every avenue of escape in case of failure, was personally desirous of peace. Had he had a diplomat for an opponent, the peace would probably have been made.[104]

99. "For God's sake what are the material Points, France and England differ about?" exclaimed Bedford. "Those two trifling ones I have mentioned (the *abri* and the slaving station), which may be easily accommodated, the evacuation of Wesel, and the assistance to be given our respective Allies, the King of Prussia and the Empress Queen." (LC Add. MSS. 32928:158–159.)

100. CAO AE CP Ang. 444:264.

101. LC Add. MSS. 32928:182–184, 187; BM Add. MSS. 32928:170–171.

102. CAO AE CP Ang. 444:332.

103. LC Add. MSS. 32928:211. He meant *"l'heure du berger."*

104. Cf. Stanley's opinion to Newcastle, in Newcastle to Hardwicke, September 26, 1761, LC Add. MSS. 32898:362–363; and Waddington, *La Guerre de sept ans,* IV, 600–601.

CHAPTER VIII

THE TREATY OF PARIS, 1763

PITT was not satisfied merely to renew the war with France: he also wished to strike immediately at Spain. But this was too much for the "precise old gentlemen" of his cabinet. In a series of cabinet meetings he laid before them the unsatisfactory state of British relations with Spain and the evidences of a Bourbon alliance inimical to the safety and the interests of Britain. He desired to open hostilities at once. But the most he could get the cabinet to do was to send Bristol instructions to demand an explanation of Spain's intentions. As an earnest of British good will, Bristol was to say that Great Britain stood ready to evacuate her establishments on the coasts of Central America, if His Catholic Majesty would permit the British logwood cutters to continue their labors until some other way of supplying Great Britain with dyewood could be found.[1] But Pitt was not satisfied. On October 5 he resigned,[2] and he was succeeded by the Earl of Egremont. As directed by the cabinet Egremont wrote to Bristol, on October 28, instructing him "gently" to insinuate, "in the most polite, and Friendly Terms," England's desire for an explanation and her willingness to evacuate the dyewood-coast establishments if Spain would guarantee England the privilege of cutting there.[3] This was no concession from the prior English position, but it was couched in far friendlier terms than most of the dispatches of Egremont's predecessor. In the meantime, however, Bristol had reported the arrival at Cadiz of the fleet from America, and a notable stiffening of Wall's attitude toward the English question.[4] Wall confessed that Spain had renewed her "family compacts," and expressed his country's fear that England was determined, after annihilating France's colonial empire, to turn on Spain herself.[5] Wall personally desired peace, and it is to be assumed that his complaints of Pitt's insatiable vindictiveness

1. "Mem^dum^s of Spanish Partialities to France," PRO Chatham MSS. XCII; LC Add. MSS. 32928:225, 233, 248–250, 259–262.

2. *Bedford Correspondence,* III, 48–50. Upon Pitt's resignation, Bute offered him the governorship of Canada. Recognizing that the governor of a colony could not sit in Parliament, Bute offered to push through Parliament a bill which would make this possible. The assumption probably was that Pitt would not go to America, in any case; but it is an interesting approach to the principle of colonial representation. (*Chatham Correspondence,* II, 146–148.)

3. LC Add. MSS. 32930:78–84.

4. Bristol to Pitt, October 21, 1761, LC House of Lords MSS.; LC Add. MSS. 32930:268–275.

5. LC Add. MSS. 32930:268–275, 276–277.

were genuine. He realized that the French alliance did not preclude peace, and apparently in the hope that Pitt's resignation might admit some moderation into the British ministry, and certainly with a desire to gain time for warlike preparations, he delayed his answer to the British demand for an explanation. He delayed until, late in November, Egremont instructed Bristol to demand a categorical answer as to Spain's intentions, and, if the answer proved to be unsatisfactory, to leave Madrid.[6] But neither the Spanish ambassadors in Paris and London nor the Spanish court looked with sympathy upon Wall's desire for peace. Nor did Choiseul, his ally, see any hope for conciliation. It was true, he said, that most of the British ministers now desired peace; but France could not accede to their demands in full, and no British minister would dare to accept less.[7] Wall was compelled to subscribe to the policy of war; and, on December 10, writing to Bristol, he replied to the British demands tersely and to the effect that their haughty and peremptory tone was in itself a declaration of war.[8] Bristol immediately left Madrid and went to Portugal;[9] and England declared war on January 4 of the new year.

Thus the war was renewed between France and England over three or four questions which, as Bedford pointed out, were tragic in their insignificance; and a new war was begun between England and Spain over a dispute that reduced itself to the question whether England should evacuate the illegal establishments on the dyewood coasts before or after Spain guaranteed the British a supply of dyewoods. But the real motive in the mind of the Spanish monarch was apparently his desire to maintain the balance of power in America in the face of the threat to Spanish dominion inherent in the anticipated elimination of France and the extension of the British North American boundary westward, and also southward toward the Gulf of Mexico. The British, he said, were on the march, and must be stopped. They had already taken all of Florida except St. Augustine and Pensacola.[10] They would soon take Louisiana; and it would not be long before they would seize Mexico. In view of this very accurate forecast of later Anglo-Saxon "manifest destiny," His Catholic Majesty urged France to take vigorous steps to defend Louisi-

6. BM Add. MSS. 32931:134–139, 140–141; AE CP Espagne 534:15–24, 35–41, 305–308. Wall wrote to Fuentes describing his negotiations with Bristol. To the Spanish ambassador in London he said, "We wait to see, whether the change of ministry will produce greater Moderation, than that court has hitherto shown. God grant it, for the Repose of Europe, which It is in such Need of!" (LC Add. MSS. 32930:276–277.)

7. AE CP Espagne 534:305–308.

8. Wall to Bristol, December 10, 1761, LC House of Lords MSS.

9. Bristol to Egremont, December 11, 1761, LC House of Lords MSS.

10. The reference is to Carolina and Georgia. Cf. Lanning, *op. cit., passim.*

ana, the last barrier between his own possessions and that expansive race, and to strengthen the barrier by moving the French population of Canada to the southern colony.[11] In his fear of British preponderance in North America, the Spanish monarch was now, if possible, more belligerent than his ally.

In any case, the campaign that followed was a parade of British victories. In the Caribbean England made a clean sweep of the French West Indies. She possessed herself of Martinique, Grenada, St. Lucia, and St. Vincent. Then the English forces turned against the possessions of Spain. They took Puerto Rico and Cuba, which gave England a strangle hold upon the routes of trade into and out of the Caribbean and the Gulf of Mexico. On the other hand, George III, who cared little about the ancestral domains of Hanover, and his minister, Bute, who cared less, decided to discontinue the Prussian subsidies. Russia had withdrawn from the war, and it appeared that Frederick could safely be left to take care of himself; besides, if the subsidies were continued, and if Frederick were given too much voice in the matter of peace, the war might go on indefinitely. This change of policy antagonized Newcastle and Hardwicke, both of whom retired from the cabinet in the spring of 1762. Its peace faction, meanwhile, had been strengthened by the addition of the Duke of Bedford, whose influence was in turn balanced by the belligerent Egremont and Grenville.

In view of these circumstances, it was easy for Bute to reopen negotiations for peace in the spring of 1762. As a matter of fact, the negotiations had never been entirely discontinued. It is indicative, probably, of Choiseul's genuine personal desire for peace that he had made a last desperate appeal to Stanley, before the British minister left Paris, for a continuation of the negotiations,[12] and that he apparently appealed to Stanley again after the latter's arrival in London, through the medium of Count Víry, the Sardinian minister to Great Britain.[13] Choiseul had to be shown that the British ministry dared to make a moderate peace. But the fall of Pitt had made the chance of success much more

11. AE CP Espagne 534:218–223, 305–308.
12. LC Add. MSS. 32928:325–328.
13. Count Víry to the Bailli de Solar de Breille, Sardinian Minister in Paris, November 17 and 27, 1761, CL Shelburne MSS. IX. This is the beginning of the famous Víry-Solar correspondence, in the course of which the preliminary negotiations between France and England were arranged. The Duke de Choiseul turned over to his cousin, the Count de Choiseul, the actual conduct of French foreign relations, with the exception of those dealing directly with Spain. Much of the Víry-Solar correspondence, therefore, passed through the hands of the Count; but the Duke was still the real director of French foreign policy, and he continued personally to conduct the relations of France with Spain. There are copies of the Víry-Solar correspondence in AE CP Espagne 536:387 ff.

likely; and toward the end of November, 1761, there appeared in London a M. de Choiseul, a cousin of the Duke de Choiseul, who was assured that Great Britain would now make every effort to negotiate a satisfactory treaty.[14] The Duke de Choiseul intimated to the Bailli de Solar that he would make a separate peace, and Solar communicated the message to Víry. Víry sent back a reply suggesting that the British ultimatum of July 29, 1761, and the French ultimatum of August 5 be made the basis of the negotiations, and that confidential agents be exchanged between the two courts.[15] Such agents were not exchanged; but on January 5, 1762, Víry improved the occasion afforded by the declaration of war on Spain to assure his correspondent that the break between Great Britain and Spain should not interfere with an Anglo-French peace, because the questions relative to Campeche logwood, and prizes made in violation of Spanish neutrality, could easily be settled at the same time.[16] Thus encouraged, Solar again communicated with the Count de Víry and the Duke de Choiseul. The latter, on January 23, wrote Solar a cautious letter to the effect that the loss of Martinique would not affect his policies and that if Great Britain genuinely desired peace, the British ministry should make France a definite offer.[17] This stand was reiterated by the French ministers at a conference with Solar a few days later, in which they again suggested that England send a confidential agent to Paris. They intimated that they did not wish to use the memorials of the preceding summer as a basis for the negotiations, but proposed that, if Great Britain did not wish to send an agent, she might send Solar a memorandum containing definite proposals, to which they promised to reply.[18]

Meanwhile, Solar had communicated to the British government a request for the release of the young Count d'Estaing, then a prisoner of war at Plymouth. Estaing was released, as requested, and a ship was provided for his return to France; and Egremont seized upon the opportunity to open direct communications with the French ministers.[19] The result of this exchange was an interview between Víry and Bute, on March 8, and a memorandum from Egremont to the Sardinian minister,

14. LC Add. MSS. 32931:347, 388, 425. This was apparently a third member of the Choiseul family.

15. Víry to Solar, November 27, Solar to Víry, December 13, Víry to Solar, December 13, December 15, 1761, CL Shelburne MSS. IX:1–18.

16. Víry to Solar, January 5, 1762, CL Shelburne MSS. IX:29–31.

17. Solar to the Count de Choiseul, Count de Choiseul to Solar, Duke de Choiseul to Solar, January 23, 1762, CL Shelburne MSS. IX:44–49.

18. Solar to Víry, February 1, 1762, CL Shelburne MSS. IX:50–58.

19. Víry to Solar, February 9, 22, 23, Solar to Víry, February 25, Egremont to the Duke de Choiseul, February 22, 1762, CL Shelburne MSS. IX:41–43, 67–68, 68–69, 71–74; AE CP Espagne 536:62–69.

two weeks later, in which the British cabinet outlined their idea of the proper terms of peace.

In general, the British agreed to boundaries for Canada and Louisiana such as had been proposed by the French ultimatum of August 5. They were willing to divide the "neutral islands" so as to give St. Lucia and St. Vincent to France, and Dominica and Tobago to Great Britain. They would allow a compromise arrangement in the case of Dunkirk, and would return the island of Goree to France. In the Gulf of St. Lawrence, they offered France both St. Pierre and Miquelon, with the right of maintaining fifty men in garrison there. Finally, on the question of Wesel and Gelderland, Bute proposed that in their case neutral garrisons be substituted for the French armies; but he would not make this a *sine qua non*. The British ministers also showed an inclination to negotiate in the case of the Spanish dispute with Great Britain, although they preferred to negotiate separately with Spain. On this subject they displayed a willingness to accept the demands of Spain with regard to the logwood coast; that is to say, Great Britain would immediately evacuate the objectionable establishments on the coast, if Spain would in return give a *bona fide* assurance that British logwood cutters might continue their work until some arrangement could be made that would be satisfactory to both parties. The Spanish demand for a share of the fisheries would not be granted; and cases of prizes made in violation of Spanish neutrality must be submitted to British courts of admiralty. If Spain were willing, negotiations might begin on this basis immediately, and it was Egremont's sanguine belief that they could be settled in a single day.[20] This beginning having been made, the British cabinet on March 29 officially sanctioned negotiations by making France a definite offer based upon the informal suggestions already made,[21] and on April 8 Víry forwarded to the Duke de Choiseul a letter from Egremont and an official declaration by the King formally proposing a reopening of the negotiations of the preceding year by a new exchange of ministers.[22]

The Duke de Choiseul, for his part, immediately notified Spain of the British overture and expressed his determination to make peace. Sweden

20. Víry to Solar, March 23, 1761, CL Shelburne MSS. IX:88–90; LC Add. MSS. 32935:249–251, 32936:1–6. An attempt was made through the Dutch ambassador in Madrid to open negotiations on this basis, but the overture was rejected. LC Add. MSS. 32935:459.

21. Great Britain, *Royal Commission on Historical Manuscripts,* Tenth Report, Appendix 1, "Underwood Manuscripts," p. 449. Hereafter cited as HMC X App. 1, Underwood MSS.

22. Víry to Solar, April 8, Egremont to Choiseul, April 8, "Declaration de Sa Majesté le Roy de la Grand Bretagne," April 8, 1762, CL Shelburne MSS. IX:100–107.

had proposed to make peace with Prussia, he said, and Russia had deserted the Allies; the German situation would now take care of itself. News had just come of the capture of Martinique and the seizure of the "neutral islands" by Great Britain; France had absolutely nothing left in America for which to continue the war, and must now accept peace on the basis of Bussy's ultimatum of the previous summer. As for Spain, the French minister proposed that the Anglo-Spanish quarrel be settled in Paris by negotiations paralleling the British settlement with France.[23]

The terms which Choiseul now proposed to Great Britain, however, in reply to her formal overture, departed sharply from at least two of the points covered in the informal preliminary conversations. In the first place, he pleaded his inability to negotiate a peace separately from Spain, and advised the British ministry of an invitation he had already extended to Spain to join in the making of the peace. For the rest, he divided the issues of the war into three groups: the differences between Spain and Britain; the colonial conflict of France and Britain in America, Africa, and Asia; and the war in Germany. In the first group, he admitted the justice of having the cases of Spanish prizes made in time of peace submitted to British admiralty courts. Spain was in the right, he said, with regard to the logwood coasts, but he believed an arrangement could be made that would satisfy both parties. As for Spain's right to a share in the Newfoundland fishery, there had not been two Spanish ships on the fishing banks in a century, and he assured his correspondent there would not be ten more, in the hundred years to come; this point, he said, was purely a point of honor, and easily settled —though he did not say precisely how.

In the second group of questions for negotiation, he took as a basis of discussion the last ultimatums exchanged in the preceding summer. He acknowledged the cession of Canada, with boundaries in the direction of Louisiana, which it would be easy to arrange. The fishery in the Gulf of St. Lawrence and on the Banks of Newfoundland he demanded, with an *abri* that would be "convenient, not illusory, as that of St. Pierre." He asked the restitution of Martinique, Guadeloupe, and Marie-Galante, and an equitable decision as to the "neutral islands." He demanded a "solid" establishment on the coast of Africa, presumably Goree, and proposed that England outline a plan for the settlement of the question of India. Minorca he proposed to return to England, and agreed to evacuate the German territory occupied by French troops, under any conditions that would protect France from any allegation of having failed in her duty to her allies. As for the third group of considera-

23. AE CP Espagne 536:60–61, 62–69; LC Add. MSS. 32936:306.

tions, those relating to the Germanic allies of France and Great Britain, he felt sure that these allies genuinely desired peace; and, ambiguously, he expressed the conviction that, if France and Britain could agree, a peace in Germany would be easy.[24]

It was over the question of the West Indies that the British cabinet was most disturbed. Choiseul's demands were staggering, for they envisaged nothing less than a restoration of all the French islands that had been seized in the war. Further, they revived the troublesome old debate over the question whether one potential "sugar island" in the West Indies was not worth more than the whole of Canada.[25] Egremont proposed to cede Martinique to France and keep Guadeloupe; but if France wished to keep both, Great Britain would then cede both, and accept Louisiana as compensation for them. Once this was settled, one might proceed to a consideration of the possible restitution of Marie-Galante and the fate of the "neutral islands."[26] At the suggestion of Bute, however, who feared these conditions would be refused by France and result in a continuation of the war, it was finally decided to offer a compromise plan, according to which Great Britain would offer France Martinique, Guadeloupe, and Marie-Galante, keeping for itself the "neutral islands" and Grenada, and demand the Mississippi River as the western boundary of the British colonies in North America.[27]

Egremont's reply to Choiseul, therefore, conformed, with some slight modifications, to the French proposals at almost every point. The three

24. Duke de Choiseul to Egremont, April 14, the Count de Choiseul to Solar, April 16, 1762, CL Shelburne MSS. IX:112–114, 115–118, 127–128, 135–142; LC Add. MSS. 32937:111–116.

25. The "Canada versus Guadeloupe" controversy entered, both in 1761 and in 1762, into the deliberations of the cabinet. It was discussed and dismissed by Choiseul and Stanley, albeit informally. The controversy is treated by William L. Grant, in "Canada versus Guadeloupe," *American Historical Review*, XVII, 735 ff. The idea of taking Guadeloupe instead of Canada now cropped up again, in a new form: the Earl of Hardwicke suggested the possibility of keeping all the West Indies and returning Canada to France. The security of the colonies in North America, he suggested, could never be assured, in any case, so long as the French remained in Louisiana. Besides, Canada, he said, "is a cold northern climate, unfruitful; furnishes no Trade to Europe, that I know of, but the Fur Trade, the most inconsiderable of all Trades. . . . It's products are mostly or nearly of yᵉ same kind with those of Great Britain, and consequently will take off not much of our's. Besides, if you remove the French Inhabitants, this Kingdom and Ireland cannot furnish, or procure, People enough to settle and inhabit it in Centuries to come; And, if You don't remove the French Inhabitants, they will never become half Subjects, and this Country must maintain an Army there to keep them in Subjection." (LC Add. MSS. 32936:311.) Cf. Grant, "Canada versus Guadeloupe," *loc. cit.*

26. LC Add. MSS. 32937:341–346.

27. *Bedford Correspondence*, III, 75–77; cf. Theodore Pease, "the Mississippi Boundary of 1763," *American Historical Review*, XL, 278–286.

points in the Spanish dispute were provided for as suggested: the cases of Spanish prizes would be submitted to British admiralty courts; Britain would give up its establishments on the dyewood coasts for a guaranty of continued cutting privileges; Egremont was sure that, as soon as this article was arranged, Spain would end her demand for a share in the Newfoundland fishery. As for the Anglo-French contest, Egremont accepted the cession of Canada with Choiseul's conditions; France was given the right to fish in the Gulf of St. Lawrence[28] and on the Banks of Newfoundland, and the island of Miquelon was added to St. Pierre as an *abri;* Goree was to be ceded to France; the British ministers promised to accept any reasonable offer France might make for the Coromandel coast; Belle Isle would be returned to France in exchange for Minorca and the evacuation of German territory occupied by French troops; Great Britain would accept the provisions of the Treaty of Aix-la-Chapelle covering Dunkirk, and would also accept the French assurance that Louis XV had no intention of retaining Ostend and Nieuport, cities in the Austrian Netherlands garrisoned by France during the war.[29] It was only on the combined point of the West Indies and the Mississippi that Egremont proposed any serious modification of Choiseul's terms. With regard to the West Indies he explained that Great Britain now held not only the islands it had held in 1761, but had added Martinique and St. Lucia, and that, while he was writing, news had come of the British seizure of Grenada and the Grenadines and of the expected occupation of St. Vincent and Tobago. His proposal for the return of Guadeloupe, Marie-Galante, and Martinique in consideration of a clear title to the "neutral islands" and the Mississippi boundary seemed modest enough. In his covering letter he urged that the French government make haste; for, he said, the anticipated success of the projected expedition against Havana would make a moderate peace more difficult, and would jeopardize even the British concessions with regard to the French islands.[30]

Up to this time, the British minister had not been explicit as to the meaning of his demand for the Mississippi River as a boundary. Did it mean the Mississippi River throughout its course, or only south of its confluence with the Ohio? When Víry pressed him for a definition, Egremont avoided going further than the language of his memorandum. Whereupon Víry turned for light to another "person of credit," and received the following statement:

28. But not to dry fish on its English-owned shores.
29. Egremont to Víry, May 1, 1762, CL Shelburne MSS. IX:164–165.
30. Egremont to Víry, May 1, 1762; same to same, same date, CL Shelburne MSS. IX:164–165.

The line of the limits of Canada to the Westward traced by M. de Vaudreuil ended at the Confluence of the Ohio and the Mississippi. From this Confluence to the sea the course of the Mississippi shall serve as limits between the two nations; but as the Mississippi has several mouths, that one is meant that is the most easterly: that is to say, the one which flows through the little Iberville River, Lakes Maurepas and Pontchartrain, and from thence communicates with the sea.[31]

Choiseul accepted the Mississippi as a boundary, but he objected strenuously to the proposed cession of all the "neutral islands" to England. St. Lucia, he said, was particularly necessary to the French because of its strategic domination of the other French islands. He proposed, as a substitute for the British demand, that St. Lucia and Grenada be allocated to France, and that Great Britain keep Dominica (or, possibly, Grenada), St. Vincent, and Tobago. As for the Mississippi boundary, he would make that river the boundary between British and French territories above its confluence with the Ohio, thus abandoning the Vaudreuil line and including the Illinois country in British territory. Below the Ohio, however, as France had settlements on both shores, he demanded sovereignty of both banks of the river and proposed that the boundary be drawn parallel to, and one league from, the left bank, through Lakes Maurepas and Pontchartrain to the sea. This, he said, would give Great Britain the port of Mobile, and would put Louisiana and Florida in an "absolute dependence" upon the British colonies.[32]

Choiseul also objected to St. Pierre and Miquelon as an *abri*. They were too small, he said; and he again proposed that Cape Breton be restored to France, with the condition that it should never be fortified. But if Britain was still unwilling to cede Cape Breton, he expressed a willingness to accept some other sizable island in the Gulf. Should the worst come to the worst, however, he would accept St. Pierre and Miquelon rather than wreck the negotiation, asking only that, in that case, the French should enjoy the same liberty to dry fish on the coasts of Cape Breton as they were to enjoy on the northern coasts of Newfoundland. As for India, he indicated that France needed nothing but certain trading stations, which would remain unfortified. Goree he ac-

31. "Note au sujet de la Limite du Cours du Mississippi entre les deux Nations," CL Shelburne MSS. IX. The boundary thus proposed would have given Mobile and Biloxi to England, but it would have left New Orleans in the hands of France. The "person of credit" was probably Bute, and the statement was apparently made without the knowledge of his colleagues. Cf. Pease, "The Mississippi Boundary," *op. cit.*, XL, 281.

32. Solar to Víry, May 12, 1762, CL Shelburne MSS. IX:208–212; Memoir of the Duke de Choiseul, May 25, 1762, CL Shelburne MSS. IX:261–279.

cepted; but he demanded, with it, the right to trade in the Senegal River. Finally, he proposed certain detailed arrangements for the Germanies, which might be modified should Great Britain so desire.[33]

To the British cabinet, in his covering letters, Choiseul appealed for a speedy peace. He predicted that the expedition against Cuba would fail, Spain would succeed against Portugal, and Spanish demands would soar. It would be a pity if the one small island of St. Lucia were to cause a continuation of the war; but he was determined to continue, if necessary. Against a cession of that small island he could cite his generosity with regard to the Mississippi. France, he said, would never have made such a concession in 1761. To cede the eastern half of the Mississippi Valley was to give away almost the whole of Louisiana, which, with the proposed boundaries, no longer had any communication with Florida. "Spain will perhaps make difficulties over this article," he wrote, "on account of her colony of Florida; but we will make her listen to reason. If she takes it badly, we will propose to her the exchange of Florida, though I know not what we should do with it, for whatever remains to us of Louisiana."[34]

Choiseul's chief desire, of course, was a speedy and generous peace. To promote it, he used all his wiles on the inexperienced Bute. But Choiseul was also too able a statesman to abandon his plans for the war simply because of the apparently favorable attitude of the British cabinet toward peace. He therefore made his arrangements for war at the same time that he was seeking peace; and, while inviting Spain to join him in his negotiations with Great Britain, he was also urging his ally to strike quickly and effectively at Portugal. His plan for war was based upon a projected invasion of England calculated to force that country to accept reasonable terms. But such an invasion would depend upon at least a temporary control of the English Channel, which, in turn, would

33. Memoir of the Duke de Choiseul, May 25, 1762, CL Shelburne MSS. IX:261–279.
34. Choiseul to Solar, May 28, 1762, CL Shelburne MSS. IX:284–297. Choiseul indulged in a lengthy exposition of his colonial views in justification of his demand for St. Lucia. With a mercantilism somewhat watered down by physiocratic doctrine, he declared himself an enemy of large colonial empires. The "American system," in particular, had been pernicious in its effects upon France; "I consider it more essential to cultivate the grain, the vines of the realm, and to sustain its manufactures, than to supply foreigners with sugar, coffee and indigo." Since these products were become necessities in France, however, he added, "I think a great power should not export any money from its own territory for these commodities . . . and, consequently, it pertains to the perfection of its constitution to have enough American possessions to supply its needs of this sort . . . [but] at the same time that the said possessions should be secure and that the commerce of the metropolis may be carried on without fear of unforeseen events, such as the effects of the illhumor of a governor, or of a sea-captain from a neighboring isle." St. Lucia was so important with regard to all these considerations, he said, that he would continue the war rather than give it up.

be possible only if British ships and men were diverted to the defense of Portugal. Thus, while urging Spain to strike, he was playing upon the disturbance in the British cabinet, caused by Newcastle's resignation, to hasten the making of an early and reasonable peace, and was at the same time suggesting to Víry, with a treacherous apparent candor, that, because a victory for Spain in Portugal would go to the heads of the Spanish, and make it difficult to bring Spain into the peace, Great Britain should rush all possible troops to Portugal, as the chief action of the year's campaign would take place there.[35]

Spain had been kept informed of the negotiations by Choiseul, and at his suggestion Great Britain had extended to His Catholic Majesty the same invitation to make peace that had been sent to Louis XV.[36] As a preliminary basis for negotiations, the British ministers had expressed a willingness to evacuate the military posts at Río Tinto, Wallis River, and Laguna Azul, in exchange for a guaranty by Spain of the right to continue cutting dyewood on the above coastal areas. The claims of Spain to a share in the codfishery were to be left as they had been by the Anglo-Spanish Treaty of Utrecht.[37]

Great Britain's invitation to make peace was forwarded to Spain by Choiseul,[38] who was already urging His Catholic Majesty both to join promptly in such negotiations,[39] and at the same time to push forward his plans for war, in order to force Great Britain to make a reasonable settlement.[40] He trusted neither the Spanish ambassador nor the ambassador's master,[41] and his distrust was intensified by the reports he was receiving from his ambassador at the Spanish court. For His Catholic Majesty, who had but recently entered the war, was still in the first flush of his enthusiasm and reluctant to make peace before there had been some signal feat of arms, such as he hoped might soon take place in Portugal.[42] In addition to this reluctance to make peace, Choiseul had

35. Corbett, op. cit., II, 298–311; Solar to Víry, June 17, 18, 1762, CL Shelburne MSS. X:18–25.

36. AE CP Espagne 536:60–61, 62–69; Solar to Víry, May 12, 1762, CL Shelburne MSS. IX:203–208; Declaration by the British King, May 19, 1762, CL Shelburne MSS. IX:217–218.

37. Víry to Solar, May 22, 1762, CL Shelburne MSS. IX:237–239.

38. Duke de Choiseul to Solar, May 27, 1762, CL Shelburne MSS. IX:281–282.

39. AE CP Espagne 536:221–222, 308–313.

40. AE CP Espagne 536:221–222; Solar to Víry, June 17, 18, 1762, CL Shelburne MSS. IX:18–25.

41. Of Grimaldi, he said, "Il n'y a pas de Sottise dont je ne crois le Bavard capable; mais Je vous prie de dissimuler jusqu'a la Fin; Nous avons besoin de Lui et nous le conduirons par son Foible Jusqu'au bout; apres quoi nous nous moquerons de Lui." (Duke de Choiseul to Solar, May 25, 1762, CL Shelburne MSS. IX:258–261.)

42. AE CP Espagne 536:281–283; Duke de Choiseul to Solar, May 28, 1762, CL Shelburne MSS. IX:283–297.

also anticipated trouble from Spain over the Mississippi boundary. True to his predictions, it came with the Spanish acceptance of the British declaration for peace, which Grimaldi handed Choiseul on June 24.[43] In this reply to the suggested terms, the Spanish ambassador merely stated that Spain would adhere, on the three vital points at issue, to the demands made upon Great Britain before the war began.[44] But when Choiseul had prepared to draft the articles which he was to forward to England, Grimaldi strenuously objected to the Mississippi boundary, as accepted by Choiseul in May, on the ground that it would bring the British into the Gulf of Mexico. Choiseul made light of the objection: the boundary he had proposed, he said, would not give Great Britain a single port large enough to receive a frigate. But Grimaldi insisted. Spain, he declared, would never admit the British to the Gulf; and as for Mobile, he demanded that that important port be not even mentioned in the negotiation. Choiseul, who was already committed to the line of the Iberville, felt constrained at least to appear to cede to the intransigent Spaniard, and, therefore, inserted in his note a vague article which apparently shut the British off from the sea.[45]

Choiseul's proposals of June 28 were little more, therefore, than a formal statement of his more informal suggestions of May 25.[46] The outstanding part of his note, of course, was that relating to the Mississippi boundary. This article, as formulated to meet the objections of Grimaldi, provided that "France will agree to the fixation of the boundaries of Canada with the greatest extent, it being understood that they will not extend beyond the Mississippi River, nor encroach upon the dependencies of Louisiana along the seacoast." This Choiseul recognized as a radical departure from the line as drawn by the British; but he explained to Solar that he had no intention of varying his preceding offer, and Great Britain had only to insist, to break down Spain's resistance.[47]

43. Grimaldi to the Duke de Choiseul, June 24, 1762, CL Shelburne MSS. X:103–107.

44. Reply of Spain to the British Declaration, June 12, 1762, CL Shelburne MSS. X:103–107; AE CP Espagne 536:389–390.

45. AE CP Espagne 536:380–382, 385–386; Solar to Víry, June 30, 1762, CL Shelburne MSS. X:139–147.

46. He again asked for Cape Breton instead of St. Pierre and Miquelon; if England insisted on retaining Cape Breton, France would acquiesce, provided only that she were granted the privilege of drying fish on the shores of Cape Breton as well as on those of Newfoundland. He insisted upon having St. Lucia for France, and asked for the privilege of trading on the Senegal River. With regard to the Germanies, he proposed that Wesel and Gelderland be garrisoned by French troops, and that England agree not to let her Hanoverian troops go to the aid of Prussia.

47. "Projet des Articles de Paix dressés par la France," June 28, 1762, CL Shelburne MSS. X:108–121; Choiseul to Solar, June 29, 1762, ibid. X:132–138; Solar to Víry, June 30, 1762, ibid. X:139–147.

Shortly after this Franco-Spanish communication was sent off, Egremont's reply to the French proposals of May 25 at long last arrived. This reply was anything but encouraging, and should have cleared Choiseul's mind of the delusion that he could play upon the divisions within the British cabinet to win British acquiescence to a generous peace. The French insistence upon St. Lucia, and Choiseul's half-refusal of the *abri* offered, had stirred the resentment of the British ministers. Bedford, to be sure, was disposed to accede to Choiseul's demands; Bute, too, was for conceding St. Lucia. But the majority of the ministers were for taking a firm stand. Egremont's answer therefore rejected all the proposed French compromises. He stood firm on St. Pierre and Miquelon, and scoffed at the *quid pro quo* offered in return for the rich "sugar islands" which Great Britain was willing to restore to France. The islands offered Britain, he said, were worth absolutely nothing; the additional lands along the upper Mississippi were "desert and useless plains," which, "if they belonged to France, make part of the cession of Canada"; and Mobile was only a "little establishment stuck in between those of France and Spain." But his strongest argument was against the proposed French *lisière* on the left bank of the Mississippi. The British intention in proposing the river as a boundary, he said, was to provide a line that would avoid forever any possible disputes in that region. Not only did the French proposal contain the germs of endless broils, but also "totally prohibits us from the navigation of the Mississippi, which we have understood should be in common for the commerce of the two nations."[48]

Bute attempted to soften the effect of this reply by informally suggesting that the Duke of Bedford, the most ardent English advocate for peace, might be the plenipotentiary who would bring the negotiations to a conclusion.[49] Bute and Egremont were both becoming genuinely apprehensive as to their success; and, finally, on June 28, Egremont, with the knowledge only of Bute, assured Víry that if France accepted the other British conditions, Great Britain would give up St. Lucia, despite the recent decision of the cabinet.[50] This concession eased the strain considerably and probably saved the negotiations from complete failure. The question of the Mississippi was still far from settled, however, and the French ministers expressed amazement that the British insisted upon

48. Egremont's memoir of June 26, 1762, CL Shelburne MSS. X:44–61; Egremont to Víry, June 26, *ibid.* X:37–44.

49. Bute to Víry, June 26, 1762, CL Shelburne MSS. X:184–189; Víry to Solar, June 27, 1762, *ibid.* X:61–92.

50. Víry to Solar, June 27, 1762, CL Shelburne MSS. X:61–92; Víry to Solar, June 28, 1762, *ibid.* X:192–194.

the Mississippi River as the boundary, from its source to its mouth, apparently without realizing that this would give New Orleans, the capital and the key to the whole of Louisiana, to Great Britain. To clarify the British ministerial mind, therefore, Choiseul sent a map to Víry, whereon was a tracing of the boundary as proposed by France, a boundary which was now extended to include everything the British demanded, except the island and city of New Orleans.[51]

The arrival of Choiseul's proposals of June 28 did not help matters in the British mind. Egremont had to express the disappointment of himself and his colleagues that the French had made no real concessions on the vital points. He reiterated the British determination to cede nothing beyond St. Pierre and Miquelon as an *abri*, made no observable concession on St. Lucia, and demanded that the Mississippi River, from its source to the sea, be the boundary in North America.[52] In the three Spanish points he saw little difficulty, except that he insisted upon a Spanish guaranty of the British privilege of cutting dyewood before England evacuated the forts on the dyewood coasts.[53] Bute worked hard with Víry over the article on the Mississippi, and finally produced a secret provision which would give New Orleans to France. Víry warned his correspondent in Paris that he must reply to the English note with great caution, as Bute and Egremont would probably be destroyed were their secret concessions on Louisiana, St. Lucia, and the Germanies to become known. Choiseul was requested to word his next communication as if the secret concessions of Bute and Egremont had never been made. He was to insist upon St. Lucia as a *sine qua non*, but he must admit the Mississippi River as a boundary, following the Iberville River outlet to the sea in order to leave New Orleans in the hands of the French, while guaranteeing the navigation of the river to both nations.[54]

Choiseul now acceded to all the British demands. And well he might, for he saw all his well-calculated schemes failing before his eyes. Charles III, unfortunately, was a gentleman and had hesitated to strike his neighbor, Portugal, without warning. He had waited so long indeed that he had given Great Britain time to send to Portugal's aid sufficient reinforcements to make Spanish success in that quarter extremely unlikely. In England, on the other hand, George Anson, First Lord of the Admiralty, had penetrated Choiseul's scheme for an invasion, and had

51. Solar to Víry, July 4, 5, 1762, CL Shelburne MSS. X:204–210, 216–224.
52. Egremont's memoir to Víry, July 10, 1762, CL Shelburne MSS. X:257–271.
53. Egremont to the Count de Choiseul, July 10, 1762, CL Shelburne MSS. X:243–246.
54. Víry to Solar, July 12, 1762, CL Shelburne MSS. X:302–320.

long since prevailed upon the cabinet to strengthen its home defenses.[55]
Finally, Víry was now persistently warning the French ministers that
they must make peace quickly. A continuation of the war would inevitably make the British terms harder, and France would lose St. Lucia; the
seizure of Cuba, which was generally expected in London, would make it
impossible for Bute to make peace without some considerable compensation.[56]

Choiseul himself was now convinced that the limit of British concession had been reached, and he made up his mind to sign the preliminaries
as Great Britain wished to have them.[57] The only obstacle in the way
was Spain; but Choiseul had now determined to make peace, regardless
of the Spanish ambassador's "verbiage." Grimaldi wrestled with the
French ministers for three successive days over the article on the Mississippi. Choiseul had tried to reassure him by saying that the British,
under the article as he proposed to draw it, would have no access to the
Gulf of Mexico, but Grimaldi would not be satisfied. He submitted his
"preliminary articles" for the Anglo-Spanish treaty, in which apparently, he did not budge from his previous demands in the matter of the
British evacuation of the posts on the dyewood coast, and the question
of Spanish participation in the Newfoundland fishery. Worst of all,
Spain refused absolutely to sign any peace that would give England a
footing on the Gulf of Mexico; and Grimaldi demanded from Choiseul a
written assurance that France would not make any such concession.[58]

Choiseul's note of July 21, therefore, was written under difficulties, to
say the least. But he did not flinch before the logical implications of his
determination to make peace. As he put it, there were now only three
points separating France and England: St. Lucia, New Orleans, and
the Prussian territories occupied by French troops; and Bute and Egremont had secretly accepted the French conditions on these three. In his
draft he traced the boundary "between Canada and Louisiana" down
the Mississippi and the Iberville rivers; he insisted upon St. Lucia as a
sine qua non, giving Grenada to England; and he submitted three different articles to cover Wesel and Gelderland, drawn up by Starhemberg,
the Austrian ambassador in Paris, from which England might choose
the one that seemed most acceptable. On the latter point, however, he
recommended the article providing for joint occupation of these places

55. Corbett, *op. cit.*, II, 315–322.
56. Víry to Solar, July 12, 1762, CL Shelburne MSS. X:302–320.
57. Duke de Choiseul to Solar, July 15, 1762, CL Shelburne MSS. X:322–325.
58. Duke de Choiseul to Solar, July 19, 1762, CL Shelburne MSS. X:325–326; Solar
to Víry, July 21, 1762, *ibid.* X:420–422; Spanish Project of Preliminaries, July 20,
1762, *ibid.* X:345–353; AE CP Espagne 536:512, 513–514, 521, 522.

by French and English troops.[59] Because of the strenuous objection of
Grimaldi, the article on the Mississippi boundary was so worded in the
draft treaty as to indicate that the line would run only to Lake Pontchartrain and that the English possessions would not extend to the shore
of the Gulf. A separate article, making it perfectly clear that the line
ran to the sea, and that the English territory included the shore line
from the Perdido River, the boundary of Spanish Florida, to Lake Pontchartrain, was to be kept secret until the signing of the definitive treaty.
If Spain still balked at the terms, France was prepared, said Choiseul,
to sign without her.[60]

To all intents and purposes, the Anglo-French peace now seemed to
be made. But it still had to be passed upon by a divided and ill-disci-
plined British cabinet. George Grenville and the Earl of Granville led
the opposition, which was determined not to give way either on St. Lucia
or on New Orleans. It took all Bute's influence and the personal inter-
vention of the King to overcome the objections of this opposition; and,
even so, Bute could not bring his colleagues to accept the French proposals in the case of Wesel and Gelderland. Reserving these questions,
therefore, for further discussion by the negotiators of the treaty in its
final form, Egremont was at last instructed to inform Choiseul that
England conceded St. Lucia and New Orleans to France, and was ready
to name an ambassador whenever France wished. He made certain new
reservations as to the Mississippi boundary, however. Since it was very
doubtful whether the Iberville River were deep enough to make English
navigation of the Mississippi a reality, he asked that England be permitted, when navigating the Mississippi, to use the same channel the
French used from the Iberville to the sea; and to forestall any possible
French fortifications below the city of New Orleans that would block
English entry to the river, he asked that any land east of the river below the island of New Orleans be included in the cession to be made to
England—thus granting France the island of New Orleans alone. As
for Spain, the British ministry were opposed to making a separate peace
without her, and requested Choiseul to attempt to bring His Catholic
Majesty to a settlement.[61]

59. "Projet d'articles Préliminaires arretés entre la France et L'Angleterre," CL
Shelburne MSS. X:376–388; Count de Choiseul to Egremont, July 21, 1762, *ibid.* X:
369–373, 402–413; Duke de Choiseul to Solar, July 21, 1762, *ibid.* X:361–365; Solar to
Víry, July 21, 1762, *ibid.* X:336–344.

60. Duke de Choiseul to Solar, July 21, 1762, CL Shelburne MSS. X:361–365; Count
de Choiseul to Solar, July 21, 1762, *ibid.* X:369–373; Solar to Víry, July 21, 1762, *ibid.*
X:428–433; "Projet d'articles Préliminaires," *ibid.* X:376–388; "Note, Art. 6," *ibid.*
X:373–374.

61. Egremont to the Count de Choiseul, July 31, 1762, CL Shelburne MSS. XI:8–16;

Choiseul was desperate. Spain was adamant on the question of the Mississippi and showed no signs of growing less so. Early in August Wall proposed to Ossun that the southern boundary of "Canada" be drawn so as to leave no doubt as to the exclusion of the British from access to the Gulf of Mexico. Spain had never recognized either France's title to Louisiana or England's title to Georgia. She would do so now, he said, if England would consent to mark the southern limits of "Canada" by a line to be drawn directly from the western boundary of Georgia to the Mississippi, leaving the territory between this line, the Mississippi, Florida, and the sea to the natives. He apparently thought nothing, in proposing this prototype of the later line of 31°–30′, of asking France and England to consent to the abandonment of such considerable places as Mobile and Biloxi.[62]

But this was too much for Choiseul, and he crisply replied that France would do as she chose with her own. Unfortunately, the latest English reply had omitted any discussion of the Spanish preliminary articles, and the French minister was under the necessity of mollifying the offended Spanish ambassador. In view of the English omission, Choiseul took it upon himself to compose a message for Spain, which he based upon Egremont's letter of July 31; and in it he tactfully suppressed all that he thought Grimaldi should not see. Then, in an effort to cajole Spain into speedy acceptance of the British terms and into naming a plenipotentiary, he sent his friend Jacob O'Dunne to Madrid to assist Ossun in his negotiations at the Spanish court. He felt sure of success, and named September 5 as the day on which the English and French ambassadors should be ready to depart.[63]

August passed while these preparations were being made. On August 21, Egremont corrected his omission with regard to Spain by saying he proposed to leave the Spanish questions in the hands of the ambassadors. But to make the British position clear, he said the British plenipotentiary would be instructed to insist that the question of prizes be left with British courts of admiralty; that Spanish participation in the Newfoundland fishery be left as provided in treaties in existence prior to the war; and that questions of the restitution of conquered territory be left to the plenipotentiaries for discussion. On the vital question of dyewoods Spain and Great Britain would exchange agreements: Great Brit-

Egremont to Víry, July 31, 1762, *ibid.* XI:32–52; Víry to Solar, August 1, 1762, *ibid.* XI:52–68.

62. AE CP Espagne 537:4–12.

63. Count de Choiseul to Solar, August 10, 1762, CL Shelburne MSS. XI:94–98; Count de Choiseul to Egremont, August 10, 1762, *ibid.* XI:146–163; Duke de Choiseul to Solar, August 12, 1762, *ibid.* XI:103–113; Solar to Víry, August 12, 1762, *ibid.* XI:114–133.

ain to evacuate its military posts, and Spain to guarantee to Great Britain the privilege of cutting.[64]

Two days later the news of a successful British action before Havana arrived in London, and a wave of national enthusiasm swept the country.[65] On August 26, Solar advised Víry that Spain's reply to the French mission was satisfactory, and that Grimaldi had been named Spanish plenipotentiary for the negotiation of the treaty in Paris.[66] On the same day Solar communicated to Grimaldi the news from Havana, and Choiseul began to talk to him in a manner to "*rabattre son caquet*,"—"to quiet his cackling." It was assumed that, if occupied, Cuba would be restored; but everybody knew that if Havana itself should fall Great Britain would not make peace without some compensation for this important conquest. As Solar put it, Spain's war had been "*plus bruyante que brillante!*"[67]

It was thus in an atmosphere of excitement and of rising British temper that the Duke de Nivernais[68] and the Duke of Bedford received their instructions as ambassadors and plenipotentiaries. They were empowered to sign preliminary articles on the basis of the British and French notes of the preceding July 10 and 21. Only one point seemed to promise much difficulty, and that was the delicate position which France occupied with regard to Spain, whose approval of a British means of access to the Gulf of Mexico, hitherto rigorously denied, must be obtained before the peace could be made. It was to be hoped that future news from Havana might bring Spain to give in on this point. On the other hand, as the mutual returning of ships and territory captured by Spain and Great Britain was to be left to the British and Spanish ambassadors for settlement, Bedford was instructed merely to make as good a bargain as he could. But he was to sign no separate peace; Spain and France must sign together, and Portugal must be included.[69]

Bedford reached Paris on September 12, and negotiations began. He had little or no trouble with the French ministers; but Grimaldi presented almost insuperable difficulties on every point, and injected a demand for new and revised commercial agreements between Great Britain

64. Egremont to Count de Choiseul, August 21, 1762, CL Shelburne MSS. XI:183–188.

65. Víry to Solar, August 23, 1762, CL Shelburne MSS. XI:214–217.

66. Solar to Víry, August 26, 1762, CL Shelburne MSS. XI:257–267; Count de Choiseul to Egremont, August 26, 1762, *ibid.* XI:277–289.

67. Víry to Solar, August 23, 1762, CL Shelburne MSS. XI:214–217; Solar to Víry, August 26, 1762, *ibid.* XI:289–294; Víry to Solar, September 4, 1762, *ibid.* XI:334–337.

68. Louis Jules Bourbon Mancini-Mazarini, Duke de Nivernais.

69. CAO AE CP Ang. 447:28–36; *Brit. Dip. Instr.*, VII, *France 1745–1789*, pp. 56–64, 64–66.

and Spain. This being a point on which Bedford had no instructions, he was compelled to refer it to London. The French ministers had not yet dared to break to Grimaldi the true import of their secret article on the Mississippi, and they begged Bedford not to jeopardize the peace by betraying the secret before the signing of the preliminaries. They assured him that if Great Britain so desired France stood ready to sign a separate and secret article guaranteeing to her everything she wished on that head.[70]

The Spanish ambassador's obstructiveness was well-nigh fatal to the negotiations. For Bedford's report to his government was received in an atmosphere already highly charged with hostility to Bute's peace. Popular clamor was mounting, cultivated and encouraged both by the opposition ministers and by the diplomatic representatives of the King of Prussia, who hated Bute. Furthermore, by his tact and address Nivernais had won certain slight concessions from Egremont that were significant only inasmuch as they increased British distrust of French sincerity. Bute himself trembled before the growing opposition, in genuine fear for both his office and his life.[71] The cabinet began to doubt the wisdom of having given Bedford plenary powers, and he was now instructed not to sign anything without first referring it to the ministry at home—a curtailment of his responsibility which he bitterly resented.[72]

At this juncture the news came of the capture of Havana, and it cleared the atmosphere. Both France and Spain now showed a willingness to close with Great Britain's terms; but, as anticipated, the British cabinet raised its demands. On October 26, a new draft treaty was sent to Bedford, one that rejected all compromises in the articles as stated, and instructed the ambassador to demand as compensation for Cuba either Florida or Puerto Rico. At the same time Bedford himself was mollified by a renewal of his full powers.[73]

Choiseul was more than ready to sign. He had asked Spain directly whether she chose to continue the war to keep England from gaining a foothold on the Gulf, and pointed out that, in that case, England would easily take both Florida and Louisiana.[74] Spain had decided in favor of the inevitable, with reservations;[75] but the news of the fall of Havana, reinforced by a personal appeal from Louis XV to Charles III, obliterated even the reservations. Louis, moved by Spain's sacrifices in a war

70. *Bedford Correspondence*, III, 103–113.

71. *Bedford Correspondence*, III, 114–116; CAO AE CP Ang. 448:83–88; Corbett, *op. cit.*, II, 358–359.

72. *Bedford Correspondence*, III, 116–117.

73. AE CP Espagne 537:227–230; *Bedford Correspondence*, III, 118–119.

74. AE CP Espagne 537:189–190.   75. AE CP Espagne 537:201.

undertaken in his behalf, foresaw a British demand for a *quid pro quo* for Havana. He therefore offered his Spanish cousin what remained of Louisiana, with New Orleans, to compensate him, in some measure, for his anticipated loss.[76] There was nothing else France could do. France was beaten, wrote Choiseul, and must submit to the English yoke, while preparing for a new war.[77] Charles, although his first impulse was to decline the offer of Louisiana, accepted the expected English conditions, and authorized Choiseul to proceed with the negotiations on that basis.[78]

The negotiators were thus prepared for the new draft treaty from London when it arrived in Paris. It came with a warning that France and Spain must sign, in view of the impossibility of getting further concession through the parliament that was shortly to meet, or continue the war.[79] The French ministers complained of certain clarifying phrases pertinent to the St. Lawrence fishery,[80] but there was nothing for them to do but sign, which both France and Spain did, on November 3.[81]

At the same time, Choiseul and Grimaldi signed an agreement by which France ceded to Spain the western half of Louisiana, with New Orleans.[82] At the last minute Choiseul had offered it to Great Britain, in order to relieve Spain of the necessity of ceding Florida, but the offer had been refused.[83] Spain had been treated harshly, wrote Choiseul; but "as for us, the conditions are better than those of last year, and those which we might expect next year."[84]

There remained only the task of arranging the final and definitive treaty. The preliminaries had first to be ratified, and this promised to be most difficult in the British Parliament. There, the great debate took

76. AE CP Espagne 537:208, 210, 215–219, 221–222.

77. AE CP Espagne 537:223.

78. AE CP Espagne 537:266–273; CAO AE CP Ang. 448:288–291.

79. *Bedford Correspondence*, III, 139, 140–142; *Brit. Dip. Instrs.*, VII, *France 1745–1789*, pp. 69–71.

80. CAO AE CP Ang. 447:388–391.   81. CAO AE CP Ang. 448:10–11.

82. Davenport and Paullin, *op. cit.*, IV, 91.

83. AE CP Espagne 537:290–291, 292–293.

84. AE CP Espagne 537:307. As finally signed, the preliminary articles provided that (1) France was to cede to Great Britain Canada, including Acadia, Cape Breton, and all the islands in the Gulf of St. Lawrence. The French inhabitants were guaranteed the right to retain and practice the Catholic religion, "as far as the laws of Great Britain permit," and were to have the privilege of selling their property and withdrawing from Canada within eighteen months. (2) France was to be free to fish and dry fish in Newfoundland as provided by Article XIII of the Treaty of Utrecht, and to fish in the Gulf of St. Lawrence, except within three leagues of the shores of the continent and the islands in the gulf, and, outside the gulf, except within fifteen leagues of the shores of Cape Breton. (3) Great Britain was to cede to France the islands of St. Pierre and Miquelon, which France undertook to leave unfortified, and with a guard of only fifty men. (4) The fortifications of the town of Dunkirk were to be left as provided in the Treaty of Aix-la-Chapelle. (5) The boundary between

place on December 9. William Pitt spoke for three hours and forty minutes against the treaty, which, he said, cast a shadow upon Britain's glory, and was both a surrender of British interests and a violation of her national good faith so far as her German allies were concerned. But a cabinet shuffle and a shameless use of bribery in Parliament by Henry Fox overcame all opposition, and the preliminaries were ratified.[85] France and Spain, not being hampered by the obstructive tendencies of representative institutions, had no such difficulties.

Meanwhile, in Paris, Bedford was working over the final draft of the treaty with Choiseul. Certain questions of language and detail had arisen in the case of the British draft treaty sent to Choiseul on December 6,[86] and one, in particular, called forth strenuous objections. With a view to sharing in the control of the mouth of the Mississippi below New Orleans, the British ministers had taken advantage of the phrase giving Great Britain the ownership of everything east of the river "except the

French and British possessions was fixed as the course of the Mississippi and the Iberville rivers to the sea. The river and port of Mobile, and all the land east of the Mississippi, except the island of New Orleans, were specifically ceded to Great Britain together with the right of navigation on the Mississippi from its source to its mouth, and especially that part of it between the island of New Orleans and the west bank below the Iberville. (6) Great Britain was to restore the former French West Indies and Belle Isle to France; and (7) France gave Grenada and the Grenadines to Great Britain. (8) The four "neutral islands" were to be divided: St. Vincent's, Tobago, and Dominica were to go to England, and St. Lucia to France. (9) England was to restore Goree to France and retain Senegal. (10) In the East Indies, England was to restore the coast of Coromandel, Malabar, and Bengal to the *status quo* of 1749, and France was to renounce conquests on the Coromandel coast made since 1749. (11) Minorca was to be restored to England. (12) The territories of Hanover, Hesse, Brunswick, and Lippe were to be restored to their rulers by France. (13) France and England were to evacuate places and areas held by their arms in the Rhineland, Prussia, Westphalia, and "the Empire," and agreed to give no further help to their respective German allies. Finally, (14) France was to evacuate Ostend and Nieuport.

With regard to Spain, the articles provided that: (1) Cases of Spanish prizes made by British ships in time of peace were to be submitted to British courts of admiralty. (2) Great Britain was to demolish its forts on the coasts of Honduras and other Spanish territories in that part of the world, but was to continue to have the privilege of cutting logwood there. (3) Spain would no longer claim any share of the Newfoundland fishery. (4) Great Britain was to restore Havana and Cuba to Spain, and (5) Spain gave up to Great Britain all it possessed on the continent of North America, east of the Mississippi River. The inhabitants of this territory (Florida) were to have the same right to practice the Catholic religion and to move elsewhere as the French inhabitants of Canada.

"His Most Faithful Majesty" of Portugal was to be included in the treaty, and France and Spain agreed to restore to him all that had been won from him during the war. Unspecified conquests or countries were to be restored to the *status quo ante bellum*. Ships taken at sea after the expiration of certain given periods were to be restored. (*All the Treaties*, II, 261–271.)

85. *Bedford Correspondence*, III, 166–167, 168–169.
86. *Brit. Dip. Instrs.*, VII, *France 1745–1789*, pp. 73–74.

town of New Orleans and the island on which it is situated," to omit provision for the demarcation of a boundary line to be drawn through the Iberville River and Lakes Maurepas and Pontchartrain. But the French saw through this sophistry; the only island east of the Mississippi and south of the Iberville, they insisted, was the island of New Orleans. Besides, the British had constantly protested that their chief desire was for a clear and unequivocal line. It was precisely to provide a line leaving no possibility of future dispute that France had accepted the line of the Iberville and had now to insist upon it. Bedford was surprised to find Grimaldi joining strenuously in the debate over this line, and he began to suspect "that the report I have heard that France intended to cede New Orleans, to Spain has some foundation."[87] Choiseul privately expressed to Nivernais his willingness to accede to the British quibble, were it not for his commitments to Spain. But his feelings of national honor, he said, compelled him to insist. A few more conferences on the subject took place, and Egremont finally gave in.[88] With this point and the arrangements as to India finally out of the way, the work was completed by the end of January, and the definitive treaty was signed on February 10, 1763.[89]

The Treaty of Paris, as finally signed, provided that Canada was to be ceded to Great Britain, and that the boundary of the British territory on the continent should henceforth be the Mississippi and the Iberville rivers. In the West Indies, Great Britain was to retain Grenada and the Grenadines, and the four "neutral islands" were to be divided, St. Lucia going to France, and St. Vincent, Tobago, and Dominica going to Great Britain. From Spain, Great Britain received Florida. The British now possessed all the land on the continent of North America east of the Mississippi River, with the exception of the island and town of New Orleans.[90]

87. *Bedford Correspondence,* III, 173–183; CAO AE CP Ang. 448:368–384, 449: 30–31.

88. CAO AE CP Ang. 449:34, 72; Egremont to Bedford, January 22, 1763, CL Shelburne MSS. XXXVIII:5.

89. *Bedford Correspondence,* III, 188; AE CP Espagne 538:72.

90. The text of the treaty is in Davenport and Paullin, *op. cit.,* IV, 92–98.

CHAPTER IX

CONCLUSION

I

MORE territory changed hands by the Treaty of Paris and its collateral Treaty of Fontainebleau than by any treaty dealing with the American hemisphere before or since. By its terms the entire North American continent, east of the Mississippi, was now British. The rest of the continent remained Spanish. The final decision in the old Anglo-French struggle for a boundary had come with the elimination of France altogether and the drawing of an entirely new line between the British and the Spaniards along the course of the Mississippi.

The diplomatic discussion of a boundary between New France and the English colonies in North America had of necessity to concern itself with three or four geographical areas: Acadia, the region south of Lakes Ontario and Erie and the St. Lawrence River, the Ohio Valley, and the lands southward from the Ohio to the Gulf of Mexico. At the beginning of the period the problem of establishing a boundary was ill-defined and only vaguely realized. It had, indeed, entered into the discussions of the diplomats for nearly a century, and certainly since 1686. But none of the conferences or the commissions which considered the question had ever made a detailed study of the boundary; nor had they ever considered the problem systematically or as a whole.

Up to the time of the Peace of Utrecht there had been little real conflict over the right of possession except in Rupert's Land and in the Iroquois country. Even after Utrecht, with the ownership of Rupert's Land and Acadia presumably settled, the assumption seems to have been that France should possess the great valleys and that the British should remain confined to their colonies along the coast. In the three decades following the peace, however, the expanding British settlements began to reach the mountains, and statesmen on both sides began vaguely and uneasily to realize the imminence of conflict. The building of Forts Toulouse, Niagara, and St. Frédéric was essentially a manifestation of the French fear of the British advance, which was most clearly exemplified by the establishment of the post at Oswego. Still, there seems as yet to have been little conscious intention in the British to expand beyond the Allegheny barrier, and, with few exceptions, they seem to have acquiesced in the French assumption that the mountains constituted the real boundary between them. Toward the mid-century, however, more and more British colonial officials and statesmen began to see the restrictive nature of the Allegheny mountain boundary and to speak of the desirability, even inevitability, of British migration beyond it. The wave of British expansiveness that followed the Peace of Aix-la-Chapelle terrified the French government and its colonial officials, and set in motion the flurry of fort building along the frontier that resulted in the erection of military establishments on the St. John River, on the isthmus of Nova Scotia, on Lake Champlain, near Toronto, at Presqu'Ile, at Venango, and at the junction of the Allegheny and Monongahela rivers. This program had begun, indeed, during the war just ended; but the founding of Halifax, with the obvious British intention of colonizing all of Nova Scotia, the reorganization of the Hudson's Bay Company, and the plans of the Ohio Company of Virginia and companies organized for the exploitation of transmontane lands farther south were evidence enough for the French that the British were no longer content to accept the old, tacitly recognized, boundary along the watershed. In all the areas of conflict the British government now began to advance claims, new or old, that threatened to carry the British boundary forward to the St. Lawrence, the Great Lakes, and the Mississippi.

The colonial governors on both sides, with and without orders from home, took the initiative in action, and the diplomats undertook their discussions to rectify—or to ratify—the actions of the colonial governors. The beginning of the diplomatic crisis over the colonies arose from the French occupation, in 1744, of St. Lucia, one of the "neutral islands" under the agreement of 1730, and Tobago, claimed by Great Britain, in 1749. The British government immediately demanded the evacuation of both these islands, under the clauses of the Treaty of Aix-la-Chapelle providing for the restoration of the *status quo ante bellum*. But the moves of the French in the West Indies were balanced by the decision of Great Britain to colonize Nova Scotia; and the West Indies were soon forgotten in the disputes over the North American boundary that started as a quarrel over the "anciennes limites" of Acadia, but soon involved the question of boundaries from the Gulf of St. Lawrence to the Gulf of Mexico. The Anglo-French joint commission of 1750 did discuss both Acadia and St. Lucia; but it was upon Acadia that its greatest efforts were expended. The commission came to its inglorious end, indeed, largely because the spread of violence in the forests of North America was too rapid to permit of any dependence upon the dilatory methods of diplomacy.

The action of the colonial governors, especially on the British side, represented not merely the desires of their home governments, but the interests of the colonists as well. The settlement of Halifax, for example, was partly at least a response to New England demands for greater protection of the fisheries and for some sort of compensation for the restitution of Cape Breton to France. The establishment of the post at Oswego had been the result of the agitation of the fur merchants of the colony of New York; and the demand for the expansion of British settlements over the divide into the Lake Champlain region was the voice of the land speculators of the Mohawk Valley. The exploitation of the lands of the Ohio Valley and the lands farther south was a project of the aristocratic land speculators of Virginia and the Carolinas. Governor Dinwiddie of Virginia, to take the clearest example, was governed in his actions largely by the interests of the men who controlled Virginia politics, as the action of the Virginia legislature in making provision for the Washington expedition shows. The settlement of Nova Scotia had been repeatedly urged by Governor Shirley of Massachusetts, and Shirley represented the interests of the fish merchants of Massachusetts as well as certain other land speculators, such as Benjamin Franklin, who hoped to profit by the exploitation of Nova Scotia territory. Similarly, the petitions for lands to the westward of the Carolinas and Georgia submitted to the Board of Trade represented a movement of population and of colonial opinion that was actually demanding military and political action. In the West Indies, it was in response to the agitation of the sugar merchants—as against the sugar planters—as well as for strategic reasons, that the British government was becoming interested in the development of the "neutral islands."

Thus colonial opinion—or more accurately, colonial interest—was joined to that of the mother country in the movements which precipitated the Seven Years' War in America. This had been true, in a measure, of every colonial war fought on American soil; and in this sense it is a mistake to speak of the American colonies as the "pawns" of European diplomacy. The effort of New York to make a treaty of neutrality and friendship with Canada during the War of the Spanish Succession, and the trade of the Albany merchants with the enemy during the War of the Austrian Succession are but exceptions that illustrate the rule that from the War of the League of Augsburg onward there were powerful interests in the colonies that actually desired war against the French for the annexation of territory or for the control of commerce or the fisheries. The power and the relative importance of this sort of colonial interest increased during the eighteenth century, with the economic expansion of the British colonies, to the point where, about 1750, it was quite possible that there might have been war between the French and British colonies, even had the French and British diplomats been successful in patching up some sort of agreement that would have kept the mother countries neutral.

In any case, both the expansiveness of the British-American empire and the war that took place as a result of it were "made in America." Colonial interests went hand-in-hand with the national mercantilist interests of the mother country; while England and France were, for mercantilist reasons, interested in the disturbance or the maintenance of the *status quo*, the colonies were interested in the fisheries, the fur trade, and more land—so much so that they were quite ready to fight for them.

II

In Acadia, the British could present their claims with a brave show of justice. The grant of Nova Scotia to Sir William Alexander had indeed included all the land between the Atlantic and the St. Lawrence. But the "anciennes limites" of Acadia, as known to the French, had never been defined as including the lands along the St. Lawrence. That, however, the French had thought of Acadia as including all the land along the Atlantic and the Gulf of St. Lawrence to the bounds of New England was true. Thus, whether or not the extreme British claim to the St. Lawrence as the northern boundary of Acadia was justified, it seems abundantly clear that the "anciennes limites" of Acadia did include all the settlements around the coasts of the peninsula and the Bay of Fundy. The British decision to build Halifax and colonize Nova Scotia could therefore have given the French no legitimate cause for concern. It was the quick imagination of La Galissonnière that envisaged the threat to the strategically important line of communications along the St. John and determined him to forestall it at all costs by the building of forts at the mouth of the river and on the isthmus. It was as a rationalization of this defensive action that the French diplomats fabricated the absurd claim, which they must have known was false, that Acadia was only a part of the peninsula. In this region, then, justice of a sort seems to have been on the side of the British; and the French would probably have done well to accept the compromise line offered by the British government which, while giving Great Britain a *lisière* along the coast, would have left the French an overland line of communications between Quebec and the Gulf of St. Lawrence.

The case is not so clear, however, with regard to the lands lying between the watershed and the St. Lawrence–Great Lakes waterway. The British could present a *fait accompli* in the shape of the post at Oswego, and they could cite numerous "deeds" from the Iroquois placing the lands of the Indians under British ownership or protection. Their strongest claim, perhaps, was that based on Article XV of the Anglo-French Treaty of Utrecht. But the real extent of the Indian lands, as the French correctly pointed out, was extremely vague and variable, and the notoriously fickle Indians themselves repeatedly denied that they had ever actually conveyed their lands to the English. With the exception of the post at Oswego, moreover, the British had never actually established themselves beyond the watershed, whereas the French could cite a long history of discovery, exploration, and actual occupation—at Forts Frontenac, Niagara, Detroit, Michilimackinac, and others in the Illinois country, to say nothing of the long-established fur trade of the *coureurs de bois* and the establishments of the French missions. By every right of discovery, use, and occupation the French claims to the lands drained by the waters that flow into the St. Lawrence seem to have been better than those of the British.

The same thing must be said of the Mississippi Valley. The French had discovered and explored it, and they had been the first to establish permanent settlements there. The boundary between Canada and Louisiana, while never clearly defined, seems to have been substantially as drawn on the "Vaudreuil Map"; the boundary between the English colonies and the great interior valley appears to have been pretty generally accepted, even by the British themselves, as lying along the Allegheny watershed. This seems to be made still clearer by the willingness of the British government to accept the Allegheny Mountains—or at least an arbitrary line only a short distance to the west of them—as the boundary in the negotiations of 1755.

As for the territory south of the Ohio, very little thought had ever been given to the boundary there before the negotiations of 1761. The general assumption seems to have been that the mountains marked the boundary down to their southern end, and that the Chattahoochee and Apalachicola rivers were the approximate boundaries of the French and British spheres of influence between the mountains and the Gulf of Mexico. Needless to say, this line was neither clearly recognized nor carefully observed by the traders of the two European rivals, and still less by the Indians living there. Yet the logic of history and geography seems to have been on the side of the French in their claim that there should be some such line.

However the justice of the case may have been, the colonial boundary conflict was a matter of grave concern to France and England, and, to a lesser degree, even to Holland and Spain. In an age of mercantilistic thinking, when the strength of a nation was thought to derive in large measure from its colonies, it was only natural that the chief protagonists should have taken the colonial question seriously. The well-being of Europe was believed to depend upon the balance of power established at the Peace of Utrecht. But that balance had its counterpart in America, and European statesmen took very seriously the possible effect of a disturbance of the colonial balance upon the balance at home. If one nation, such as England, were allowed to increase its colonial holdings at the expense of one of its rivals, the European balance would inevitably be disturbed. Because it suited British interests to do so, Great Britain scoffed at the idea of an American balance of power in the decade following the Peace of Aix-la-Chapelle. But Great Britain had been one of the guarantors of the balance of colonial power established at Utrecht. At that time it was England that feared lest France might disturb the American balance by annexing some part of the colonial possessions of Spain. In 1739, Great Britain, while frankly recognizing this principle of the colonial balance of power, had attempted to seize a part of the Spanish empire, and France had intervened to maintain the American equilibrium. Now Great Britain was offending again, and this time threatening to disturb the balance at the expense of the possessions of France herself. It was only natural for France to turn to Spain, as Spain had turned to her in the War of Jenkins' Ear, for assistance in the defense of the colonial equilibrium. Holland, colonial power and ally of England, was also vitally interested; but Holland refused to be drawn into the war against France because of the well-founded Dutch fear of a French invasion by land. Nevertheless, The Hague did serve as a meeting place for French and British diplomats negotiating for colonial peace throughout the war.

Such was the international significance of the dispute over the Canadian boundary in the eight years between the Peace of Aix-la-Chapelle and the declaration of war in 1756. Had France then been willing to accept even the extreme British claim, Canada at worst would have been bounded, along its southern frontier, by a neutral zone, or series of zones. Such a zone would have stretched along the southern shore of the St. Lawrence and Lake Ontario to Niagara, and thence along the western shore of the Ohio River as far as the Wabash. Presumably such a zone would have been established to the west of the mountains south of the Ohio. But Canada, as far as the Ohio and the Mississippi rivers, would have remained French; and the British would have been committed not only to a recognition of French ownership but also to a clearly marked boundary line which would have placed a definite limit upon British expansion westward.

But the French diplomats demanded the watershed or nothing, along with the entire course of the St. John River, and the war was fought to determine the ownership of the St. John, the southern half of the St. Lawrence Valley, the Ohio Valley, and the eastern half of the Mississippi Valley, as well as of the "neutral islands." Once the war had begun, and as the tide gradually turned in favor of the British, the logic of historical justice gave way to military power as the ultimate determinant in the diplomatic adjustment of the North American boundary. As might have been expected, the British demands now progressed from the mountains, acceptable as a boundary in 1755, to the Wabash and to a "protectorate" over the southern Indians in Pitt's negotiations of 1761. Then, with the victories of 1762, they advanced still farther, to the line as finally established, to the course of the Mississippi River itself.

III

Among the forces that had driven the three chief colonial powers into the great struggle for the final decision, at least four were of major importance. In the minds of both colonial and British leaders, one of the most powerful motives in the rivalry with France was the preservation of British dominance in the great northeastern fisheries. There the Peace of Utrecht had given the British a dominant position by its recognition of Britain's ownership of Newfoundland and the cession of Acadia. But it had also given the French fishermen a strong base in the island of Cape Breton, from whence proceeded rivalry, quarrels, and even armed clashes, both at sea and on land. The shortsightedness of the restitution of Cape Breton in 1748, from the point of view of the New England fishing interests, became immediately apparent, and the founding of Halifax was undertaken, in part at least, for the rectification of that error. At the end of the Seven Years' War, Choiseul tried desperately to recover Cape Breton, but Pitt knew where the British fishing interest lay, and the failure of his negotiations was in considerable measure due to his deliberate determination to reduce the French fishery to practically zero, and to put it beyond all possibility of being a serious challenge to the British monopoly for the future. Bute, who followed Pitt in the negotiations with France, simply did not dare to affront British public opinion by a reduction of Pitt's demands in this direction.

A second major motive in the diplomatic history of the Canadian boundary had been the consideration of strategic position. For such a man as Governor Shirley of Massachusetts, the desire for control of the coast of the Bay of Fundy was largely a matter of freezing the French out of the Atlantic fisheries; but for such a man as La Galissonnière, the chief consideration had been a strategic one, represented by the effort to establish, from the Gulf of St. Lawrence to the Gulf of Mexico, a defensive line to halt the British advance at the only points where, as he correctly estimated, it was strategically possible to do so. His argument for the preservation of the Allegheny boundary at all costs was based upon strategic considerations, and almost nothing else: the French had no settlements to protect along the line he proposed; his point was simply that if the British were once allowed to break through that line, they would be in a position to destroy New France. As the event proved, his idea of the strategic factor in the boundary situation was substantially correct.

A third major motive among those leading to war over the boundary had been the centuries-old dispute over the control of the fur trade. From the time of the clashes in the sixteen eighties between fur traders on the shores of Hudson Bay, in "Norumbega," and in the St. Lawrence Valley, the British and French fur traders and merchants had been at swords' points over the profits from this lucrative business. After the Peace of Utrecht, as the trade moved ever farther westward, this rivalry centered about the control of the bottleneck of the Niagara–Lake Ontario route over which passed the trade both of the French and of the British, the control of the deer-hunting Indians of the gulf coastal plain, and the fur trade of the Indians of the Ohio Valley. The fur merchants stood behind the British diplomats in the effort to keep the western tribes and the routes leading to them open to British traders. And the first British interests to take advantage of the conquest of Canada were the British fur merchants who rushed in to establish themselves in Quebec and Montreal.

The strongest motive of all, perhaps, in the developments that made an Anglo-French conflict in North America inevitable, had been the rapid expansion of British settlements westward. The filling up of the great valley of the Alleghenies had begun as early as 1726, and during the next decade the migration of British-American people southward and westward had been a steady and swelling stream. By 1750 this stream had begun to spread out beyond the mountains, southward into the Carolina-Georgia piedmont and westward along the occidental slope of the Allegheny massif. Similarly, the Mohawk Valley in New York had begun to fill up, and settlers were beginning to cast their eyes upon the green pastures on the Lake Champlain–St. Lawrence side of the divide. It was this population movement that the great land speculators had hoped to exploit. They were, in this sense, the agents of a great sociological phenomenon, land hunger. And, as they had the ear of the British government, it had become easy for their governmental agents to precipitate first diplomatic action, and then a war, in behalf of their interests.

All these considerations were of major importance in the diplomatic history of the Canadian boundary, both before the Seven Years' War and at its conclusion. France was defeated in each and all of the four issues, and eliminated from the contest. The final decision was of enormous significance for both the "Americans" and the "Canadians," for it determined that future developments in both areas were to follow Anglo-Saxon rather than French lines. The elimination of France opened the fisheries and the fur trade to a joint Canadian and British-American monopoly. The annexation of the eastern half of the Mississippi Valley, in which lay half of Canada, brought about a territorial and political overlapping of Canada and the seaboard colonies, opened these lands to a westward flow of British-American population, and initiated a new phase in the Canadian-American westward movement.

BIBLIOGRAPHY

I. MANUSCRIPT SOURCES

ADDITIONAL MANUSCRIPTS. British Museum.

ADDITIONAL MANUSCRIPTS. Transcripts of documents in the British Museum deposited in the Library of Congress, Washington.

CHATHAM MANUSCRIPTS. Correspondence and papers of William Pitt, Earl of Chatham, in the Public Record Office, London.

CORRESPONDANCE POLITIQUE: Angleterre. Transcripts of documents in the Archives du ministère des affaires étrangères, Paris, deposited in the Archives of the Dominion of Canada, Ottawa.

—— Espagne. Archives du ministère des affaires étrangères, Paris.

DOCUMENTS DES COLONIES. Archives nationales, Paris.

FOREIGN OFFICE PAPERS [British]. Transcripts of documents in the Public Record Office, London, deposited in the Archives of the Dominion of Canada, Ottawa.

HOUSE OF LORDS MANUSCRIPTS. Transcripts and photostats of documents in the Library of the House of Lords, London, deposited in the Library of Congress, Washington.

MÉMOIRES ET DOCUMENTS: Amérique. Archives du ministère des affaires étrangères, Paris.

—— Transcripts and photostats of documents in the Archives du ministère des affaires étrangères, Paris, deposited in the Library of Congress, Washington.

MILDMAY PAPERS. The personal papers of William Mildmay. William L. Clements Library, Ann Arbor, Michigan.

SHELBURNE MANUSCRIPTS. The papers of the Earl of Shelburne, William L. Clements Library, Ann Arbor, Michigan.

STOWE MANUSCRIPTS. British Museum.

II. PRINTED SOURCES

AKINS, THOMAS B., ed. Selections from the public documents of the province of Nova Scotia. Halifax, 1869.

ALBEMARLE, GEORGE THOMAS KEPPELL, 6th earl of. Memoirs of the Marquis of Rockingham and his contemporaries. With original letters and documents now first published. London, 1852. 2 vols.

ALMON, J., comp. A collection of all the treaties of peace, alliance, and commerce, between Great Britain and other powers, from the revolution in 1688, to the present time. London, 1772. 2 vols.

THE ANNUAL REGISTER, or A view of the history, politics and literature of the year 1758 [etc.]. London, 1760 sqq.

ARREDONDO, ANTONIO DE. Arredondo's historical proof of Spain's title to Georgia; a contribution to the history of one of the Spanish borderlands. Edited by Herbert E. Bolton. Berkeley, Calif., 1925.

BEDFORD, JOHN RUSSELL, *4th duke of*. Correspondence of John, fourth duke of Bedford: selected from the originals at Woburn Abbey. With an introduction by Lord John Russell. London, 1842–1846. 3 vols.

BRITISH DIPLOMATIC INSTRUCTIONS, 1689–1789, II, France 1689–1721; IV, France 1721–1727; VI, France 1727–1744; VII, France 1745–1789. In: Royal Historical Society, *Publications,* Camden third series, XXXV, XXXVIII, XLIII, XLIX. London, 1925, 1927, 1930, 1934.

BRITISH DIPLOMATIC REPRESENTATIVES, 1689–1789. In: Royal Historical Society, *Publications,* Camden third series, XLVI. London, 1932.

BURKE, EDMUND. The works of the Right Honourable Edmund Burke. London, 1808–1813. 12 vols.

CAMPBELL, JOHN, *1st baron Campbell.* "Life of Lord Chancellor Hardwicke," Lives of the lord chancellors and keepers of the great seal of England, from the earliest times till the reign of King George IV. 5th ed. London, 1868. 10 vols.

CANADA ARCHIVES. Report concerning Canadian archives for the year 1905. Ottawa, 1906–1907. 3 vols.

CARROLL, B. R., *ed.* Historical collections of South Carolina. New York, 1836. 2 vols.

CHALMERS, GEORGE. A collection of treaties between Great Britain and other powers. London, 1790. 2 vols.

CHARLEVOIX, PIERRE FRANÇOIS XAVIER DE. Histoire et description générale de la Nouvelle France. Paris, 1744. 6 vols.

CHESTERFIELD, PHILIP DORMER, *4th earl of.* The letters of Philip Dormer Stanhope, earl of Chesterfield, with the characters. Edited with introduction, notes, and index by John Bradshaw. London, 1892. 3 vols.

—— Private correspondence of Chesterfield and Newcastle, 1744–46. Edited with introduction and notes by Sir Richard Lodge. In: Royal Historical Society, *Publications,* Camden third series, XLIV. London, 1930.

CHOISEUL, ETIENNE FRANÇOIS, *duc de.* Mémoire historique sur la négociation de la France & de l'Angleterre, depuis le 26 mars 1761 jusqu'au 20 septembre de la même année, avec les pièces justicatives. Paris, 1761.

—— Mémoires du Duc de Choiseul, 1719–1785. Ed. by Fernand Calmettes. Paris, 1904.

COBBETT, WILLIAM, *ed.* The parliamentary history of England from the earliest period to the year 1803. London, 1806–1820. 36 vols.

COLLECTION DES MANUSCRITS RELATIFS À LA NOUVELLE FRANCE. Quebec, 1883, 1884. Four volumes in two.

COXE, WILLIAM. Memoirs of Horatio, lord Walpole, selected from his correspondence and papers and connected with the history of the times, from 1678 to 1757. 3d ed. London, 1820. 2 vols.

—— Memoirs of the kings of Spain of the house of Bourbon from the accession of Philip the Fifth to the death of Charles the Third: 1700 to 1788. 2d ed. London, 1815. 5 vols.

DAVENPORT, FRANCES GARDINER, *ed.* European treaties bearing on the history of the United States and its dependencies. Washington, 1917–1937. 4 vols. Vol. IV edited by C. O. Paullin.

DOUGLASS, WILLIAM. A summary, historical and political, of the first progressive settlements, and present state of the British settlements in North America. Boston, 1755. 2 vols.

DUMONT, JEAN, *comp.* Corps universel diplomatique du droit des gens, comprenant un recueil des traitez d'alliance, de paix, de trêve, de neutralité de commerce, et d'échange. Amsterdam, 1726–1731. 8 vols. *Also* Supplement. Amsterdam, 1739. 5 vols.

FORCE, PETER, *ed.* American archives: consisting of a collection of authentick records, state papers, debates, and letters and other notices of publick affairs, the whole forming a documentary history of the origin and progress of the North American colonies; of the causes and accomplishment of the American revolution; and of the constitution of government for the United States. Series 4, 5. Washington, 1837–1853.

FRANCE: Commission des archives diplomatiques au ministère des affaires étrangères. Recueil des instructions données aux ambassadeurs et ministres de France depuis les traités de Westphalie jusqu'à la révolution française, XI, XII, XII bis, Espagne.

FREDERICK II, *the Great, King of Prussia.* Politische correspondenz Friedrich des Grossen. Berlin, 1879–1900. 31 vols.

FRENCH, BENJ. F., *ed.* Historical collections of Louisiana. New York, 1846–1853. 5 vols.

THE GENTLEMAN'S MAGAZINE. London, 1731 sqq.

THE CORRESPONDENCE OF GEORGE THE THIRD from 1760 to December 1783 . . . edited by Sir John Fortescue. London, 1927. 6 vols.

GIST, CHRISTOPHER. Christopher Gist's journals. . . . Edited by William M. Darlington. Pittsburgh, 1893.

GREAT BRITAIN: Board of Trade. Journal of the commissioners for trade and plantations. London, 1920.

—— Privy Council. Acts of the Privy Council of England. Colonial series. Vols. I–VI, London, 1908–1912.

—— Public record office. Calendar of state papers, colonial series . . . America and West Indies. London, 1922—.

—— Royal commission on historical manuscripts. Reports I–XX. London, 1870–1928.

HARRIS, GEORGE. The Life of Lord Chancellor Hardwicke, with selections from his correspondence, diaries, speeches, and judgments. London, 1847. 3 vols.

JEFFERYS, THOMAS. The Conduct of the French, with regard to Nova Scotia; from its first settlement to the present time. In which are exposed the falsehood and absurdity of their arguments made use of to elude the force of the treaty of Utrecht, and support their unjust proceedings. In a letter to a member of Parliament. London, 1754.

KEENE, SIR BENJAMIN. The private correspondencé of Sir Benjamin Keene, K.B.; edited with introduction and notes by Sir Richard Lodge. Cambridge, 1933.

LOUIS XV. Correspondance secrète inédite de Louis XV sur la politique étrangère avec le comte de Broglie, Tercier, etc., et autres documents . . . précédés d'une étude sur le caractère et la politique personelle de Louis XV par M. E[dgard] Boutaric. Paris, 1866. 2 vols.

MAINE HISTORICAL SOCIETY. Collections of the Maine historical society. Portland, 1831—.

MARGRY, PIERRE, ed. Mémoires et documents pour servir à l'histoire des origines françaises des pays d'outre-mer. Découvertes et établissements des Français dans l'ouest et dans le sud de l'Amérique Septentrionale (1614–1754). Paris, 1879–1888. 6 vols.

MÉMOIRES DES COMMISSAIRES DU ROI et de ceux de Sa Majesté Britannique, sur les possessions et les droits respectifs des deux couronnes en Amérique; avec les actes publics et pièces justificatives. Paris, 1755. 3 vols. A fourth volume, containing memorials restating the French claim to Acadia and setting forth the French title to Tobago, which had not been presented because of the rupture of diplomatic negotiations, was added in 1757.

MÉMOIRES DES COMMISSAIRES DU ROI et de ceux de Sa Majesté Britannique. Paris, 1756. 6 vols.

MOREAU, JACOB NICHOLAS, comp. Mémoire contenant le précis des faits, avec leurs pièces justificatives. Pour servir de réponse aux observations envoyées par les ministres d'Angleterre, dans les cours de l'Europe. Paris, 1756.

NEW YORK, state of. Report of the regents of the university on the boundaries of the state of New York. Albany, 1874, 1884. 2 vols.

O'CALLAGHAN, E. B., ed. Documents relative to the colonial history of the state of New York. Albany, 1853–1887. 15 vols.

OBSERVATIONS SUR LE MÉMOIRE DE LA FRANCE envoyées dans les cours de l'Europe, par le ministère Britannique, pour justifier la réponse faite à la requisition de S.M.T.C. du 21 décembre 1755. Bound in with Moreau's Mémoire contenant le précis des faits, avec leurs pièces justificatives, Paris, 1756, but not printed with it.

PAPERS RELATIVE TO THE RUPTURE WITH SPAIN laid before both houses of parliament on 29th of June 1762 by His Majesty's command. London, 1762.

PAULLIN, C. O. See Davenport.

PEASE, THEODORE CALVIN, ed. Anglo-French boundary disputes in the West, 1749–1763. Collections of the Illinois state historical library, vol. XXVII. Springfield, Ill., 1936.

PENNSYLVANIA ARCHIVES. Philadelphia, Harrisburg, 1852—.

PENNSYLVANIA COLONIAL RECORDS. Philadelphia, Harrisburg, 1852–1853. 16 vols.

Pitt, William, *1st earl of Chatham*. Correspondence of William Pitt. Ed. by William Stanhope Taylor and Capt. John Henry Pringle. London, 1838–1840. 4 vols.

—— Correspondence of Wm. Pitt, when secretary of state, with colonial governors and military and naval commissioners in America. . . . Ed. by Gertrude Selwyn Kimball. New York, 1906. 2 vols.

Quebec, legislature of. Nouvelle France: Documents historiques: correspondance échangée entre les autorités françaises et les gouverneurs et intendants. Quebec, 1893. 2 vols.

Rowland, Dunbar, *and* A. G. Sanders, *eds*. Mississippi provincial archives, 1729–1740; French dominion. Jackson, Miss., 1927.

Serrano y Sanz, Manuel. Documentos históricos de la Florida y la Luisiana, siglos XVI al XVIII. Madrid, 1912.

Shirley, William. Correspondence of William Shirley, governor of Massachusetts and military commander in America, 1731–1760. Edited by Charles Henry Lincoln. New York, 1912. 2 vols.

Smith, William Henry, *ed*. The Pelham papers: Loss of Oswego. In: American historical association papers, vol. IV, pt. 4, pp. 367–379. New York, 1890.

Spotswood, Alexander. The official letters of Alexander Spotswood, lieutenant-governor of the colony of Virginia, 1710–1722. Ed. by R. A. Brock. Richmond, 1882–1885. 2 vols.

Stock, Leo F., *ed*. Proceedings and debates of the British parliaments respecting North America, 1542–1727. Washington, 1924–1930. 3 vols.

Temple, Richard Grenville, *2d earl of*. The Grenville papers: being a correspondence of Richard Grenville, Earl Temple, K.G., and the Right Honourable George Grenville, their friends and contemporaries. . . . Ed. by William James Smith. London, 1852–1853. 4 vols.

Thackeray, Francis. A history of the Right Honorable William Pitt, earl of Chatham. . . . London, 1827. 2 vols.

The Memorials of the English and French commissaries concerning the limits of Nova Scotia or Acadia [and St. Lucia]. London, 1755. 2 vols.

Thwaites, Reuben Gold, *ed*. The Jesuit relations and allied documents, 1610–1791. Cleveland, 1896–1901. 73 vols.

Tyrell, J. B., *ed*. Documents relating to the early history of Hudson Bay. In: Publications of the Champlain Society, vol. XVIII. Toronto, 1931.

United States. Journals of the Continental Congress, 1774–1789. Edited by Worthington Chauncey Ford, Gaillard Hunt, et al. Washington, 1904—. 13 vols.

—— Secret journals of the acts and proceedings of Congress. Boston, 1820–1821. 4 vols.

Walpole, Horace, *4th earl of Orford*. Memoirs of the reign of King George the Second. Ed. by the late Lord Holland, 2d ed., rev. London, 1847. 3 vols.

—— The letters of Horace Walpole, fourth earl of Orford; chronologically arranged and edited by Mrs. Paget Toynbee. Oxford, 1903–1905. 16 vols.

III. SECONDARY MATERIALS

ADAMS, JAMES TRUSLOW. The founding of New England. Boston, 1921.

AITON, ARTHUR SCOTT. The diplomacy of the Louisiana cession by France to Spain. *American Historical Review,* XXXVI, 701–720.

ALVORD, CLARENCE WALWORTH. The Illinois country, 1673–1818. Chicago, 1922.

—— The Mississippi valley in British politics. Cleveland, 1917. 2 vols.

BARTHÉLEMY, JOSEPH. Le traité de Paris entre la France et l'Angleterre. *Revue des questions historiques,* XLIII, 420 ff.

BEER, GEORGE LOUIS. British colonial policy, 1754–65. New York, 1907.

BEMIS, SAMUEL F. The diplomacy of the American revolution. New York, 1935.

BLART, LOUIS. Les rapports de la France et de l'Espagne après le pacte de famille, jusqu'à la fin du ministère du duc de Choiseul. Paris, 1915.

BOURGUET, ALFRED. Le duc de Choiseul et l'alliance espagnole. Paris, 1906.

—— Études sur la politique étrangère du duc de Choiseul. Paris, 1907.

BREBNER, J. BARTLET. New England's outpost. New York, 1927.

BREEN, HARRY HEGART. Saint Lucia: historical, statistical and descriptive. London, 1844.

BRIDGES, GEORGE WILSON. The annals of Jamaica. London, 1828. 2 vols.

BROGLIE, JACQUES VICTOR ALBERT, *duc de.* Histoire et diplomatie. Paris, 1899.

BROWN, VERA LEE. Anglo-Spanish relations in America in the closing years of the colonial era (1763–74). Baltimore, 1923.

CORBETT, [SIR] JULIAN STAFFORD. England in the seven years' war; a study in combined strategy. London, 1907. 2 vols.

COULTER, ELLIS MERTON. A short history of Georgia. Chapel Hill, N. C., 1933.

CRANE, V. W. The southern frontier, 1670–1732. Durham, N. C., 1928.

DANVILA Y COLLADO, MANUEL. Reinado de Carlos III. Madrid, 1893–1895. 6 vols.

DAUBIGNY, EUGÈNE THEODORE. Choiseul et la France d'outre-mer après le traité de Paris. Paris, 1892.

DODSON, LEONIDAS. Alexander Spotswood, governor of colonial Virginia, 1710–1722. Philadelphia, 1932.

DONIOL, HENRI. Histoire de la participation de la France à l'établissement des États-Unis d'Amérique. Paris, 1886–1892. 5 vols.

EDWARDS, BRYAN. The history, civil and commercial, of the British colonies in the West Indies. 5th ed. London, 1793–1794. 5 vols.

EGERTON, H. E. British foreign policy in Europe to the end of the 19th century. London, 1918.

FITZMAURICE, EDMOND GEORGE PETTY. Life of William, Earl of Shelburne, afterwards first marquess of Lansdowne, with extracts from his papers and correspondence. 2d ed. London, 1912. 2 vols.

FLASSAN, GAËTAN DE RAXIS DE. Histoire générale et raisonnée de la diplomatie francaise, ou de la politique de la France, depuis la fondation de la monarchie, jusqu'à la fin du règne de Louis XVI ; avec des tables chronologiques de tous les traités conclus par la France. Paris, 1811. 7 vols.

FRANZ, ALEXANDER. Die Kolonisation des Mississippitales bis zum Ausgange der französischen Herrschaft. Leipzig, 1906.

FROUDE, JAMES A. The English in the West Indies. London, 1888.

GARDNER, WILLIAM JAMES. A history of Jamaica from its discovery by Christopher Columbus to the year 1872. London, 1909.

GARNEAU, F. X. Histoire du Canada. Paris, 1913, 1920. 2 vols.

GIPSON, LAWRENCE H. Zones of international friction: North America, south of the great lakes region, 1748–1754. New York, 1939.

GRANT, WILLIAM LAWSON. La mission de M. de Bussy à Londres en 1761. Paris, 1906.

—— Canada versus Guadeloupe. *American Historical Review*, XVII, 735 ff.

HANNA, CHARLES A. The Wilderness Trail. New York, 1917. 2 vols.

HASSAL, ARTHUR. The history of British foreign policy from the earliest times to 1912. Edinburgh and London, 1912.

HILL, DAVID JAYNE. A history of diplomacy in the international development of Europe. New York, 1905–1914. 3 vols.

HOTBLACK, KATE. Chatham's colonial policy; a study in the fiscal and economic implications of the colonial policy of the elder Pitt. London, 1917.

—— The Peace of Paris, 1763. In: Royal Historical Society, *Transactions*, 3d series, II, 235–267. London, 1908.

HUNT, WILLIAM. Pitt's retirement from office, 5 October 1761. *English Historical Review*, XXI, 119–132.

INNIS, H. A. Cape Breton and the French régime. In: *Transactions of the Royal Society of Canada*, Section II, 1935, pp. 51–87.

—— The cod fisheries. New Haven, 1940.

JOHNSON, JAMES G. The colonial southeast, 1732–1763; an international contest for territorial and economic control. In: University of Colorado *Studies*, XIX. Boulder, 1932.

LANNING, J. T. American participation in the war of Jenkins' ear. *Georgia Historical Quarterly*, XI, no. 3, pp. 191–215.

—— The American colonies in the preliminaries of the war of Jenkins' ear. *Georgia Historical Quarterly*, II, no. 2, pp. 129–156.

—— The diplomatic history of Georgia. Chapel Hill, N. C., 1936.

LECKY, WILLIAM EDWARD HARTPOLE. A history of England in the 18th century. New York, 1892–1893. 7 vols.

LOUNSBURY, RALPH GREENLEE. The British fishery at Newfoundland, 1634–1763. New Haven, 1934.

MASSEY, WILLIAM NATHANIEL. A history of England during the reign of George the Third. London, 1855–1863. 4 vols.

MURDOCK, BEAMISH. A history of Nova Scotia or Acadia. Halifax, 1865–1867. 3 vols.

NAMIER, L. B. England in the age of the American Revolution. London, 1930.

OSGOOD, HERBERT E. The American colonies in the eighteenth century. New York, 1924. 4 vols.

PARES, RICHARD. Colonial blockade and neutral rights, 1739–1763. London, 1938.

PARKMAN, FRANCIS. Montcalm and Wolfe, France and England in North America. Boston, 1897–1898. 2 vols.

PAULIAT, LOUIS. La politique coloniale sous l'ancien régime d'après des documents empruntés aux archives coloniales du ministère de la marine et des colonies. Paris, 1887.

PEASE, THEODORE. The Mississippi boundary of 1763. *American Historical Review,* XL, 278–286.

PEÑARANDA Y DE ANGULO, AGUSTÍN DE. Consideraciones generales sobre el segundo Pacto de Familia . . . 1761, entre Francia y España y las dos Sicilias. Madrid, 1906.

PENSON, LILLIAN M. The colonial agents of the British West Indies: a study in colonial administration, mainly in the 18th century. London, 1924.

PITMAN, FRANK WESLEY. The development of the British West Indies, 1700–1763. New Haven, 1917.

PROWSE, D. W. A history of Newfoundland, from the English, colonial, and foreign records. 2d ed., rev. and corr. London, 1896.

RAYMOND, REV. W. D. History of the River St. John, A.D. 1604–1784. St. John, N. B., 1905.

—— Nova Scotia under English rule from the capture of Port Royal to the conquest of Canada, A.D. 1710–1760. In: Royal Society of Canada, *Proceedings and Transactions,* 3d series, vol. IV, sec. II, pp. 55–84.

RENAUT, FRANCIS PAUL. Le pacte de famille et l'Amérique; la politique coloniale franco-espagnole de 1760 à 1792. Paris, 1922.

ROSE, J. HOLLAND, A. P. NEWTON, *and* E. A. BENIANS, *eds.* The Cambridge history of the British Empire: Vol. I, The old empire from the beginnings to 1783. New York, 1929.

ROUSSEAU, FRANÇOIS. La règne de Charles III en Espagne, 1759–1788. Paris, 1907. 2 vols.

RUSSELL, NELSON VANCE. The reaction in England and America to the capture of Havana, 1762. *Hispanic American Historical Review,* IX, 303–316.

RUVILLE, ALBERT VON. William Pitt, earl of Chatham. London, 1907. 3 vols.

SCHAEFER, H. Geschichte von Portugal. Hamburg, 1836–1854. 5 vols.

SCHÖNE, L. La politique coloniale sous Louis XV et Louis XVI. Paris, 1907.

SHEPHERD, WM. R. The cession of Louisiana to Spain. *Political Science Quarterly,* XIX, 439–458.

SOLTAU, ROGER H. The duke de Choiseul. Oxford, 1909.

SOULANGE, BODIN. La diplomatie de Louis XV et le pacte de famille. Paris, 1894.

TEMPERLEY, H. W. V. Pitt's retirement from office, 1761. *English Historical Review,* XXI, 327–332.

TERRAGE, MARC VILLIERS DU TERRAGE, BARON DE. Les dernières années de la Louisiane française. . . . Paris, 1903.

TURNER, F. J. "The diplomatic contest for the Mississippi Valley." *Atlantic Monthly,* XCIII, 676–691, 807–817.

VOLWILER, ALBERT T. George Groghan and the westward movement, 1741–1782. Cleveland, 1926.

WADDINGTON, RICHARD. Louis XV et le renversement des alliances. Paris, 1896.

—— La guerre de sept ans. Paris, 1899. 5 vols.

WILLIAMS, ARTHUR FREDERICK BASIL. The life of William Pitt, Earl of Chatham. 2 vols.

WILLSON, BECKLES. The great company (1667–1871). London, 1900. 2 vols.

WINSOR, JUSTIN. The Mississippi Basin. Boston, 1898.

WRONG, GEORGE McKINNON. The rise and fall of New France. New York, 1928. 2 vols.

INDEX